'PLEADING FOR A REFORMATION VISION'

Life and Selected Writings of
William Childs Robinson
(1897–1982)

By the same author:

Princeton Seminary, Vol. 1: Faith and Learning
Princeton Seminary, Vol. 2: The Majestic Testimony
'Our Southern Zion': Old Columbia Seminary (1828–1927)

'PLEADING FOR A REFORMATION VISION'

Life and Selected Writings of
William Childs Robinson
(1897–1982)

DAVID B. CALHOUN

THE BANNER OF TRUTH TRUST

THE BANNER OF TRUTH TRUST

The Grey House, 3 Murrayfield Road, Edinburgh, EH12 6EL, UK

P.O. Box 621, Carlisle, PA 17013, USA

*

© David B. Calhoun 2013

*

ISBNs
Print: 978-1-84871-356-7
EPUB: 978-1-84871-357-4
Kindle: 978-1-84871-359-8

*

Typeset in Adobe Garamond Pro 11/13 pt
at the Banner of Truth Trust, Edinburgh
Printed in the USA by
Versa Press Inc.,
East Peoria, IL

We plead for a Reformation vision of the King in His beauty, God in His majesty and a sense of our absolute dependence upon Him. We depend upon Him for light and He gives us His Word with the illumination of the Spirit, we anchor in Him for life and the everlasting arms of our Maker sustain us, we look to Him for redemption and behold the Lamb of God that taketh away the sins of the world, we cry to Him for salvation and the Holy Spirit raises us up with Christ and makes us sit with Him in the heavenlies, we raise our bruised hopes and our bleeding hearts to Him and He opens the portals of the blessed hope of the glorious appearing of our great God and Saviour Jesus Christ—bringing with Him the New Jerusalem, the new heavens and the new earth in which dwelleth righteousness.

WILLIAM CHILDS ROBINSON
Southern Presbyterian Journal
December 2, 1946

William Childs Robinson (1897–1982)

CONTENTS

'PLEADING FOR A REFORMATION VISION'

SELECTED WRITINGS OF WILLIAM CHILDS ROBINSON

Dedicated to the Memory of

WILLIAM CHILDS ROBINSON
(1897–1982)

Believer
Student of Church History
Witness

and

G. ALLEN FLEECE
(1910–1996)

My father-in-law
Student of William Childs Robinson
Southern Presbyterian Pastor
President of Columbia Bible College
Missionary Statesman

As an exponent and a champion of the Reformed faith, William Childs Robinson sought to sound again and again the vital affirmations of the Protestant Reformation. He has emphasized always the authority of the Word of God and the Lordship of Jesus Christ. For him the fact of the sovereignty of God was central, and he constantly taught and preached the doctrine of justification by faith.

J. McDOWELL RICHARDS, Formerly President of Columbia
Theological Seminary, Decatur, Georgia

I have often said that Dr. William Childs Robinson was the greatest scholar I had the privilege of studying under. I believe that I took every elective that he offered and would say that his theological influence on my thinking was greater than that of any other teacher. I have quoted him more than probably all of my other professors combined.

D. JAMES KENNEDY, Formerly Senior Pastor,
Coral Ridge Presbyterian Church, Ft. Lauderdale, Florida

Dr. Robinson lived in the presence of the living God. He honored his convictions against the pressures of the time and the lure of career ambitions . . . Even though his work was against the times, this very fact is perhaps the best reason for taking his work seriously. It is likely that his work as a churchman and teacher of ministers was more lasting than can now be estimated. In any case, the final judgment, as he knew so well, belongs to God. Few of Robinson's critics have been able to match his brilliance, his diligent churchmanship and scholarship, his commitment to the faith and to participation in the organized life of the church.

JOHN H. LEITH, Formerly Professor of Theology
Union Theological Seminary, Richmond, Virginia

William Childs Robinson was a key figure in the history of Presbyterianism in the South, and in the whole country. When the struggle in the Southern Presbyterian Church was at its height, Dr. Robinson was right there. If you asked the "founding fathers" of the Presbyterian Church in America, they would all point to him as the stalwart of the faith in those critical days.

O. PALMER ROBERTSON, Director and Vice Chancellor,
African Bible College, Uganda

PREFACE

I am so glad that David Calhoun has written this biography of William Childs Robinson! For years I had hoped that a competent historian would undertake this important task because Dr. Robinson was more influential on my own theology and pastoral work than any other. I am delighted that, through this book, his life and ministry can become better known to future generations.

I had first come to know of Dr. Robinson through my college classmate Julius Scott who had always spoken of this professor in glowing terms. So, although I was from Long Island, New York, I went to Columbia Theological Seminary in Decatur, Georgia, for my seminary work. Why? I went to Columbia in order to sit at the feet of William Childs Robinson. At a time when the classical Reformed Faith was fading from most of the seminaries of the mainline Presbyterian Church, Dr. Robinson believed and taught the old faith "once delivered to the saints" with passion and enthusiasm. And I hungered for that kind of teaching.

I first met Dr. Robinson informally. I had just arrived at the seminary and had gone to check my mailbox. As I walked back down the hall, an older man approached me. "Good evening," he said. "I'm William Robinson." And he offered his hand. I almost fainted! "Dr. Robinson, you are the reason I've come to Columbia! I am so honored to meet you." We chatted for a few moments.

As I sat in his classes, I was not disappointed. In addition to taking the required courses he taught, I eagerly soaked up every elective he offered. A few of the electives I especially remember were The Westminster Confession of Faith, Southern Presbyterian Worthies, The Doctrine of the Atonement, and The Reformed Doctrine of

Justification. I went to Columbia as a "general evangelical." From Dr. Robinson I learned and embraced the classical Reformed Faith, and came to understand what J. Gresham Machen had meant on his deathbed when he exclaimed, "Isn't the Reformed Faith grand!" I shall be eternally grateful.

Every now and then, when a guest preacher would be introduced to the seminary in chapel, something like this would be said: "Now, Brother, speak to us from your heart." "Dr. Robbie," as many students affectionately called him, would fume afterwards in class, "We don't want to hear what is in his heart! Jesus told us what is in the human heart: 'For out of the heart come evil thoughts, murder, adultery, sexual immorality, theft, false witness, slander' (Matthew 15:19). We don't want to hear this from the pulpit! We want to hear the Word of God!"

Dr. Robinson was an excellent expositor of Scripture himself. He had a high view of preaching and believed that worship should be "with reverence and awe" (Hebrews 12:28). He had little patience with frivolous, trivial and "light" forms of worship. He also believed that church architecture for Presbyterian buildings ought to reflect the Reformed theology of the church.

Dr. Robinson held to the full authority of Scripture because he believed that it is "God's infallible Word." He preferred the word *infallible* to *inerrant* because *infallible* was the word used in the ordination vows, and he thought the word *inerrant* might be too easily misunderstood.

Dr. Robinson never tired of quoting the Rev. Thomas Goulding, first professor of Columbia Seminary, who started teaching there in 1829. Prof. Goulding often told his students, "Let every sermon preached contain so much of the plan of salvation that should a heathen come in who never heard the gospel before, and should depart never to hear it again, he should learn enough to know what he must do to be saved." Dr. Robinson urged us to keep this in mind every time we preached.

To my great benefit, Dr. Robinson and I became friends. He came and preached for me in two of the churches I served in the early days of my ministry – Dahlonega Presbyterian Church, Dahlonega,

Georgia, and Lakemont Presbyterian Church in Augusta, Georgia. I shall never forget a magnificent sermon he preached on the sixth chapter of Isaiah. I cherished the times I heard him pray. He was always generous in replying to my inquiries about some pastoral concerns.

LOWELL BEACH SYKES
Pastor Emeritus
Rivermont Evangelical Presbyterian Church
Lynchburg, Virginia
May 2013

FOREWORD

Sometimes a tall slim man came to our home place about a mile east of Decatur, Georgia. I had not yet entered the first grade. He was daddy's guest. The two of them walked around our yard, talking as they went. Daddy frequently introduced him to us children, "This is Dr. Robinson. He teaches at Columbia Seminary."

Sometimes my brother and I accompanied daddy to the little Ingleside Presbyterian Church in the Textile Mill village where Dr. Robinson frequently preached. The older we grew the more significant it was for us to sit and listen to his sermons.

In the fall of 1956, I started my first term as a student at Columbia Seminary. I'd been warned that the institution was not conservative in its theology. But Dr. Robinson was there. I knew that he was a conservative and that I would learn a great deal from him. I was disappointed to discover that Dr. Robinson was on leave that term. There was nothing for me to do but take the required courses and an elective course in Greek, and await Dr. Robinson's return.

Sometime after Christmas the second term began! When I entered the classroom at the right end of the hall, there sat Dr. Robinson! The conservative students were delighted. Others were able to control their excitement!

There were four parts of the seminary curriculum—Systematic Theology, Biblical Theology, Historical Theology, and Practical Theology. Dr. Robinson taught Historical Theology. His method included: (1) Lectures, usually while sitting, but with frequent trips to the black board and around the room. (2) Textbooks, including Philip Schaff's *History of the Christian Church* and James Hastings Nichols' *History of Christianity 1650-1950*. (3) Student Papers, and

(4) Class discussions. Class sessions were often spiced with Dr. Robinson's own brand of humor.

Just before the beginning of my third and final year at the seminary I stood before the altar in a church in Atlanta, beside a lovely bride who has now stayed with me for almost fifty-five years. The bride's father and Dr. Robinson, a long time friend of both families, presided at the ceremony. After graduation my wife and I frequently visited the Robinsons.

Years later, when we heard that Dr. Robinson was in an infirmary in Clinton, South Carolina, we went to see him. We had a pleasant visit, and as I stood to leave he said, "Wait, I want to tell you what I understand to be the meaning of justification." I listened as he explained what he had taught in his classes at the seminary. He asked if that was what I understood to be the meaning of the doctrine. I refrained from saying, "Yes sir, that is exactly what I learned from you in your class." I simply said, "Yes sir, that is exactly what I understand it to be." He leaned back on his pillow and, with a smile, said, "Good. That is what I am dying on."

J. Julius Scott, Jr,
Emeritus Professor of Biblical and Historical Studies,
Wheaton College Graduate School,
Wheaton, Illinois

ACKNOWLEDGEMENTS

As always, Wayne Sparkman, Director of the Historical Center of the Presbyterian Church in America, has helped me with his friendship, his knowledge of Presbyterian history, his diligence in collecting material, and his insights and suggestions. Chris Paton, Archivist, Campbell Library at Columbia Theological Seminary, assisted in locating photographs and several writings of William Childs Robinson.

Iain Murray kindly (and voluntarily) read the manuscript for this book and made valuable suggestions that resulted in a major revision. I thank him for his wisdom and encouragement. And thanks to all the staff at the Banner of Truth Trust for their guidance and the skillful production of this book.

I am grateful for personal accounts of William Childs Robinson from a number of his students: Julius Scott, W. Wilson Benton, Samuel S. Cappel, Thomas T. Ellis, Ben Haden, D. James Kennedy, Charles E. McGowan, John C. Neville, Paul G. Settle, Lowell B. Sykes, Henry Lewis Smith, and Kennedy Smartt. Information from these men came in the form of letters, emails, and telephone conversations. Julius Scott and Lowell Sykes have provided their own memories of Dr. Robinson in their prefaces to this book.

Joel Belz, Founder of WORLD Magazine, granted me "full permission to quote anything from Dr. Robinson's writings in the (Southern) Presbyterian Journal." Permission to use published material from Robinson was also given by Wm. B. Eerdmans Publishing Company and by Columbia Theological Seminary. Permission has been sought for the use of several writings from other sources.

I regret that I have been able to provide little information about Mary McConkey Robinson, surely a lively and interesting woman.

I have searched unsuccessfully for personal correspondence that perhaps would have greatly expanded my remarks about her, which have been based largely on the memories of Dr. Robinson's seminary students. In the dedication of one of his books, William calls Mary "the light of the home, with whom 'the best is yet to be.'" They had been married for sixty-one years when he died in 1982. Mary died in 1993.

My wife, Anne, happily read my work, correcting mistakes and improving my writing. Her father, Dr. G. Allen Fleece, often spoke of the influence of William Childs Robinson upon his life and ministry.

INTRODUCTION

William Childs Robinson was a minister in the Presbyterian Church in the United States (the Southern Presbyterian Church) from 1920. In 1926 he became a professor at Columbia Theological Seminary, a post which he held until his death in 1982. Robinson's career spanned the Great Depression, the two World Wars, the Korean War, the Vietnam War, and the Civil Rights movement. These were difficult years for America and for Protestant Christianity in America. Robinson saw his beloved Southern Presbyterian Church slowly move toward a more liberal theological position. He gave himself to preserving the old Calvinism that had marked the church from its beginning in 1861 when Southern Presbyterians began their own separate denomination. His voice was heard in seminary classrooms, in pulpits across the South and beyond, and in the courts of the Southern Presbyterian Church, "pleading for a Reformation vision" based on faithfulness to Scripture and supported by the Reformation of the sixteenth century and its notable followers.

Most of William Childs Robinson's life was spent as a teacher of seminarians. In 1948 James E. Moore, pastor of Mount Washington Presbyterian Church in Baltimore, Maryland, wrote to young Morton Smith, who had asked him whether or not he should go to seminary. Moore gave three reasons why a person going into the Christian ministry should go to seminary. First, to study the Bible, which alone contains "God's message of salvation for a lost world." Second, to study the entire Bible so that one is able to declare the "whole counsel of God." Third, to learn how to "convey the truth of the Bible to others." Moore wrote that he wanted Smith to be so prepared that he could go into any community and be able to present "the riches of God's grace in Christ Jesus" to everyone—to all classes and all races of people. The Baltimore pastor added that he could recommend no Southern Presbyterian seminary because of the presence of liberal teachers in each of them. Instead he suggested that Morton Smith consider Westminster Theological Seminary in Philadelphia, which, he said, fulfilled all the requirements of a seminary in a "biblical, scholarly way." Moore also deplored the lack of scholarship in the four Southern Presbyterian seminaries, adding that there was "only one man who is a scholar of the first rank" in those seminaries—William Childs Robinson at Columbia Theological Seminary.[1]

William Childs Robinson is not a recognized name among American Christians today—not even among those who would be glad to know about him. His books are seldom read. His struggle to preserve the historic Reformed orthodoxy of his denomination has been largely forgotten. Southern Presbyterian scholar John Leith has written, "In the years after World War II Dr. Robinson's influence waned. If the impression is correct that he is not given the credit in the church to which his career entitles him, it is a great pity." Leith believed, however, that it was likely that Robinson's "work as a churchman and teacher of ministers was more lasting than can now be estimated."[2] It is my prayer that this book will serve to further Dr. Leith's hope.

William Childs Robinson had a lifelong connection with Columbia Theological Seminary.[3] He was born into a Columbia, South Carolina, family who worshiped at First Presbyterian Church, the "mother church" of the seminary. He was a student at Columbia Seminary from 1917 to 1920. After serving as a pastor in Pennsylvania, he returned to Columbia Seminary in 1926 as a member of the

[1] Letter in the Historical Center of the Presbyterian Church in America, St. Louis, Missouri.
[2] Leith, *The Presbyterian Outlook,* January 10, 1983, 15. In one of his books, Leith lists the seminary professors that most influenced him—including Dr. Robinson at Columbia Theological Seminary, the only Columbia professor that Leith mentions. John H. Leith, *Crisis in the Church: The Plight of Theological Education,* (Louisville: Westminster John Knox Press, 1997), xii.
[3] For the history of the "Old" Columbia Seminary, see David B. Calhoun, *"Our Southern Zion": Old Columbia Seminary (1828-1927),* (Edinburgh: Banner of Truth Trust, 2012).

faculty and remained there until his retirement in 1967. In his forty-one years as a seminary professor he taught close to 1,500 students, and his influence reached across the Southern Presbyterian Church and beyond.

Dr. Robinson was a professor of church history and polity. He was also a theologian, a preacher, and a pastor. Introducing his lectures at the Free Church College in Edinburgh in 1938, Robinson stated that he came "as a believer to advocate the Word of the Cross as it is stated in the Holy Scriptures, as a student of church history to remind the hearer and reader of the testimony of the Christian centuries in confirmation of the Word, and as a witness endeavouring to stand where the great Christian witnesses have stood and testify to Him who loved us and delivered Himself up for us."[1] Dr. Robinson was indeed a believer, a student of church history, and a witness. This is abundantly evident in his life, his preaching and teaching, and in his writing. He powerfully and often eloquently combined Bible and personal faith, theology and church history, literature and pastoral concerns.

[1] WCR, *The Word of the Cross* (London: The Sovereign Grace Union; and Zondervan Publishing House, 1938), preface.

WILLIAM CHILDS ROBINSON
(1897–1982)

William Childs Robinson at his graduation from Columbia Theological Seminary in 1920 (provided by the Archives of the Campbell Library at Columbia Theological Seminary)

1. CHILD OF THE CHURCH

William Childs Robinson was born in Lincolnton, North Carolina, on December 4, 1897, the son of Edith (Childs) and David Robinson. The Robinsons were faithful members of the Presbyterian church in Lincolnton, whose pastor was the Reverend Robert Z. Johnston, an 1861 graduate of Columbia Theological Seminary. When Edith and David Robinson moved to Columbia, South Carolina, they worshiped at First Presbyterian Church, where William grew up under the ministries of Samuel M. Smith and James O. Reavis.[1]

David Robinson was a deacon and later an elder at First Presbyterian and a member of the Board of Directors of Columbia Theological Seminary. He conducted a Sunday school mission in the Waverly suburb of Columbia. At his retirement in 1967, William Childs Robinson told the story of how a professor at Columbia Seminary was "recruited" to help in the Sunday school. One Sunday morning "a tall, distinguished looking gentleman," Dr. R. C. Reed, visited that Sunday school. The secretary of the Sunday school announced that "the superintendent and the assistant superintendent" were both present that day. Dr. Reed turned to Mr. Robinson and asked, "Just who is the superintendent of this Sunday school?" "Why, you are," answered David Robinson, who had just appointed himself "the assistant superintendent." Dr. Robinson added, "So from early years I have lived in the shadow of Columbia Theological Seminary."[2]

---

[1] For Smith and Reavis, see David B. Calhoun, *The Glory of the Lord Risen Upon It: First Presbyterian Church, Columbia, South Carolina, 1795-1995* (Columbia: R. L. Bryan Company, 1994), 151-81.

[2] *Columbia Theological Seminary Bulletin*, December 1967. In 1906 the Sunday school became the Woodrow Memorial Presbyterian Church.

3

William Childs Robinson's first book was dedicated to his father—"David Wallace Robinson, A lifelong representative of those Presbyterian Elders and Deacons whose gifts of time, means, business and professional abilities have made possible the institutions of our Church."[1]

In another of his books Robinson described the time a doctor told Robinson's father that it was necessary to amputate his right leg in an effort to prolong his life. When the doctor stepped out of the room, the father, a Presbyterian elder, and the son, now a minister, repeated together the twenty-third Psalm. "As we did so," the son wrote, "the voice of the minister shook, but the voice of the elder never quavered." His faith was riveted in the living God by His Holy Word. The faith of which he loved to sing in life sustained him in death:

> How firm a foundation, ye saints of the Lord,
> Is laid for your faith in His excellent Word!
>
> The soul that on Jesus has leaned for repose,
> I will not, I will not desert to his foes;
> That soul, though all hell should endeavor to shake,
> I'll never, no never, no never forsake.[2]

Dr. Robinson's second book, *The Certainties of the Gospel*, was dedicated to his mother, Edith Childs Robinson, in whom dwelt, he wrote, "an unfeigned faith in the certainties of the Gospel."[3]

---

[1] WCR, *Columbia Theological Seminary and the Southern Presbyterian Church, 1831-1931: A Study in Church History, Presbyterian Polity, Missionary Enterprise, and Religious Thought* (Decatur, Georgia: Dennis Lindsey Printing Company, 1931).
[2] WCR, *What is Christian Faith?* (Grand Rapids: Zondervan Publishing House, 1937), 79.
[3] WCR, *The Certainties of the Gospel* (Grand Rapids: Zondervan Publishing House, 1935).

2. CALLED INTO THE MINISTRY

William Childs Robinson graduated from Roanoke College in 1917. Forty years later he paid tribute to one of his teachers, Dr. L. A. Fox, who took the time to show his students carefully, from the New Testament records, that Jesus Christ really rose from the dead. And "the living Christ, the risen Christ, called some of us into His ministry," Robinson said.[1] Robinson often told his seminary classes that Dr. Fox said to him, "William, always be faithful to the theology of the Confession of Faith of your church. Your Presbyterian Church and my Lutheran Church are among the few Protestant churches to have a theology."

To prepare for the ministry Robinson attended Columbia Seminary in his hometown. He received his Bachelor of Divinity degree in 1920, also fulfilling requirements for a Master of Arts degree from the University of South Carolina. William cherished the training he received at Columbia Seminary from William McPheeters, Professor of Old Testament Literature; R. C. Reed, Professor of Ecclesiastical History and Church Polity; Henry Alexander White, Professor of New Testament Literature and Exegesis; James O. Reavis, Professor of Bible, Homiletics and Pastoral Theology; Edgar D. Kerr, Professor of Greek and Hebrew; and Thornton C. Whaling, President and Professor of Didactic and Polemic Theology.[2]

Robinson was licensed as a Presbyterian minister in April 1920 by Congaree (South Carolina) Presbytery and ordained in July by Greenbrier (West Virginia) Presbytery of the Presbyterian Church in the United States (the Southern Presbyterian Church).

[1] *The Southern Presbyterian Journal* [afterwards *Presbyterian Journal*], September 26, 1956, 5.
[2] See Calhoun, *Our Southern Zion: Old Columbia Seminary (1828–1927)* (Edinburgh: The Banner of Truth Trust, 2012), 333-40.

In 1921 Robinson earned the Master of Theology degree from Princeton Theological Seminary. The Princeton faculty comprised at that time B. B. Warfield, John D. Davis, William Brenton Greene, Geerhardus Vos, William Park Armstrong, Robert Dick Wilson, Caspar Wistar Hodge, Charles Erdman, Frederick Loetscher, Joseph Ross Stevenson, Jonathan Ritchie Smith, J. Gresham Machen, and O. T. Allis.[1] Dr. Warfield, especially, impressed the young Robinson, who paid tribute to Warfield's teaching and writings in the foreword to *Our Lord: An Affirmation of the Deity of Christ.* Robinson wrote: "The writer studied [Warfield's *Lord of Glory*] in the classroom of its learned author and has since taught the book to a number of his own classes." Robinson stated that his thinking was so permeated by Warfield's book that he drew upon it "without being prepared to cite definite passages."[2]

Robinson was present for Warfield's last lecture on February 16, 1921. Twenty-eight years later Robinson described the scene. Because of his physical weakness, Dr. Warfield asked to be excused from his usual custom of standing to lead the opening prayer. He then "plunged into a glowing exposition of the third chapter of First John. The discourse quickly gathered about the sixteenth verse as a center: 'Hereby perceive we the love of God, because he laid down his life for us: and we ought to lay down our lives for the brethren.' All the eloquence of Dr. Warfield's Christian heart," stated Robinson, "all the wisdom of his ripened scholarship focused on the interpretation of that text." "The laying down of His life in our stead was a great thing," said Warfield, "but the wonder of the text is that He, being all that He was, the Lord of glory, laid down His life for us, being what we are, mere creatures of His hand, guilty sinners deserving His wrath." "The more fully we realize His glory and His gift and our sinfulness," Dr. Warfield continued, "the deeper becomes our wonder at His grace and our wish to glorify His name."[3]

[1] See David B. Calhoun, *Princeton Seminary: The Majestic Testimony, 1869-1929* (Edinburgh: The Banner of Truth Trust, 1996), 313-43.
[2] WCR, *Our Lord: An Affirmation of the Deity of Christ* (Grand Rapids: Wm. B. Eerdmans Publishing Company, 1949), [11]; Benjamin Breckinridge Warfield, *The Lord of Glory: a study of the designations of our Lord in the New Testament with especial reference to his deity* (New York: American Tract Society, 1907; repr. Grand Rapids: Zondervan, 1974).
[3] WCR, *Our Lord,* [11].

3. PASTOR IN GETTYSBURG

On June 22, 1921, William Childs Robinson married Mary McConkey of Salem, Virginia. That same year he transferred his ecclesiastical membership to the Presbyterian Church in the United States of America (the Northern Presbyterian Church) and became pastor of the Presbyterian church in Gettysburg, Pennsylvania, an unusual post for a South Carolinian. One imagines the feelings of the earnest young Southerner living in the place of the famous 1863 defeat of the Confederate army. Robinson often visited the battlefield, drawing sermon illustrations from the stories and monuments of "our grandfathers in grey and in blue."[1]

In one sermon he described the North Carolina monument at Gettysburg that depicted a young soldier, terrified by the dangers of battle, being encouraged by a friend who had placed his hand on the young man's shoulder, and by another companion who held the colors before his face, while a falling officer was calling him to go forward.[2]

Robinson used a story that an elder in the Gettysburg church told him to illustrate the power of God in answering prayer:

> A Yankee soldier, a member of Cole's Maryland Calvary, was wounded and carried as a prisoner to Andersonville, Georgia. Fever set in and one night the doctors gave him up as hopeless. But the next day, to their surprise, he was greatly improved. When the war was over and the prisoner returned to his home, he told the incident to his sisters. They immediately got out the calendar and, checking the time, said, "That was the night our mother walked the floor all night praying for you."

[1] WCR, *Presbyterian Journal*, March 1944, 8.
[2] WCR, *Presbyterian Journal*, August 1942, 4.

A mother praying up near the Mason-Dixon Line and the Lord Christ putting on the healing staunch in Andersonville, Georgia.

Preaching during the dark days of World War II, Dr. Robinson went on to say:

We can and should pray, and the Lord Jesus Christ can and will hear our prayers, and keep our loved ones in the hollow of His hand whether that keeping be for time or for eternity. No, I did not say they would all return, but that He would hear our prayers for each and for every one.[1]

In a sermon on Matthew 10:29—"Sparrow-Soldier-Sailor: Not One Shall Fall Without Your Father"—preached in 1943, Robinson said:

On one of the monuments at Gettysburg is a tree, its limbs torn by shot and shrapnel, but nestled against its trunk the sculptor has carved a nest with a mother bird nestling her fledglings under her wing. The men of that regiment remembered just this scene and had it carved upon their memorial. God, our Father, does care for His birds of the heaven and no one is forgotten by Him.[2]

For five years Robinson served the church in Gettysburg. He loved his Northern congregation, and the people of his church held for him a deep affection. He was, a later colleague wrote, a "highly successful and much loved pastor."[3]

[1] WCR, *Presbyterian Journal,* August 1942, 5.
[2] WCR, *Presbyterian Journal,* June 1943, 11.
[3] J. McDowell Richards, *As I Remember It: Columbia Theological Seminary 1932–1971* (Decatur, Georgia: CTS Press, 1985), 43.

4. PROFESSOR OF CHURCH HISTORY

In 1926 William Childs Robinson was called to teach at Columbia Theological Seminary. Robinson's first year on the faculty of the seminary was spent mainly on leave of absence for study at Harvard University, where he earned the Doctor of Theology degree. Robinson's first book—*Columbia Theological Seminary and the Southern Presbyterian Church, 1831–1931*—was based on his Harvard doctoral dissertation. It was published in 1931, the centennial year of the Society of Missionary Inquiry at Columbia Seminary, Robinson noted. The book contains chapters on the history of Columbia Seminary and the characteristics of the Southern Presbyterian Church—its polity, missionary enterprise, and thought.[1]

Paul Woolley, Professor of Church History at Westminster Theological Seminary in Philadelphia, praised Robinson's book in a lengthy review in *The Evangelical Quarterly*. He wrote:

> The genial professor of Church History and Polity at Columbia Theological Seminary here publishes what is in effect a centennial history of Columbia Seminary ... Should the reader imagine, however, that the book contains only a dry-as-dust compilation, he will be most agreeably disappointed. Not only does the genial humour of the author show itself, but the matter of the volume is far from being a catalogue of historical events in the life of an institution. Rather it is a study of the vital questions of life and thought which have animated Columbia Seminary and the whole Southern Presbyterian Church during the last one hundred years ... Here, as elsewhere, Dr. Robinson shows that incisive ability to get to the heart of a matter, which is one of the characteristics of this book upon which he is most highly to be

[1] For a portion of Robinson's material on the theology of Columbia Seminary see *Selected Writings*, 1.

congratulated ... In this volume Robinson has given us a concise, clear and scholarly survey of the development and present state of Presbyterian doctrine and life in one of the great areas of our Lord's vineyard.[1]

A twenty-five-page section in Robinson's book dealt with "Natural Science in Connection with Revealed Religion." Here Robinson surveyed "the evolution controversy" at Columbia Seminary and in the Southern Presbyterian Church in the 1880s and offered an appreciative judgment of Dr. Woodrow, who held to a kind of theistic evolution of the body of Adam.[2] Robinson's views on evolution shifted during his lifetime. In 1946 he asked "What will one need to do to please the followers of Darwin? To suit them shall we surrender creation, the miracles, and the fall to the fancied demands of evolution?"[3] In 1962 he contributed a chapter for the book *Science and Religion: Twenty-Three Prominent Churchmen Express Their Opinion*, in which he hopefully claimed that there was "a lessening of the dominance of the dogma of evolution with the passing years of the twentieth century." He wrote: "There are rifts in the fog, or, if you please, the mirage seems to be lifting." In commenting on the views of James Woodrow, Robinson wrote, "Personally, I have never found the arguments for organic evolution sufficiently strong to accept that hypothesis as being probably true." He stated that the sharp cleavage in the theory of Woodrow's "between body and soul better befits the dichotomy of Hellenistic thought than the unity of man presupposed in the Hebrew Scriptures."[4]

* * * * *

William Childs Robinson's full-time service at Columbia Seminary began in the fall of 1927 in the seminary's new location in Decatur, Georgia. The seminary opened its first session there on Wednesday, September 14, at 10:00 a.m. in the new chapel. Two distinguished

[1] Paul Wooley, *The Evangelical Quarterly*, January 15, 1932, 84-89.
[2] See Calhoun, *Our Southern Zion*, 265-80.
[3] WCR, *Presbyterian Journal*, September 16, 1946, 2.
[4] John Clover Monsma, ed., *Science and Religion: Twenty-Three Prominent Churchmen Express Their Opinion* (New York: G. P. Putnam's Sons, 1962), 165, 168-69.

members of the faculty had died a short time before—R. C. Reed in the summer of 1925, and the next summer, Henry Alexander White. Robinson joined the senior member of the faculty, Dr. William McPheeters, who taught Old Testament, Apologetics, and Preaching; Dr. E. D. Kerr, Professor of Greek and Hebrew; Dr. Melton Clark, Professor of English Bible, Christian Education, and Preaching; Dr. James Benjamin Green, who taught Theology, Bible and, from time to time, Preaching. Joining these men in 1930 was S. A. Cartledge, who graduated from Columbia Seminary and earned a Ph.D. in New Testament from the University of Chicago. In the seminary's history its professors had come to their posts after experience in the pastorate—in some cases quite extensive—but Cartledge came directly to the classroom from his academic studies.

The General Assembly of the Southern Presbyterian Church met in Atlanta in 1928 and joined in the ceremonies celebrating the centennial of Columbia Seminary, including a banquet honoring Dr. McPheeters and the inauguration of Dr. Robinson. Robinson's inaugural address was on "Columbia Theological Seminary and the Southern Presbyterian Church."[1] He described the life and teaching of the first hundred years of "the grand old seminary" and closed with a plea to Southern Presbyterians:

> But just because the Columbia tradition is a scriptural tradition, a spiritual tradition, our human efforts are not sufficient to guarantee its perpetuation. We earnestly ask the prayer support of every one who loves this great heritage. In this year of removal [to Atlanta] we ask the prayers of those who have so faithfully held the lines and proven the bulwark of support for the seminary. One of the seminary's most devoted supporters recently suggested that the attention of its friends be called to the gracious promise recorded in Isaiah 40:31. Will every lover of the seminary lay to heart this year our spiritual need and plead to God His promise, "They that wait on the Lord shall renew their strength"? Will you ask Him to renew Columbia Seminary this year in the great tradition of loyalty to Himself? Will you ask for her a regirding with strength by the Lord for service in His vineyard? In this crucial moment we earnestly appeal to you, who are "the Lord's remembrancers," to make mention of Columbia in prayer: that the

[1] See Selected Writings 2.

Lord may renew His heritage, revive His work, regenerate with a rich baptism of redeeming grace every soul that comes in any way into contact with the seminary you own and love.[1]

Dr. Robinson transferred back into the Southern Presbyterian Church and was received by Congaree Presbytery (South Carolina) in 1928. After the stock market crash of 1929, it was by no means certain that Columbia Seminary would survive. Faculty salaries—already inadequate—had to be drastically reduced. At the funeral of J. B. Green in 1967, the seminary president, James McDowell Richards, said that Green was part of the little group of professors who carried forward the work of the seminary during the depression years of the early 1930s, "laboring under discouraging circumstances, at tremendous personal sacrifice and at a salary so small that I prefer not to mention it in public today." During their first year in Decatur, the Robinsons spent all their money furnishing their house, so that several times their car ran out of gas. The students "humorously complained" to the faculty that Dr. Robinson ran out of money by the middle of every month and that they "had to push him around until the first!"[2]

During these difficult years the seminary directors considered various options, including combining the seminary with another institution. Dr. Robinson was firm in his conviction that Columbia Seminary had a mission to the southeastern United States, and that it should decline offers to merge with seminaries elsewhere. Robinson dramatized his determination that the seminary remain in Georgia by "sinking some anchor stones." There were no sidewalks, and the dirt stretch from the street curb to Robinson's house was "a bit over ten feet." One day a wagon came by with several granite blocks from Stone Mountain. Robinson bought them and got the driver to help him place them, reaching from the curb to the walk of his house. They became, he said, his "anchor stones."[3]

David W. Robinson Jr., Dr. Robinson's brother, and his sister, Mrs. R. C. (Alice Robinson) Johnson, served the seminary "ably and

[1] WCR, "The Columbia Tradition," *Columbia Theological Seminary Bulletin,* January 1928.
[2] *Columbia Theological Seminary Bulletin,* December 1967.
[3] *Columbia Theological Seminary Bulletin,* December 1967.

unselfishly in legal and business relationships during the difficult days of the Great Depression."[1]

Among the students that entered the seminary during Robinson's first years was Peter Marshall. Marshall came to the United States from Scotland in 1927. He worked for some months in construction in New Jersey, but homesickness and the summer heat made him think that he would have to go home. Just in time, a special delivery letter arrived from a boyhood friend, Dave Wood, who had come the year before from Scotland to Birmingham, Alabama. Dave encouraged Peter to come to Birmingham. "You would like the South," he wrote, "and I feel pretty certain I could get you a job with me on *The Birmingham News.*"[2] Peter came to Birmingham, worked for the newspaper, and attended the First Presbyterian Church where he heard powerful and picturesque preaching by the Welsh pastor, Dr. Trevor Mordecai. Peter was accepted by the session as a candidate for the ministry, taught the Men's Bible Class, and planned to go to Columbia Seminary in the fall of 1928 to prepare for the ministry, his long-time goal. Peter did not have six dollars for the train fare to Atlanta. The problem was solved when he was invited to travel by car with James A. Bryan, the pastor of Third Presbyterian Church in Birmingham, and his son, Harry, who was a student at the seminary. Birmingham's beloved "Brother Bryan," as everyone called him, delivered the opening lectures at the seminary that year.[3]

During Dr. Robinson's early years on the seminary faculty, Dr. Melton Clark was Professor of English Bible and Pastoral Theology and acting president for two years.[4] Robinson said that Clark

taught the Reformed faith from the Bible. When I first came to the faculty I was under the impression that one could perhaps teach this faith better by logical reasoning. But ere long I found myself asking admission to the position taken by my friend and elder brother in the

[1] Richards, *Soli Deo Gloria,* 4.
[2] Catherine Marshall, *A Man Called Peter: the Story of Peter Marshall* (New York: McGraw-Hill, 1951), 25.
[3] See David B. Calhoun, "Brother Bryan of Birmingham: 'He Went About Doing Good,'" *Presbyterion,* Fall 2012, 65-73.
[4] Calhoun, *Our Southern Zion,* 355-59. Clark resigned from the seminary faculty in 1932 to become pastor of the First Presbyterian Church in Anniston, Alabama. He served this church until 1944. He died May 2, 1946.

faith, Dr. Melton Clark, that is, seeking to present the truth as it is in Christ Jesus *from God's Holy Word.*

"No one who studied under Dr. Clark," Robinson said, "failed to get worthwhile lessons on courtesy and tact together with the valuable content derived from his courses." "So judicious a colleague as Dr. McPheeters," Robinson added, "remarked that no man showed more of the spirit of Christ than did Dr. Melton Clark."[1]

Robinson admired and loved William McPheeters, his teacher and now colleague at Columbia Seminary. "For such a man the truth and authority of the Word of God demanded the utmost diligence in scholarship, and one could hardly come out of his class without a higher concept of the responsibility resting upon anyone who would undertake to interpret and present the truths of Scripture." McPheeters took a strong stand against what he saw as signs of theological decline in the denomination. He said to the seminary president, J. McDowell Richards, that he did not wish to enter the presence of the Lord without having borne witness to the truth as best he could. [2]

One of Robinson's prized possessions was a Greek New Testament that was always in the hand or at the side of Dr. McPheeters during his latter years and final sickness.[3] Robinson wrote:

> As he faced man's last great enemy and felt the frail bark of his earthly life going to pieces, this man of God was continually fortifying his soul with the Word which was immediately inspired by God. When I last saw that tiny frame [who] was the Gibraltar of Southern Presbyterian loyalty to the Word, lying beside him on the bed were this Testament and the current copy of a popular religious weekly. Referring to the latter, he remarked, "Why will our ministers try to feed immortal souls on such chaff?" Turning to the former, he declared he had been impressed anew with the determination of the apostles to give themselves to prayer and the ministry of the Word (*Acts* 6:4). "If we could only realize," said the dying saint, "the utter reasonableness of doing just that—preach the Word of God and pray the Holy Spirit

[1] *Presbyterian Journal,* July 16, 1952.
[2] Richards, *As I Remember It,* 40.
[3] McPheeters ended his career as a member of the faculty in 1933, was elected Professor Emeritus, and lived in Charlotte, North Carolina, until his death in 1935.

to bless it!" The last messages I received from this father in Israel were two. For himself he asked, "Pray that Satan may not buffet me too hard." To [me] he gave this admonition, "Hold on to the sufficiency of the Word."[1]

On August 14, 1935, Dr. McPheeters died. Every detail of the funeral service was conducted as he had directed. There was no address, only the singing of hymns of triumph, prayers, and the reading of passages he had selected from the Bible.[2]

A memorial bulletin issued by Columbia Seminary quoted the Rev. S. C. Byrd, who wrote that Dr. McPheeters "was regarded by some as a meddler and criticized by others as a heresy hunter. But in spirit and in purpose he was not either merely. His efforts and his zeal were for truth's sake, and so he was undeterred by criticism, censure and rebuff. He was of the spirit of which martyrs are made."[3] Dr. Robinson gladly took up the mantle of his teacher and friend as one who also was determined to bear witness to the truth.

Robinson's main field was Church History, in which he followed Dr. R. C. Reed—his teacher and "distinguished predecessor." He also taught Church Polity and Apologetics, and, from time to time, Preaching and Missions.[4] J. McDowell Richards, who became president of Columbia Seminary in 1932, described Robinson as "an ardent and able defender of Protestant orthodoxy. A scholar by instinct, he brought a fresh emphasis upon scholarship into his classroom, and his influence was quickly seen in the new volumes which were secured for the library and in the requirements which he made for their use."[5]

---

[1] WCR, *What is Christian Faith?*, 80-81.

[2] Dr. McPheeters' son, Thomas McPheeters of Charlotte, North Carolina, left a trust in 1961 to Columbia Theological Seminary amounting to approximately five million dollars, the largest gift in the school's 162-year history. According to John Leith, J. McDowell Richards, president of the seminary, was troubled in conscience each year when he signed a statement that the seminary was teaching the doctrines of the Westminster Confession of Faith, because he was uncertain that the teachings at Columbia were "as faithful to the Westminster Confession as the [McPheeters] trust required." Leith, *Crisis in the Church*, 86 and ft.13, pages 122-23.

[3] Ernest Trice Thompson, *Presbyterians in the South*, 3 vols. (Richmond, Virginia: John Knox Press, 1963), 3:214.

[4] WCR, *Presbyterian Journal*, May 1942, 6.

[5] Richards, *As I Remember It*, 43-44.

William Childs Robinson's approach to Church History is illustrated by his 1962 Columbia Alumni Lectures (repeated as the R. L. Robinson Lectures at Erskine Theological Seminary in 1967). The lectures were published as *The Reformation: A Rediscovery of Grace* and "affectionately" dedicated to the students and graduates of the seminary. Robinson's book was recognized by *Christianity Today* as one of the choice evangelical books of 1962.

Dr. Robinson was concerned that the true message of the Reformation was being lost among Protestant Christians. "Frequently, the theme for Reformation Sunday," he wrote, "is some subject that stands on the periphery rather than at the center of the movement." Robinson presented his lectures and his book with "the prayer that as we hear the witness of the Reformers, the Voice [of God] they heard may call us anew into the obedience of Christian faith."

Robinson began the book with seven affirmations summarizing the central themes of the Christian faith as set forth by the Reformers.

1. Grace. The Reformation was a revival of Augustinianism. Its cutting edge is formulated in the slogans of grace, thus, *sola gratia, solo Christo, sola fide, soli Deo Gloria, sola scriptura.*

2. God. The Reformation was a rediscovery of God, as He revealed Himself in His majesty and His holiness, in His mercy and His love, in His power and His acts.

3. The Gospel. "The Reformation was a deeper plunge into the meaning of the Gospel than even Augustine had made" (Schaff). It proclaimed Christ—not as insufficient—but as all-sufficient. For the Reformation is Jesus Christ clothed with His gospel.

4. Justification. The article of the Reformation was justification: "We have only one doctrine—*Christ is our righteousness*" (Bugenhagen).

5. Theology. The Reformation was a theological revival, and the Reformers witnessed to a biblical theology as the very life of the Church.

6. The Word. "The genius of the Reformation is best described as the rediscovery of the Holy Spirit as the dynamic presence of God in Jesus Christ under the veil of the preached Word" (H. A. Oberman).

7. The Church. The sociological principle of the Reformation was

the priesthood of all believers. Luther transferred concern from the Church Triumphant in Heaven and the Church Patient in Purgatory to the Church Militant here on earth, and made every Christian under God a king for himself, a priest for others.[1]

There are seven chapters in *The Reformation: A Rediscovery of Grace*: 1. The Slogans of Grace: The Heart of the Reformation; 2. The Significance of the Reformation: Luther Rediscovers God; 3. The Gospel of the Reformation: Christ All-Sufficient; 4. The Article of the Reformation: Justification; 5. The Theologian of the Reformation: John Calvin, Interpreter of God's Word; 6. The Instrument of the Reformation: The Preached Word; and 7. The Root and Fruit of the Reformation: The Evangelical Church. In these chapters, as in all William Childs Robinson's teaching, history is saturated with Bible and theology, and Bible and theology are illustrated and applied by history.

In these lectures, Dr. Robinson, as always, preached the gospel as he taught history and theology. He said:

> For the Reformers, God was speaking. God was making Himself their God. God was daily forgiving their sins. Thus did the Reformation advance. How can a sinner know that God is gracious to Him? Only on the authority of God's own Word. How can I be assured that God is truly reconciled to me, a guilty, hell-deserving sinner? Only because God tells me in His own Word that He has made peace by the blood of Christ's Cross. How can one be sure that his sins are forgiven? On the authority of the Word: "Son, be of good cheer, thy sins are forgiven thee." Can one be sure that only faith, faith alone—simply to Thy Cross I cling, naked come to Thee for dress, casting myself helpless and undone on the mercy of God, on the merit of Christ— is sufficient? Yes, sinner, you can, I can, be sure—for God graciously says so. God declares forgiveness in the proclamation of His Word and seals it in the fellowship of His people as they continue in the unity of Christ's body and true members of His church. We have put our trust in Jesus Christ that we may be justified by faith in Him, apart from the works of the law. Luther needed but one thing to live by: the assurance that God was gracious to him, the assurance which God gave him by His own Word. Calvin knew God's tender love toward us, for He has plainly uttered in

[1] WCR, *The Reformation: A Rediscovery of Grace* (Grand Rapids: William B. Eerdmans Publishing Company, 1962), ix-x.

His gospel that He will be both a Father and a Saviour unto us through the means of Jesus Christ.[1]

Dr. Robinson sought a Reformation vision for himself and all the church with these words of benediction:

May the Hand that wrought in Luther, the Hand that lifted Calvin, the Hand that used Knox to bring Scotland to Himself, and Wesley to save England from rationalism, act in His living power in your life and mine, in your ministry and mine, in the hearts and lives, in the faith and worship, of your people and of mine.[2]

[1] WCR, *The Reformation*, 126-27.
[2] WCR, *The Reformation*, 58.

18

5. THE CERTAINTIES OF THE GOSPEL

From the beginning of his career to the end, William Childs Robinson taught and defended the doctrines of Christian orthodoxy. In one of his earliest books, *The Certainties of the Gospel*, Robinson called for a recovery of certainty, which had become, he said, "the lost chord in modern Protestantism." He wrote:

> "Faith is a certainty," declared Patrick Hamilton, the man whose martyr flames lit the Reformation fires in Scotland. A glorious sense of certainty was characteristic of the Protestants of the Reformation. "God cannot be worshipped in doubt," cried Calvin and Cop as they publicly proclaimed the Protestant faith in France. To the end of his life Calvin insisted upon the necessity that "we be assured of our salvation in order to invoke God as our Father in full liberty."

Robinson deplored the loss of conviction in modern Protestantism and stated that "the Apostle [Paul] has placed a series of stepping stones to the goal of this lost certainty. At each of the focal points in the gospel Paul has erected not an 'I think,' not an 'I hope,' not an 'I wager'; but an 'I KNOW.'" Robinson stressed those "certain definite facts, certain things which God did for men, certain historical events with the meaning of those events ... 'Christ died for our sins according to the Scriptures; He was buried; He hath been raised on the third day according to the Scriptures.'" He urged his seminary students to major on these foundational truths:

> In simple faith, the faith of a child, I beg you to make the death and resurrection of Christ the ABCs of your Christian life. In all the depths of your devotion build with these stones. They were beautiful enough to shape that pure poem of the Middle Ages which we call Francis of Assisi. In all the flights of your eloquence hold fast these facts and

truths. They earned for John of Constantinople the title "Chrysostom, the golden-mouthed." In all the heights of your philosophy do not despise these mighty words. They made the theologies of Athanasius, of Augustine of Hippo, of Anselm, of Aquinas, of Luther, of Calvin, of Wesley, and of Spurgeon. Lay the foundation of your faith here; build with these tried and precious stones, and the gates of hell shall not prevail against you.[1]

In the chapters of the book Robinson laid out six certainties: "The Certainty that God is the Author of the Gospel"; "The Certainty of Jesus Christ, the Substance of the Gospel"; "The Certainty of the ABCs of the Gospel" [the death and resurrection of Christ]; "The Certainty of Grace, the Fundamental Characteristic of the Gospel"; The Certainty of Justification by Faith, the Gospel Way of Salvation"; and "The Certainty of God's Love and Care, the Comfort of the Gospel."

R. A. Finlayson wrote a review of *The Certainties of the Gospel* for the *Evangelical Review* in which he heartily commended "the volume to all who can appreciate a warm, fresh, and scholarly presentation of 'those things that are most surely believed among us.'" Finlayson noted especially Robinson's definition of sovereign grace as "the doctrine of the mastery or lordship of the Holy Spirit," and his impressive declaration that "wherever men have modified the sovereignty of divine grace, they have detracted from the sole glory of God and have robbed His people of that comfort and certainty of salvation which is properly theirs."[2]

Robinson followed *The Certainties of the Gospel* with *What is Christian Faith?*[3] He began with the words:

The question which an age ponders is a true index to the seriousness, or the levity, of that era and a valuable forecast of that which is to follow. Current American religious and philosophical thought is discussing the question, What do I think of God? Two centuries ago Jonathan Edwards made our intellectual leadership aware of a deeper question, What does God think of me?—and the Great Awakening followed.

[1] WCR, *The Certainties of the Gospel*, 9, 10, 58, 75.
[2] R. A. Finlayson, *The Evangelical Quarterly*, January 1938, 99-101. "The Meaning of Grace," from *The Certainties of the Gospel* (88-98) is Selected Writings 3.
[3] WCR, *What is Christian Faith?* The following quotations are from the "Introduction."

Modernism asks, How can I know that God is? Luther's spirit agonized with this other query, How can I know that God is gracious to me? Liberalism's quandary wrought agnosticism; Luther's question brought in the Reformation.

Robinson explained that by omission of the article "the" in the title of his book, he was directing attention to the nature of faith rather than to its content. In other places he had "sought to present and defend the mighty acts of God which constitute the gospel," he wrote, but this "study is primarily directed to defining the nature of the faith which relates us to the glorious gospel of the blessed God."

Dr. Robinson often dealt with these two questions: "What is Christian Faith?" and "What is *the* Christian faith?" He wrote an editorial in *The Southern Presbyterian Journal*—"What is the Essence of the Faith?"—in which he asked how a minister could deny the objectivity, the historicity, and the corporeality of Christ's resurrection and yet maintain that he held to "the essence of the faith." Such "idealism," wrote Robinson, turns God's revelation into the interior experience of the individual. The transcendence of God and the objective truthfulness of the Bible are gone, and Christian theology is dissolved in the general philosophy of religion. Robinson continued:

> The fundamental error of idealism is in not recognizing that man is a fallen and a guilty sinner. Idealism may be a good religion for sinless angels, but general truths can only spell the eternal doom of sinners such as we are. We need divine intervention—we need God to become man and do something—to do enough—to save us from the just punishment due for our sins. And thus the Christian religion must have not merely general truths, but definite events at its very heart and essence. We are saved by God's becoming man for us men and for our salvation, by Christ's dying for our sins according to the Scriptures, by His rising again for our justification, by His ascending to the right hand of the Father, by His intercession for us.[1]

In another article, Robinson asked, "What is left after theological liberals have rejected the essentials of the Christian faith?" He answered, "If what is left be labeled 'the essence of Christianity,' will

---

[1] WCR, *Presbyterian Journal,* June 15, 1946, 2.

not the word be used in the apothecary sense of *essence*—the faint odor left in the bottle when the liquid is all evaporated?"[1]

Foundational to a correct understanding of the Christian faith, Dr. Robinson insisted, are the great themes of the first two chapters of the Westminster Confession of Faith—"Of the Holy Scripture" and "Of God, and of the Holy Trinity."

The doctrine of the triune God is celebrated in Robinson's article "The Theocentric Theology Implicit in the name of the Trinity." He quoted the nineteenth-century Columbia Seminary professor John L. Girardeau, who wrote, "Everything has a tongue that proclaims the being of God, and the union of these tongues makes a course of unbroken and perfect harmony."[2]

In "God—Or Man's Idea of God?" Robinson asserted the Christian view of God against human ideas of "god."

> When we use the word God in the Christian sense we are speaking of the Living One who made the heavens and the earth and all things therein, who upholds all things by the word of His power, who rules in the armies of heaven and among men, who bowed the heavens and came down in Christ for us men and our salvation, who translated us from the kingdom of darkness into the kingdom of the Son of His love by the power of the Holy Spirit. He is the high and lofty One that inhabiteth eternity, whose Name is holy. He is glorious in holiness, fearful in praises, doing wonders. His Name is Jehovah, gracious and merciful, slow to anger and plenteous in lovingkindness and truth, forgiving iniquity and transgressions and sin, but who will by no means clear the guilty. God is a Spirit. God is light and in Him there is not one bit of darkness. God is love. He is a just God at the same time as He is a Saviour. He commendeth His love for us in that while we were yet sinners Christ died for us. And we are justified freely by His grace through the redemption that is in Christ Jesus, whom God set forth a propitiation to declare His righteousness or justice in the passing over of sins. We worship Him in the Name of the Father, and of the Son, and of the Holy Ghost.[3]

In a short article, "The Trinity: God in Action," Robinson argued that "God is the living God, and as such He may be expected to

[1] WCR, *Presbyterian Journal,* September 16, 1946, 2.
[2] WCR, *The Evangelical Quarterly,* July 14, 1934, 225-26.
[3] WCR, *Presbyterian Journal,* November 15, 1946, 4.

reveal Himself primarily in action, not formula. This He has done in the incarnation of God the Son and in the outpouring of God the Holy Spirit."[1] This self-revelation of God is set forth in the Word of God, the Bible.

The inspiration and authority of the Bible were beginning to be questioned in the South (long after it was in the North and in Europe) during Robinson's years as a seminary professor. In 1944 Robinson wrote the article "Full Inspiration" in the *Christian Observer*, in which he sought to state "the truth, the substantial truth, the simple truth, the trustworthiness of the Word." He showed how in the hands of careful scholars such as A. A. Hodge, B. B. Warfield, and W. M. McPheeters, "inspiration becomes the sovereignty of God carried to a high degree." They used the word "verbal" to show that God's supervision did not stop with the thought but reached to the expression of that thought in the very words of Scripture. Furthermore, the Westminster Confession implies the same truth when it speaks of the Holy Scriptures as "the Word of God written." The Bible itself teaches verbal inspiration, stated Robinson, when "our Lord used a word of the Psalmist dropped almost incidentally for an argument with the Jews (John 10:34-36)," and when the Apostle Paul spoke of combining spiritual thoughts with spiritual words (1 Corinthians 2:13).

Robinson explained that the great Dutch Calvinists, Kuyper and Bavinck, used the expression "absolute inspiration." And a Scottish writer defined inspiration as, "Divine authorship by means of human authorship." Divine authorship by means of human authorship throws the emphasis on God and treats the Bible as His work or product, which is the point of view of 2 Peter 1:21. Dabney stated his view of inspiration in this way: "The sacred Scriptures possess plenary inspiration, and are infallible truth in every word ... To the dictates of these Scriptures, interpreted according to the fair and customary sense of human language, all philosophy, all speculations and all inferences must implicitly bend, and ... the Holy Spirit, to be obtained by constant prayer and holy living, is the only sufficient interpreter of God's Word."

[1] WCR, *Presbyterian Journal*, August 6, 1975, 9. See Selected Writings 4.

Robinson ended the article "Full Inspiration" by stating that to treat any part of the Bible

> as fraudulent is to make the Divine Author party to the fraud and so to destroy the only foundation we have for truth. Whether one uses the adjective "plenary" or "verbal" or "absolute" or "authoritative," let us agree with our Confession: The authority of the Holy Scripture, for which it ought to be believed and obeyed, dependeth not upon the testimony of any man or church, but wholly upon God—who is truth itself—the Author thereof.[1]

Increasingly at Columbia Seminary, in the Southern Presbyterian Church, and throughout American Christianity, the battle was for the deity of Christ, for the authority and inerrancy of Scripture, and for the biblical message of salvation by faith alone. In this time of growing uncertainty Dr. Robinson dedicated himself to teaching, preaching, and writing about the certainties of the gospel.

---

[1] WCR, *Christian Observer,* September 20, 1944, 6.

6. THE DOCTRINE OF THE CHURCH

D r. Robinson contributed a chapter on "The Nature of the Church" to the volume *Christian Faith and Modern Theology*.[1] He discussed the meaning of the church and her history, ministry, and mission. "The Church is the spiritual family of God," he wrote, "the Christian fellowship created by the Holy Spirit through the testimony to the mighty acts of God in Christ Jesus. Wherever the Holy Spirit unites worshiping souls to Christ and to each other, there is found the mystery of the Church." Robinson summed up his treatment of the history of the church by stating:

> Throughout the history of the church the reciprocal interaction of this inward power and outward direction has been essential to a healthy church life. Where the inward work of the Spirit has been forgotten, the external forms have yielded to formalism, scholasticism, rationalism, carnal security, and a timeless metaphysics. Where the Word, the sacraments, and ministration have been neglected and only the inner aspect has been magnified, the church has drifted toward unbalanced subjectivism, unregulated mysticism, and even to fanaticism.

"The one essential ministry of the church," Robinson affirmed, "is the ministry of her Lord and Saviour Jesus Christ."

> By Christ's heavenly ministration, all of God's people have access to the throne of grace ... God uses this priesthood of all believers to choose those whom He has equipped and called to be the ministers of the churches. Likewise each officer and member is to receive grace from the Head of the Church and use it for the communion of the saints, that the body may grow up into all things in Christ.

[1] Carl F. H. Henry, ed., *Christian Faith and Modern Theology* (New York: Channel Press, 1964), 389-99.

'PLEADING FOR A REFORMATION VISION'

To the church God has given the Scripture, which contains what Christians believe and have expressed in creedal statements. In a short article for the *Christian Observer* Dr. Robinson discussed the Apostles' Creed.[1] "As the Holy Scriptures was the rule of faith or canon of truth in the broad compass," he wrote, "so the creed became the same rule in its compressed form ... The Apostles' Creed preserved the distinctive elements of the Christian faith in these early centuries [of church history], namely, the creation of heaven and of earth, the incarnation and death of Christ, and the resurrection of the body (or flesh). It was these distinctive doctrines that kept Christianity from decomposing into Platonism, and made it a definitely theocentric faith."

Robinson continued:

> The use of the Apostles' Creed in our worship gives people a chance to express their Christian faith. It serves to keep the sermon and each part of the service within the ambit of the Christian point of view and to make the Christian truth the point of reference.
>
> While the creed was composed long before the Reformation, it is gloriously Protestant in throwing all the emphasis upon what God did for us. Thus it implicitly teaches justification by faith alone. It presents God the Father as first in creation, God the Son as first in redemption, God the Holy Spirit as first in regeneration. Its stress falls not on the teaching or the example of Christ, but it locates the glory of our redemption in His death and His resurrection. There is first a fourfold beat on His humiliation, then a like mighty emphasis on His victory. It keeps in close compass the mighty works of Christ in the past, the present, and the future.

Robinson concluded with the exhortation: "Let us never say we are not saved by creeds but by Christ. Of course Christ saves us. But in the creeds we gloriously confess the Christ who saves us. The Apostles' Creed is richer in Christ than are most of our sermons, prayers, or hymns."

Dr. Robinson was pleased that the use of the Apostles' Creed was increasing in Southern Presbyterian churches, but believed that "this great affirmation" was being blunted by the way in which it was often introduced. He wrote, "We are called to confess our faith, or to

---

[1] WCR, *Christian Observer*, July 26, 1944, 5.

unite in our confession of faith. Thus the primary attention is turned toward us and from God." He suggested that we use a different introduction, such as, "Let us confess our great and gracious God; or let us confess the mighty God in His gracious acts for our salvation; or let us confess God who in His mercy and His might has acted to save us in Christ."[1]

Robinson vigorously defended the statements of the Apostles' Creed, believing that they faithfully summarized biblical truth. Two assertions of the creed increasingly came under attack during his lifetime—"born of the Virgin Mary" and "the third day he rose again from the dead."

Robinson insisted on the truth and the necessity of the doctrine of the virgin birth of Christ:

> The virgin birth is the Church's God-given safeguard for the essential fact of the incarnation. When the safeguard is dropped, men will not long maintain that Jesus Christ is God manifest in the flesh ... "Brother Bryan of Birmingham" used to say that Jesus Christ was the only person who ever lived before he was born. The denial of the virgin birth logically leads to the denial of Christ's eternity, of His pre-existence, of His divine person and makes Him only a temporal, human person in whom God did something ... We shall all give account to the Head of the Church for the witness we bear or fail to bear to Him, to His eternal deity, to His virgin birth, to His actual objective resurrection and to His cleansing blood.[2]

Robinson took up this topic again in an article in the *Evangelical Quarterly* and another in *Christianity Today*. He stated that "the birth accounts in the first and third Gospels articulate the Spirit-wrought faith always in the heart of the primitive community, which comes to expression also in sacramental worship and in sundry creedal statements." Matthew and Luke give, Robinson wrote, "two simple dignified accounts of the virgin birth of Jesus. Their naturalness, delicacy and sobriety indicate their historic reality. The Matthaean one is evidently based on Joseph's testimony and cites Isaiah 7:14; the Lukan rests on Mary's witness and 'the throne of David' (in *Luke* 1:32) and echoes Isaiah 9:6-7. These things which Mary treasured in her

---

[1] WCR, *Christian Observer*, May 31, 1961, 7.
[2] WCR, *Christian Observer*, September 5, 1945, 6.

heart are here transmitted to us." Robinson dealt with the fact that John and Paul, "the chief New Testament expounders of the faith," do not mention the virgin birth. He argued that "what is explicit in Matthew and Luke is implicit in Paul and John." In Paul there is the argument from silence, Robinson claimed. Paul writes four times of the birth of Jesus "including the assertion that God's own Son was born, made of a human mother; but four times Paul avoids asserting the birth of Jesus by means of a human begetting ... As he had no divine mother, so also he had no human father." In John's Gospel Robinson finds the argument from analogy. As Jesus was conceived by the Holy Spirit and born of the virgin Mary, "so Christians are born from above, not of a human father but of the Spirit, as is set forth in John 3:5." Robinson concluded:

> When God called Mary to be the mother of His Son, He wrought the conception in her by the power of the Holy Ghost and so filled her with the grace of the Spirit that she yielded herself to His Word as the bondmaid of the Lord. In turn Joseph listened to the admonition of the angel of the Lord that the child conceived in Mary was of the Holy Spirit. Likewise ... Elizabeth, filled with the Holy Spirit, sang the *Benedicta*, Zacharias the *Benedictus*, and Simeon the *Nunc dimittis.* And the angels sounded the *Gloria in excelsis* and
>
> > ... the happy morn
> > Wherein the Son of Heaven's eternal King,
> > Of wedded Maid and Virgin Mother born,
> > Our great redemption from above did bring.
>
> May the Lord who confronted Mary and Joseph ... grant to His present Church the grace of humility that we may not use our critical historical science to master God's intervention in the birth of Jesus. May the risen Lord in the power of His Spirit so encounter us that in this matter also our hearts may be mastered by the obedience of faith and our minds brought into captivity to Christ.[1]

"The Reformed Doctrine of the Bodily Resurrection of Christ" was an address given by Dr. Robinson on August 15, 1956.[2] He began

[1] WCR, "A Re-Study of the Virgin Birth of Christ," *Evangelical Quarterly,* October-December 1965, 198-211; and "The Virgin Birth—A Broader Base," *Christianity Today,* December 8, 1972, 6-8.
[2] WCR, *Presbyterian Journal,* September 26, 1956, 5-10. A fuller presentation

by stressing the necessity of a renewed emphasis upon Christ's bodily resurrection. "In Latin Christianity," he wrote,

> the profusion of crucifixes focuses the eye upon the crucified, dead Jesus, leaving to the evangelical church a special responsibility for proclaiming the risen living Lord. In American Protestantism the weight of old liberalism still swings many away from the bodily "physical" resurrection of Christ witnessed in the New Testament to … a myth whose meaning is real only in faith. The pessimism resulting from inadequate presentations can be lifted only by the proclamation of the bodily resurrection of Jesus Christ as a factual occurrence, an act of God's self-disclosure in truly divine dimensions.
>
> By the resurrection of the Lord Jesus as the summation of His whole ministry, God brought the blessings which Israel looked for only in the future into the present. Since Christ died for our sins and rose for our justification, in Him we have today the forgiveness of sins and the peace which passes human understanding. Since the risen Christ breathed upon His disciples and poured upon them at Pentecost His Holy Spirit, therefore, God's Spirit bears witness with our spirits that we are the children of God. Since God raised up Jesus our Lord from the dead, He has raised us from the death of sin to the newness of life with Christ, and His resurrection is the measure of the exceeding greatness of God's power to work in believers. As our faith receives the mighty work of God in the resurrection of Christ, we share in the Christian hope of the new heaven and a new earth. We believe in the Almighty who makes the dead alive and creates the things that are from nothing. The God who raised Jesus the Lord from the dead is able to save and keep and raise those who are Christ's. Each of these blessings comes from the nail-pierced hands of the risen Redeemer. The whole New Testament gospel is inseparably one in the proclamation of the Risen One as the crucified. The present exalted one is expressly the crucified, the sympathizing High Priest, the Lamb in the midst of the throne.

Robinson ended his long discourse with the words:

> May I say this in closing? I have here before me a full discussion of Paul's treatment in 1 Corinthians 15, but there is not time to present it. Paul does not teach that our resurrection will not be physical. There is a translation to that effect in the RSV, but it is an erroneous rendering

---

of this topic appeared in April 1957 in *Theologische Zeitschrift*, the journal of the theological faculty of the University of Basel.

of the Greek. Paul says that our present body is psychical, not physical as the RSV gives. The future body will be spiritual, but not in the sense that it is non-physical. This body is psychical, that is, its life-principle is soul or psychology. The resurrection body will be spiritual in the sense that it will be raised by the Holy Spirit and of it the Spirit will be the life principle.

Neither does Paul say that the future body will not be flesh and blood, as a hasty reading of 1 Corinthians 15:50 may signify. "Flesh and blood" is the subject of that sentence, not the predicate. And "flesh and blood" does not mean the physical or material side of man as against his intellectual or spiritual side. In the Bible it means the whole man, human nature, as against God and His Spirit. This fallen human nature cannot inherit eternal life. It must be changed by the Spirit from its enmity against God and its corruption. Paul is talking Christian salvation in 1 Corinthians 15; not Hellenistic dualism. When by God's grace through Jesus Christ the Spirit changes our corrupt human nature and takes away our opposition to God, we shall live with God in our spiritual bodies in a new heaven and a new earth. Paul believed in the bodily resurrection of Christ and of His people. He said, "He shall come and change our vile bodies and make them like unto His glorious body."

The resurrection is God's "yes" to life, God's declaration that not death but life is the last word. The resurrection of Christ's body is God's "yes" to the body. Jesus Christ was crucified publicly as a malefactor. That is not God's last public word about Christ. He shall come in His glory—publicly. As the resurrection reveals God's "yes" to the body and "yes" to life, so the resurrection reveals God. Only God can raise the dead. Those that believe in the resurrection of the body have a God-centered faith and a God-centered hope.

Robinson also defended the literal second coming of Christ against those who were insisting that the Enlightenment science of Copernicus and others made such a view impossible. In an editorial in *The Southern Presbyterian Journal* he wrote:

It is as well to note that many of those who reject the personal second coming of Christ on the ground that it implies a pre-Copernican view of heaven, for the same reason reject the ascension of Christ. And when one denies that Christ ascended to the Father, there seems little reason for thinking that He will come again and receive us unto Himself and place us in the many mansions of the Father's house.[1]

[1] WCR, *Presbyterian Journal,* September 16, 1946, 2.

In his classes, writings, and sermons, Dr. Robinson upheld the orthodox doctrine of the full deity and humanity of Christ. In the opening address to the students of Columbia Seminary in the fall of 1943, Robinson reviewed briefly the work of the early church councils:

The nature of the unchanging Christ is revealed in the Christian Scriptures. From this holy deposit of truth the ancient church, through four centuries of careful work, formulated her God-given faith. The first Ecumenical Council declared that Christ is eternal God, the second that He is also complete man, the third that He is one person, the fourth that this one person is in two natures, the fifth that the person is divine and that the human nature became personal in union with the eternal Word, the sixth that in Christ there are two wills or willings. In this long process one group magnified one set of facts, another a different emphasis until each aspect had found its true niche and the whole picture was set so simply that even childhood can apprehend it. Christ "being the eternal Son of God, became man, and so was and continueth to be, God and man, in two distinct natures and one person, forever." "Christ, the Son of God, became man by taking to Himself a true body and a reasonable soul, being conceived by the power of the Holy Ghost, in the womb of the Virgin Mary, and born of her, yet without sin."[1]

Five of Dr. Robinson's published books treat Christology—*Our Lord, An Affirmation of the Deity of Christ; The Word of the Cross; Christ—The Bread of Life; Christ—The Hope of Glory;* and *Who Say Ye That I Am?* The last of these contained six chapters written by Robinson's Columbia Seminary students in competition for the Robert A. Dunn Award. Dunn was a Christian businessman of Charlotte, North Carolina, whose life's goal was "that the gospel of our Lord Jesus Christ be taught and preached in its divine revelation and power." Dr. Robinson wrote an introductory chapter to the book and "voiced his gratitude that 'I and the children God has given me' unite in this testimony to the glory and the grace of our great God and Saviour, Jesus Christ."[2] Christology, it has been said, is the measure of any theology. Dr. Robinson's attention to this essential pillar of the

[1] WCR, *Presbyterian Journal,* November 1943, 5.
[2] WCR, *Who Say Ye That I Am? Six Theses on the Deity of Christ* (Grand Rapids: Wm. B. Eerdmans Publishing Company, 1949).

Christian faith is indicative of his understanding of its importance, especially in a time when it was being undermined in various ways.

On the first page of *Our Lord, An Affirmation of the Deity of Christ,* Robinson quoted words from Dostoevsky's *The Possessed:* "The most pressing question in the problem of faith is whether a man, as a civilized being, as a European, can believe at all, believe, that is, in the divinity of the Son of God, Jesus Christ, for therein rests, strictly speaking, the whole faith."

Robinson wrote: "No one who is aware of the trends in American Christianity can doubt that this is an appropriate time to state one's faith in our Lord Jesus Christ and to set forth the reasons for and the implications of that faith." He credited B. B. Warfield's *The Lord of Glory*—which he had studied in the Princeton professor's classroom—with shaping and strengthening his own understanding of the deity of Christ.[1]

In *Our Lord: An Affirmation of the Deity of Christ,* Dr. Robinson moved from treatment of the Bible's and the Christian church's affirmation of the deity of Christ to equally impressive chapters on the results of such a faith. If Christ is God, then we must worship Him.[2]

Dr. Robinson carefully followed the theological developments of his time that threatened the orthodox view of Christ. He reviewed the new *Revised Standard Version of the New Testament* when it appeared in 1946. This is a very worthwhile translation, he wrote, "made in the light of fresh studies in the Greek and Aramaic and the background out of which the New Testament was written"; and he praised it for its "rich command of ... English." He pointed out, however, that the translators "have taken liberties with the text in accord with their premise that they are translating ideas rather than words." "Sometimes these are their own ideas" and not the ideas of the writers of the New Testament. Robinson was especially concerned with "the lowered Christology" of the new translation and noted numerous passages where it appeared. *"The Revised Standard Version of the New Testament* is a good book," he wrote, but "it would be a better book

---

[1] WCR, *Our Lord, An Affirmation of the Deity of Christ.*
[2] Selected Writings 5, "The Blessings of Worshiping Jesus" is from *Our Lord: An Affirmation of the Deity of Christ,* 146-52.

if it had rendered more closely the Greek New Testament and spoken more definitively from faith to faith."[1]

Robinson reviewed the *Westminster Study Edition of the Holy Bible*, published by the Board of Christian Education of the Presbyterian Church in the United States of America and charged that it used "one method after another to avoid giving Christ the term 'God.'" "We are impressed by the Christological declension of this Westminster Edition of the Bible," Robinson wrote,

> as compared with the Christology of Warfield's *The Lord of Glory* and *Christology and Criticism* and that of Machen's *God Transcendent*. The last named said: "There is no such thing as almost God ... The next thing less is infinitely less." And we are also impressed by the fact that current Continental scholarship ... gives more support to the Christological positions of Warfield and of Machen than to those of this Presbyterian Bible that boasts of its modern knowledge. Is it just possible that Warfield and Machen are not as much out of date as some would like to make them?[2]

In "Christ: True God and True Man or: Is Presbyterianism to Surrender the Faith Formulated at Chalcedon?" Robinson wrote that the faith of the church set forth in the Chalcedonian Definition resulted from "three centuries of careful work during which every other statement was sifted and its weaknesses revealed. This has all the marks of survival value. It does justice to all the facts of Biblical revelation."[3]

---

[1] WCR, *Presbyterian Journal,* October 1, 1946, 6-7.
[2] WCR, *Presbyterian Journal,* August 15, 1949, 3.
[3] WCR, *Presbyterian Journal,* October 1, 1949, 8.

7. THE WORD OF THE CROSS

Dr. Robinson's stature as an evangelical Christian scholar was recognized by an invitation to deliver the Free Church Lectures in Edinburgh in 1938. Robinson was delighted to be in Scotland. He said:

> One who comes from a younger country, culture and Church, particularly one who comes from one of the daughter churches of Scottish Presbyterianism to the mother city of Edinburgh, is embarrassed by the greater age, prestige and position of the host city. And the recollection of the scholarship, eloquence, and piety with which the Gospel has been proclaimed in the Presbyterian churches and colleges of Scotland heightens the sense of one's inadequacy. In this hallowed place, the privilege of hearing lectures is more appropriate than that of delivering them.

Robinson was encouraged, however, by remembering that he was there in Scotland "not as an initiator, but as a witness to a Gospel that is prior in time, higher in source, and holier in content than any human prestige." "And in presenting the Word of the Cross," Robinson said,

> one remembers that it was not a man of age, but a lad burned at the stake ere he became twenty-five, who established in Scotland personal "assurance of emancipation and peace through living faith in the atonement of Christ." As one who has been blessed by the expositions of the gospel set forth by that noble young martyr and his Scottish successors, the lecturer counts it a privilege and an honour to bring back to his land another testimony to the Evangel for which Patrick Hamilton was burned four hundred and ten years ago.

Speaking later of his visit to Scotland Robinson said,

> I was a guest in the very gracious home of Principal John Macleod.

There I was privileged to share in the devout life and worship of the Free Church, which goes back to Chalmers and the revival fires kindled in his day. Later we were privileged to have Dr. Macleod and one of his daughters as our guests for lectures at Columbia Theological Seminary, and in our home we invited him to lead our worship after his Free Church custom—something that was a blessing to us.[1]

Robinson remembered that Principal Macleod told him of the radiant faith of his wife. Yet, said Robinson in a sermon, when "this good Scottish woman came to die she spoke of herself as sinful all through, waiting the touch of the Great Physician." The preacher added: "Blessed be God, the same precious Saviour who convicts us of sin, says, 'Son, Daughter, be of good cheer, thy sins are forgiven thee.'"[2] When John Macleod's *Scottish Theology in Relation to Church History since the Reformation* was published in 1943, Robinson wrote that "Dr. Macleod is writing as a lover who has clothed the story of Scottish theology in the vestments of romance and in the majesty of truth."[3]

Robinson began his Free Church lectures by asserting that "the cross is not a compromise, but a substitution; not a cancellation, but a satisfaction; not a wiping off, but a wiping out in blood and agony and death."[4] He then explored the centuries and the continents to capture apt illustrations and quotations in prose and poetry. His lectures were filled not only with references to the church fathers, medieval theologians, sixteenth-century Reformers, Puritans and Scottish Presbyterians, but his hearers also heard mention of Samuel Lapsley, the Southern Presbyterian missionary to Africa, and quotations from Sidney Lanier, the Georgia poet, as well as references to Southern churchmen. "In my own communion," Dr. Robinson said, "Dabney, Thornwell, Plumer, Palmer, Stuart Robinson, Strickler, and Baker have ploughed the cross deep into our hearts."[5]

Principal John Macleod said that Robinson's lectures "set forth

---

[1] [Thomas Ellis], "A Biographical Tribute to William Childs Robinson from a Former Student," *The Banner of Truth* 182 (November 1978), 5.

[2] WCR, *Presbyterian Journal*, August 1942, 5.

[3] WCR, *Westminster Theological Journal*, November 1944, 48.

[4] WCR, *The Word of the Cross*, 2.

[5] WCR, *The Word of the Cross*, preface, 23. This book was translated and published in Korean.

faithfully the truth of the apostolic message" and strike "a clear Gospel note … of that teaching which is the heart's core of the good news from God."[1]

"The word of the cross"—that Christ is our righteousness and we are justified by his death—was the major theme of Robinson's ministry. In 1925, the year before he was called to teach at Columbia Seminary, he wrote an article defending the continuing importance of the Reformation doctrine of justification by faith alone for modern Christianity.[2] He described "the heart of the Reformed faith" as "the single clear statement that Christ with His precious blood has fully satisfied for our sins and that His righteousness is imputed to us and received by faith alone."[3] Robinson quoted William S. Plumer, pastor of the First Presbyterian Church of Richmond and later professor at Columbia Seminary: "Justification by Christ's imputed righteousness is the centre arch of that bridge by which we pass out of time into a blessed eternity."[4]

In his last book, *The Reformation: A Rediscovery of Grace,* he traced the "cardinal place" of justification from the Reformation to his own Southern Presbyterian Church.

> The Protestant doctrine of justification is ably set forth in the Thirty-nine Articles, in a Sermon of Salvation in the Homilies of 1562, in Hooker's work on justification in 1585, as well as in the Westminster Confession and Catechisms. According to Hooker, "Christ has merited righteousness for as many as are found in Him. And in Him God finds us if we be believers: for by believing we are incorporated into Christ." Even the man who is full of sin, "being found in Christ through faith and having his sin in hatred through repentance, him God beholds with a gracious eye and accepts him in Jesus Christ as perfectly righteous as if he had fulfilled all that is commanded in the holy law of God." For John Owen of Oxford, justification gave the first occasion to the whole work of the Reformation. According to *Grace Abounding for the Chief of Sinners,* John Bunyan found peace for

---

[1] "The Cross in Church History" and "The Lamb of God Enthroned" are Selected Writings 6 and 7.
[2] WCR, *The Presbyterian,* 12 February 1925, 6-7, 30. This article appears in Selected Writings 8.
[3] WCR, *Christianity Today,* February 27, 1961, 43.
[4] WCR, *Presbyterian Journal,* October 18, 1961, 6.

his troubled heart in a vision of Christ as our righteousness at God's right hand. E. Fisher wrote *The Marrow of Modern Divinity* in about the middle of the seventeenth century, and Thomas Boston with the Erskines defended it in Scotland in the next century. These Marrow Men insisted on the free offer of the gracious Gospel of the imputation of the righteousness of Christ to needy sinners, against the tenet that the sinner must first prepare himself by forsaking his sin before coming to Christ. For Robert Traill, faith justifies as a mere instrument receiving the imputed righteousness of Christ. Thomas Adam taught the evangelicals to see "sin and Christ, ill desert and no condemnation" at one and the same time.

In England the evangelical emphasis was continued in John Wesley's *The Lord Our Righteousness,* by Charles Simeon of Cambridge and by Charles Spurgeon of London; in Scotland by William Cunningham in *The Reformers and the Theology of the Reformation,* by James Buchanan in *The Doctrine of Justification,* and by Alexander Whyte in *A Commentary on the Shorter Catechism.*

In America, Jonathan Edwards's sermons on justification in 1734 led to the Great Awakening, which was carried forward by George Whitefield. John Witherspoon and Archibald Alexander brought the torch to Princeton with their writings on justification. The light was lifted in Charles Hodge's *Systematic Theology* and in the works of his two sons and grandson, and by B. B. Warfield.

At Columbia Theological Seminary, Thomas Goulding regarded the doctrine of justification as the epitome of the Christian system and James H. Thornwell made it the architectonic principle of all theology. It occupies large space in Wm. S. Plumer's *The Grace of Christ,* in John L. Girardeau's *Calvinism and Evangelical Arminianism,* in Thornton Whaling's *Questions on Theology,* in J. B. Green's *Harmony of the Westminster Standards,* as it does in this series of lectures. R. L. Dabney of Union Theological Seminary (Richmond, Va.) delivered his final addresses at Columbia on the theme "Christ Our Substitute and Sacrifice for Imputed Guilt." That this note is typical of the great institution with which Dabney's name is indissolubly connected is seen in the excellent words to be cited later from Thomas Cary Johnson's *John Calvin and the Genevan Reformation;* while for R. A. Webb (Presbyterian Seminary, Louisville, Ky.) "there is no more important doctrine, no more distinguished blessing, in all the Christian system than justification."[1]

[1] WCR, *The Reformation,* 82-83.

In a series of short articles in *The Presbyterian Journal* during October 1975 Robinson wrote on "Calvin on Justification," "Bunyan on Justification," and "Wesley on Justification." He noted that Calvin, "the second patriarch of the Reformation, was always conscious of being heir to Luther." "All the merit is in Christ, or, as Calvin put it, 'The name of Christ excludes all merit' in ourselves." "Perhaps the most moving scene in *Pilgrim's Progress* occurs," Robinson wrote, "as Pilgrim comes up to the cross. The burden of his sin falls from his back and tumbles into the emptied sepulcher while he sings, 'Blest cross! Blest sepulcher! Blest rather be the Man that there was put to shame for me.'" Robinson wrote that John Wesley, in his sermon "The Lord Our Righteousness," agreed with Calvin on the doctrine of justification when he said that "the righteousness of Christ, both His active and passive righteousness, is the meritorious cause of our justification, and has procured for us at God's right hand, that upon our believing, we should be accounted righteous by Him."[1]

Not long before he died Robinson wrote:

> In our Westminster Standards the eyes of faith are focused upon Christ offering Himself a sacrifice to satisfy divine justice and to reconcile us to God. They refer to His making satisfaction perhaps seven times, about the same number of references as found in the Heidelberg Catechism of 1563. In that catechism the term sometimes translates the German *genug tun*, to do enough, which is exactly what satisfy means. Jesus Christ did enough, bore enough, suffered enough, obeyed enough to save me from the wrath of God.[2]

For Dr. Robinson, "the righteousness of Christ is never something merely legal, but is Christ's personal presence in the believer through faith and by the Holy Spirit."[3] Robinson was always careful to make the connection between doctrine and life, between what we believe and how we live. Doctrine to him was the most practical thing in the world. He wrote about how John Calvin offered his wife, Idelette de Bure, "doctrine and prayer" when she lay dying. "No, this

---

[1] WCR, *Presbyterian Journal*, October 15, 1975, 13; October 22, 1975, 10; and October 29, 1975, 10.
[2] WCR, "How to Hold Our Theological Heritage," unpublished sermon, Historical Center of the Presbyterian Church in America, St. Louis, Missouri.
[3] WCR, *Westminster Theological Journal*, May 1955, 213.

does not mean that he was heartless. She was going into eternity and he pillowed her dying head on the precious promises of God—doctrine—and prayed for the Holy Spirit to illumine these promises with the dying grace He gives."[1]

Robinson wrote a summary of a pamphlet by John Witherspoon in which Witherspoon outlined the connection between the doctrine of justification by the imputed righteousness of Christ and holiness of life. The Reformation doctrine of justification by the imputed righteousness of Christ was attacked on the grounds that it loosened the obligations to practice Christian living. Dr. Witherspoon replied, "On the contrary, the belief and acceptance of justification by the grace of God through the imputed righteousness of Christ makes men greater lovers of purity and holiness and fills them with a greater abhorrence of sin."[2]

---

[1] WCR, *Christian Observer*, January 9, 1935, 8.
[2] WCR, *Presbyterian Journal*, September 22, 1976. See Selected Writings 9.

8. ROBINSON AND BARTH

William Childs Robinson spent the summer session of 1938 as a student under Karl Barth at the University of Basel. During the several seminars, "open-evenings," and private interviews in which he participated, Robinson came to appreciate certain features of Barth's theology, but found himself opposed to others. Prior to interviewing Professor Barth, Robinson drew up a series of questions, in some cases with answers or partial answers from Barth's lectures, conversations, and recent writings, and gave them to Barth on a Wednesday with the understanding that either questions or answers, or both, might be modified in any way that he suggested. The interview was conducted on the following Saturday and Professor Barth gave his approval for its publication in America. Robinson summed up his evaluation of Barth's theology:

> In estimating a theologian one may consider his position, direction, and attitude. As indicated below, the interviewer holds a somewhat different position from Professor Barth. However, he rejoices in Barth's movement in the Reformed direction; and even with reference to some doctrines in which he does not regard Barth's present position as satisfactorily settled, such as sanctification and inspiration, notes that Barth has projected a further study in sanctification as a course for the ensuing semester, and that he finds verbal inspiration in 1 Corinthians 2:13, while his colleague, Pfarrer W. Vischer, speaks of the Holy Spirit as the hidden author of Holy Scripture. Barth's attitude toward the church and her doctrines is indicated by the title which he has chosen for his volumes on theology—*Kirchliche Dogmatik*.
>
> Barth's approach to, and consequently his formulation of, theology is different from our classical Calvinism. One ought neither to obscure the distinctions between the two, nor to become so absorbed in these variations as to overlook the great testimonies in which both concur.

For example, our approach has stressed the beginning; his, the end; both affirm that God is the Alpha and the Omega. We take more the viewpoint of God, the Creator; he, more that of God, the Redeemer; we both worship the Triune God. We are more historical; he, more eschatological; in this day of battle we agree in the Christian Confession—the Apostles' Creed. We preach the Law and the Gospel; he, the Gospel and the Law; we both proclaim justification by faith alone without abrogating either the Law or the Gospel. Our Biblicism has issued from a higher doctrine of inspiration; his, from a deeper sense of the sufficiency—yea, exclusiveness for us—of the revelation attested in Holy Scripture; we both insist that Christian preaching is the church's faithful exposition of Scripture. Our concern is more to maintain the Biblical faith against destructive criticism; his more to purge it from philosophical adulteration; we both testify to the Lord Jesus Christ as the theme of the Bible and look to Him to own that testimony by the power of the Holy Spirit. We hold that the Bible is the Word of God; he, that by the free grace of God, the Bible as expounded in the Church becomes the Word of God; both that by His Word and Spirit Christ reveals to us the will of God for our salvation. We have given human reason wider scope; he, perhaps more intensive exercise; both agree that God's thoughts are higher than our thoughts, and that our reason must be brought into captivity to the obedience of Christ.

For the maintenance of His truth the Lord Jesus Christ is dependent neither upon the one nor upon the other of us. "All flesh is as grass … but the word of the Lord abideth forever." And yet by His grace He raises up and uses witnesses to Himself who often differ greatly one from another. One remembers that Athanasius welcomed the Neo-Orthodox even when they did not agree with him in every particular, *e.g.,* the use of hypostasis. And one notices that the European Calvinistic Congresses are graced by some of Barth's closest associates—Peter Barth, G. T. Thompson, W. Vischer. The way in which the Confessional Church of Germany—of which Barth is no insignificant factor—has lifted the Christian Symbol has strengthened the faith of many. It is a stimulus to observe how the influence of Barth has turned the preaching of many back to the exposition of God's Word and the proclamation of the gospel of the apostles and Reformers; and an inspiration to note the joy Barth shows in the unfolding of Holy Scripture, particularly as it sets forth the Risen Christ and the Christian hope.[1]

[1] *Bulletin: Columbia Theological Seminary,* November 1938, 8.

Robinson, like other evangelical Christians, rejoiced in the way Barth demolished the old liberalism that had reigned for a generation or more among scholars. Ten years before Robinson's summer at Basel, J. Gresham Machen found in much of Barth's theology what sounded like "a simple return to evangelical Christianity."[1] John Macleod helped to articulate the response of traditional Reformed theology to neo-orthodoxy as one of "mingled hope and fear."[2]

For several years Robinson taught a course on the theology of Barth at Columbia Seminary. Paul Settle, who studied at the seminary from 1956 to 1959, remarks that Dr. Robinson was "truly a Barthian scholar who, while rejecting Barth's obvious errors, appreciated him for his attempts to retain some commitment to the Scriptures as the Word of God and to Christ Jesus as the Savior of His people." Robinson agreed with a European scholar who said that even "the later Barth is still too much infected with Plato and Kierkegaard" in not taking the events of the Bible history seriously enough.[3]

Robinson's quotations of liberal and neo-orthodox writers (sometimes positively, often negatively) in his theological and biblical writings do not suggest an acceptance of those writers' views. As a conscientious seminary professor, Robinson kept up with the latest European and British scholarship, but used it carefully, always subjecting it to biblical scrutiny and theological orthodoxy. Like John Murray, Robinson did "not refuse any of the parcels of enlightenment on many aspects of truth which even this confused generation may bring us."[4]

Paul Settle describes Dr. Robinson as a

> Reformed scholar who had sifted through the theological heresies and idiosyncrasies of the centuries and advocated Reformation theology as the only successful polemic against them and the only consistent foundation for biblical ministry, theological scholarship, polity, witness, and outreach.

[1] J. Gresham Machen, *J. Gresham Machen: Selected Shorter Writings,* ed. D. G. Hart (Phillipsburg, New Jersey, 2004), 537.
[2] *Dictionary of Scottish Church History & Theology* (Edinburgh: T&T Clark, 1993), 531.
[3] WCR, *Presbyterian Journal,* September 16, 1946, 2.
[4] John Murray, *Collected Writings of John Murray* (Edinburgh: The Banner of Truth Trust, 1976) 1:22.

A photo of the Columbia Seminary faculty taken in the 1950s (courtesy of the Archives of the Campbell Library at Columbia Theological Seminary). Seated left to right: James Benjamin Green, J. McDowell Richards, and William Childs Robinson. Manford George Gutzke is standing second from the right.

43

9. ROBINSON AND GUTZKE

In 1939 Manford Gutzke and his wife, Sarah Bernstein Gutzke, came to Columbia Seminary. The two names—William Childs Robinson and Manford George Gutzke—are linked in the memories of several generations of Columbia Seminary students.

The two men were very different. Robinson was born into a stalwart Presbyterian family and embodied Presbyterian polity and Reformed theology in every fiber of his being. Gutzke grew up in a moral but non-Christian home and came to Christ later in life. He loved the Bible with all his heart and taught it powerfully in plain language.

Gutzke was born in Ontario, Canada in 1896, into a family that insisted on good conduct, including church attendance. "On the whole," he wrote, "we felt that religion was related somehow to decency." As a boy he believed "that God was real and yet in some sense he was not our God. He was our creator and he was our judge … but the idea that God would forgive you and be gracious to you" never once occurred to him. Church meant for him that "you dressed up in your best and that you acted your best." But "if anybody believed in the Lord in our church," Gutzke wrote, "they certainly kept it a secret." As a boy and young man, he did not feel uneasy about his unbelief, but was concerned that he had nothing else to take the place of God. He felt "altogether alone in the universe."[1]

When Manford was nine or ten years old, Mr. Caruthers, a farmer who lived nearby, intrigued the young boy because he seemed really to believe and practice what he believed. Before he retired from farm-

---

[1] Quotations in this chapter, unless otherwise indicated, are from the booklet *Out of Darkness* (Atlanta, Georgia: The Bible for You, n.d.), by Manford George Gutzke, 1.

ing and moved away, he made a point of visiting all of his neighbors and asked each one "Do you know how to be saved?" He then told them the gospel story. On Mr. Caruthers' last day at the church, seven of the people he had visited joined the church on profession of faith. Gutzke was not one of them, but "later this man's personal testimony was used of the Lord in bringing me to faith," he wrote.[1]

Young Gutzke had no confidence in the Bible at all, accepting Darwin's theory of evolution rather than the Genesis story. He soon came to reject evolution, however, believing that it was a theory without facts to back it up. Gutzke lived a moral life. He did not smoke or drink or swear. But he did not become a Christian. He felt, he recalled, "like a little boy in a great big warehouse, about midnight, in the dark ... alone and with noises."

One night as Manford was bringing in the cows after a day's work on the farm, the thought hit him, "If God is real, he sees me right now. I am in his presence."

> So I stopped there in the wheat field and the cows went on toward home, and I stood and looked up into the starry sky. I remember I reached up and took off my cap, and I felt like a fool, because maybe there wasn't anything up there ... And I said, "If you are there, you know I don't know, but if you're there, and if heaven is real, if anything a man can do here on earth will help him get there, if there is any kind of condition to meet and he can make it, if you show me what to do, I'll do it."

Manford felt good about what he had done, but wondered how God would show him. He thought that there was no way that God could reach down to him. Suddenly he had "an amazing idea. Maybe this is what church is about!" Then it dawned on him that maybe this is what the Bible is about. So he began to go to church and to read the Bible. He read through Genesis and Exodus, got bogged down in Leviticus, and turned to the New Testament. Every night he read a chapter of the Bible, recited the Ten Commandments, and prayed the Lord's Prayer.

One Sunday a visiting preacher ended his sermon with the words, "If anybody wants to know how to get to heaven, you just come and

[1] Manford George Gutzke, *Plain Talk About Real Christians* (Grand Rapids: Baker Book House, 1972), 7-8.

see me at my home." Manford and two friends went to his house. Manford told the preacher, "I don't know how to get to heaven and I wish you would tell me." The preacher seemed to have "a bit of trouble getting started," so he asked the young man some questions. When he found out that Manford didn't drink, didn't smoke, didn't gamble, didn't use profanity, lived a clean life, went to church every Sunday, read the Bible and prayed, he said, "Why, you don't have anything to worry about. Everything is all right. You just keep right on that road and you'll get there." Disappointed, Manford told his friends on the way home, "He doesn't know either."

Later Manford met a postmaster "who believed that Jesus Christ was alive." He was amazed to find someone who really believed that. One evening the postmaster asked him, "Are you a Christian?" When Manford could not answer that question, the man told him that salvation was a free gift of God. Manford answered that he could not believe that because it was too good to be true. The postmaster asked him some questions.

> "If there is a God, how big is he?" I said, "He's infinite." "If he is God, how strong is he?" "He's infinite." "How wise would he be?" "He's infinite." "Well," he said, "how good would he be?" I said, "He would be infinitely good."

Still Gutzke hesitated. He asked, "Why would God want to do it? Why would he want to do this wonderful thing for me?"

> Then he gave me John 3:16 in a way that I'll never forget: "For God so loved the world that He gave His only begotten Son; that whosoever believeth in Him should not perish but have everlasting life." And so the first promise of light began to shine in my soul.

Dr. Gutzke wrote:

> Now from this time on my story is very simple. Since I already knew the gospel and God was real, it only remained for me to believe it for myself. It wasn't easy, for I couldn't be sure he meant *me*. Finally, I looked up into the heavens one night while I was walking on a country road all by myself, and I just spoke to God. I said, "I believe now that you are there, and I believe that Jesus Christ is your Son, and I believe that he died for me. And I know that I need salvation, but I believe that he has it prepared for me, and I want to believe it was for me.

Help me." And suddenly I was able to believe. It was just as though everything had been completely settled. And I could truly say, "My Lord and my God."

Someone might ask me, "How is it with you now?" Many is the time in life I still feel like a small boy—alone in a warehouse in the middle of the night and it is dark and there are noises all around me. But there is Someone holding my hand. I am never alone anymore. Now I walk in the presence of the Lord, and he holds me in grace and mercy.

Manford Gutzke began to prepare for a career in law but soon became convinced that God was calling him into Christian ministry. He studied at the Bible Institute of Los Angeles, and earned a Master's degree in theology from Southern Methodist University. For eight years he was pastor of Westminster Presbyterian Church in Dallas, then taught Bible at Austin College for four years. He completed a Ph.D. in education at Columbia University in New York City.

On May 13, 1940, Dr. Gutzke gave his inaugural address as Professor of English Bible and Religious Education at Columbia Seminary. In a time of "fearful war," "moral, social, and spiritual collapse," and "a sleeping church," Gutzke said that many people, "fascinated by material prosperity, and drunken with human achievement, have left their Bibles unopened, their knees unbent, their heads unbowed." He reviewed briefly "what the Christian believes about God ... the Creator, the Sustainer, the Sovereign [and] the Savior." The "revelation of the grace of God is the particular burden of all Scripture," he said, "as it was the great work and mission of Christ, as it is today the cardinal truth of the gospel, preached by Christians to the ends of the earth."

The new professor then outlined his own duties at the seminary. Religious education, an expression of "doubtful significance," was defined by Gutzke as "the whole range of educational work carried on by our church ... The basic purpose involved is as old and familiar as the Great Commission: 'Go ye into all the world and *teach* all nations.' The making and culturing of Christians has ever been the heartfelt purpose of Spirit-filled witnesses for Christ." Gutzke warned that the Southern Presbyterian Church "has been in imminent danger of incorporating a far more naturalistic viewpoint in its educational program than our hearts desire, our convictions imply, or our Bibles warrant." He concluded his address by discussing the task confronting the church in three points.

One, "we must study the Bible. It is not enough to have confidence that the Scriptures are the Word of God. It is essential that we have knowledge of what the Word of God says … Formal study under definite guidance will yield results. But living with it, reading it, hearing it, thinking it, until it becomes 'second nature,' until our thoughts couch themselves in its terms and use its ideas—that will give one a grasp of the Bible that will be truly powerful and practical in life and experience."

Two, "we must interpret the Bible in contemporary language." Gutzke explained:

> Inasmuch as our gospel is a living message we cannot hesitate to present it in the language of the hour. Hudson Taylor made a distinct contribution to foreign mission technique when he adopted Chinese customs, language, dress, manners as a means to facilitate the presentation of the universal gospel to the Chinese. Since there is a 20th century cast of mind wherein we live, let us not falter in "translating" our Scriptures into the 20th century "vernacular."

Three, "we must teach believers the truth about Christian living. Our generation needs to be taught that salvation is of God by His grace. There is an ineptitude in human nature," Gutzke concluded,

> a disinclination in the natural heart, an unfitness in the soul that disqualifies man as he is from fellowship with God. But Christ Jesus died for our sins, He was raised for our justification, He lives for our sanctification. He waits for our glorification. The Holy Spirit has been given to comfort, to guide, to teach, to show, to empower our regenerated beings in fellowship and communion with a living, indwelling, personal Christ. We can walk with Him, and we can talk with Him. We can pray to Him and He will answer us. The Lord Jesus is living now and our fellowship with Him personally should be intimate, personal, and constant. "Christ in you, the hope of glory" needs to be etched into the consciousness of every believing soul. And to this task we must set ourselves with diligence and vigor at once.[1]

[1] Manford George Gutzke, *Bulletin: Columbia Theological Seminary,* September 1940, 3-24.

The directors, faculty, alumni, students, and friends of the seminary who listened to Gutzke's long address realized that the new professor was a man of strong convictions and plain speech, who would faithfully teach the Bible.

Dr. Gutzke did not become deeply involved in the theological issues at the seminary and in the denomination as did Dr. Robinson, but he supported and defended his colleague. One day Gutzke told his class,

> You know many people assume that Dr. Robinson and I are close personal friends because we hold similar views, but we are not really close personally. However, I want to tell you that some time ago I became aware that Dr. Robinson had been treated very unjustly. He could have retaliated, but he did not. I really admired him for that.

Gutzke was a man of gentle spirit and gracious, friendly disposition. Students loved him. Gifted in the simple presentation of Scripture and use of appropriate illustrations, Gutzke was soon in wide demand throughout the Southern Presbyterian Church for Bible conferences. He produced radio programs and wrote numerous books, including commentaries on many of the Bible books and several Christian doctrines, the titles of which began with the words "Plain Talk."

After two years at Westminster Seminary, Kennedy Smartt transferred to Columbia Seminary to take Church History, under Dr. Robinson, and English Bible, under Dr. Gutzke. He writes about Gutzke:

> His deep knowledge of the Scriptures, his sincere and abiding confidence in scriptural inerrancy, his tremendous ability to make profound things simple, his graphic way of illustrating truth with stories from his own life and background, and his way of making the gospel understandable, make him one of the most unforgettable characters I have ever known. He had been a champion prize fighter in the Canadian Army during World War I, and was a big man both physically and spiritually. And, when I was in seminary, I had the privilege of sitting under his ministry sometimes twice a day. He gave me more material to preach than I had opportunities to speak.[1]

[1] Kennedy Smartt, *I Am Reminded: An Autobiographical, Anecdotal History of The*

Paul Settle compares Gutzke and Robinson, "While Dr. Gutzke introduced us to the devotional and practical riches of the Word, it was Dr. Robinson who convinced us of the intellectual and spiritual integrity of the Reformed faith."

Presbyterian Church In America, 13.

10. THE BREAD OF LIFE AND
THE HOPE OF GLORY

*C*hrist—*The Bread of Life* contains Robinson's lectures delivered at Fuller Theological Seminary in the winter of 1949. He had been chosen by the Fuller faculty to inaugurate the Payton Lectures. Robinson began by saying that he knew that he was speaking "in the presence of more gifted and dynamic teachers," but that he found some consolation "in remembering that he [spoke] as a representative of an older to one of the newer theological seminaries of America." When the lectures were published, Fuller's president, Harold John Ockenga, wrote in the foreword: "Dr. Robinson represents that unqualified allegiance to Biblical truth, that positive ecclesiastical outlook, that scholarly attainment, that personal devotion and zeal at which Fuller Seminary aims."

"Christ is the only and the indispensable answer," Dr. Robinson told his listeners. "He is the bread from heaven for our hungry human hearts." Robinson explained:

> For the Marxian communist, Christ is a *drug*, an opiate to lull the worker to sleep with dreams of a good time coming, while others profit from his labors. For the Nazi, He is a *poison* to sap the strength of Nordic manhood. For the culture religion of "modern man" He is a *cake*, which one may or may not order as a dessert after an otherwise adequate meal served by the Enlightenment. For the Christian believer, Jesus Christ is *the bread*, the staff of life.

Thomas Ellis, who studied with Dr. Robinson at Columbia Seminary, wrote that before he heard Robinson teach and preach, he had first "heard" him while reading *Christ—The Bread of Life*. Ellis described the impact this book made on his life.

'PLEADING FOR A REFORMATION VISION'

I believe that it was in the second chapter, entitled "The Savior of Sinners," that I first came to feel I was indeed a lost, undone sinner without any hope save in God's sovereign mercy. Words quoted from Augustine, Luther, Calvin, Bunyan, Thomas Adams, Warfield and many others became arrows from God's bow that struck and stuck in my heart. As I sat alone reading late into that night, tears began to run down my face. I cried to God to save a poor sinner who could not save himself but who must forever rest upon Christ and His righteousness alone for salvation. Had I never heard the gospel before? Yes, all my life. Yet never had the truth been applied to my condition as God did that night through the lucid, penetrating language of those pages. How clear and how necessary that I should not be found in my own righteousness, but that I should continually be found clothed in the righteousness of Christ alone! May I forever be thankful that our gracious Sovereign ... saw fit to bring together that most excellent, honest book and my poor ignorant, guilty, and enslaved soul![1]

In the chapter "The Saviour of Sinners," referred to by Thomas Ellis, Robinson gave a deeply moving presentation of "God's accusation against man, the certainty of His judgment, and above all the forgiveness of sins" by collecting testimonies in church history from the Apostle Paul to John "Rabbi" Duncan.[2]

Robinson contrasted the Catholic and Protestant concept of the church in the following words:

Now the church carries out her commission as she bears witness to the lordship of Jesus Christ, not as she seeks to substitute her own authority for His Lordship. We are not to pin our hopes on human institutions that ignore Him. We are not to set up our programs in lieu of His program, which is the preaching of the crucified Saviour, the risen, reigning Lord. The difference between the Roman Catholic and the Protestant faith is right here. True Protestantism subordinates the church to her Lord and the church's word to His Word. Romanism assumes that she is the vicegerent of the Christ and that what her Pope speaks *ex cathedra* has Christ's own infallibility. According to Boehme in *On the Road to Reformation*, the high-water mark of Luther's titanic struggle came when at Eyster Gate the Reformer cast into the flames the canon law. The lawyers stood aghast, Luther returned to the

[1] [Ellis], "Biographical Tribute," 1-2.
[2] See Selected Writings 10.

classroom to tell his students that to stand any longer with him meant martyrdom, but that since they understood the gospel, to depart from it meant hell. The challenge is flung, the chips are down, the issue is: martyrdom or hell![1]

In another chapter of *Christ—The Bread of Life,* Dr. Robinson explored the biblical witness to Christ as the Shepherd of Israel, the Good Shepherd, the Great Shepherd, and the Chief Shepherd.[2]

In his preface to *Our Lord: An Affirmation of the Deity of Christ,* Robinson stated that "in giving an affirmation to the deity of Christ in the face of modern denials," he had necessarily emphasized "the Christ of history. An adequate balance calls for an equal consideration of the risen, present, living, reigning Christ and of His coming in glory." This he did in *Christ—The Hope of Glory: Christological Eschatology*—the 1941 James Sprunt Lectures at Union Theological Seminary in Virginia.

Robinson introduced *Christ—The Hope of Glory* with an illustration and a quotation from R. A. Webb's *The Christian's Hope*:

> In the First Presbyterian Church of Charlotte there are two windows depicting Christian hope. One represents a woman whose feet are in chains, whose head and shoulders are shrouded in mists, but who is reaching through the clouds into the light of heaven. The other shows the Holy City, New Jerusalem, coming down out of heaven from God. God has let down His gracious promises of a new heaven and a new earth which our Lord will bring with Him when He comes in His glory. Though our feet be chained by the sordidness of earth and our heads lost in the smoke of battle and the turmoil of trivialities, we can still grasp the promises of God that are yea in Christ. For, "everywhere hope looks out of the windows of the Christian Scriptures."[3]

Robinson drew from church history to describe the Christian's hope in the hour of death:

> Since angels rejoice over the sinner that repenteth (Luke 15:10) and witness the believer's fidelity to his charge (1 Tim. 5:21), it is easy to

---

[1] WCR, *Christ—The Bread of Life* (Grand Rapids: Wm. B. Eerdmans Publishing Company, 1950), 87-88.

[2] See Selected Writings II.

[3] WCR, *Christ—The Hope of Glory: Christological Eschatology* (Grand Rapids: Eerdmans, 1945), 16.

infer that they often welcome the pilgrim of the night into the gates of light. As the Reverend William Ross was preaching in Glasgow … he suddenly declared, "The hosts of God are twenty thousand. This room is full of angels, I see them all around. The Lord has laid His hand on me." And so this man of God died and was buried in Edinburgh.[1]

All Christian history is redolent with the testimony of His presence in that eventful hour. Stephen saw such a vision of the Son of Man as he received the crown of martyrdom that his face shone like the face of an angel. Polycarp needed not to be tied to the stake, but drew strength to endure the flame from the King he had served eighty and six years. To steady her in the approaching ordeal a triumphant vision was vouchsafed to that heroic young mother Perpetua. When Walter Milne, the last and oldest of the Martyrs of St. Andrews, was drawn up from the bottle dungeon he was too weak to stand. Men said he would be unable to testify. But God so strengthened His witness with His grace and with the refreshing air providentially permitted between the dungeon and cathedral, that Milne made the arches of that vast edifice ring with his testimony. John Owen welcomed death as the long-wished-for day in which he should see the glory of Christ in a manner in which he was incapable of doing in this world; Alexander Henderson said "there was never a school boy more desirous to have the play than I am to leave this world"; Robert Bruce breakfasted with his children and went to sup with the Lord Jesus Christ. Grimshaw grieved that he had done so *little* for Christ, and rejoiced that Christ had done so *much* for him. For Andrew Fuller there was no rapture, no despondency, but this word of a calm mind, "My hope is such that I am not afraid to plunge into eternity." And time would fail me to tell of Hus and Hamilton, of Ridley and Cranmer, of Wesley, of Erskine, and [John and Betty] Stam.

In the chapter "The Judgment Seat of Christ," Robinson showed how "the judgment seat of Christ lends a seriousness to all life."[2] Under the title *"Regnum Gloriae"* Robinson described the glory of Christ—the glory of his grace, the glory of holiness, the glory of happiness, and the glory of beauty.[3]

---

[1] Account given by Principal John Macleod of Edinburgh.

[2] "The Judgment Seat of Christ" from *Christ—The Hope of Glory* appears in Selected Writings 12 (as abridged in *The Banner of Truth* 178 and 181).

[3] See Selected Writings 13.

In *Christ—The Hope of Glory*, Robinson referred to James Buchanan Hutton, pastor of the First Presbyterian Church, Jackson, Mississippi, from 1896 to 1940. Hutton was born in Washington County, Virginia, on March 19, 1866. After graduating from Union Theological Seminary in Virginia, he was ordained in November 1892 by Central Mississippi Presbytery. He served the churches in Lexington and Durant, Mississippi, until called to First Church, Jackson, in 1896. Hutton invited J. Gresham Machen and Cornelius Van Til to speak at the Synod of Mississippi youth conferences in the 1930s and encouraged Westminster Seminary graduates to serve churches of Central Mississippi Presbytery. Hutton died on September 22, 1940. Robinson wrote:

> When Jackson, Mississippi, mourned the death of her first citizen, Dr. J. B. Hutton, the city remembered his testimony to the sufficiency of God for life's most tragic moment. On that former day Dr. Hutton was seated with his sorrowing loved ones in the front pew of the church he had so long and faithfully served. In front of the pulpit from which his many eloquent messages had been uttered was a sombre casket holding the cold and silent form of his first-born son, a boy whom he passionately loved because a physical infirmity deprived him of a fair chance in life. Humanly speaking, the death of that young man had been a tragic blunder. The doctor had given the antitetanic serum to a patient suffering with asthma without making a preliminary test; and death had ensued instantaneously. The choir was softly singing the final stanza of "Lead, Kindly Light," when Dr. Hutton slipped quietly from the pew, placed his hand tenderly on the casket, and in a voice choked with emotion, said: "My friends, what I have been telling you through all these years is true. Only faith in God can bring us consolation in hours of deepest sorrow. I have preached this to you from this pulpit many times, I have been with you in your own hours of grief and bereavement, and I now know that my Redeemer liveth and He is able to keep that which I have committed unto Him against this day."[1]

As Dr. Hutton preached Christ, God bore in upon the preacher's soul the assurance that the Captain of our salvation will lead on 'till

> The night is gone
> And with the morn

---

[1] Sullens, Major Frederick, in *The Jackson Daily News,* September 23, 1940, 4.

'PLEADING FOR A REFORMATION VISION'

Those angel faces smile
Which I have loved long since and lost awhile!

11. REFORMED THEOLOGIAN

Dr. Robinson's main area of teaching at Columbia Seminary was church history, but he expanded his courses to include much more. Julius Scott said that he learned from Robinson "something of the content of virtually every other theological field in addition to church history and historical theology." John Leith wrote that in addition to church history, Dr. Robinson also taught "an excellent course on the history of doctrine." Some of the faculty objected to this course, an indication that the new emphasis at the seminary was on contemporary, not historical, theology.[1]

Dr. Robinson believed that theology must be formed and reformed, if necessary, by the Word of God. He invited others to "show us our slips and errors. And as lovers of truth we will seek to correct the errors that are shown us—that the lamp of truth may burn the more brightly."[2] He was not ignorant of modern thought, but tested it by Bible truth. He was not disturbed when people criticized him as a narrow-minded conservative. He liked to quote G. K. Chesterton, "The Church of the second century almost died of broad-mindedness," adding, "Our age is gravely menaced by the same dread malady."[3]

Robinson pointed out the fallacy of assuming that when a truth is dated it is thereby dissolved, the notion that a thing is untrue because it is old. As a young scholar at Columbia Seminary, he wrote that one of the best answers to this popular idea was to be found in the work of a French philosopher, Professor Jacques Chavalier, who said, "We

[1] Leith, *Crisis in the Church,* 47.
[2] WCR, *Presbyterian Journal,* March 1, 1950, 5.
[3] WCR, *Presbyterian Journal,* November 15, 1946, 5. Here Robinson is quoting the inaugural address of W. W. Bryden as principal of Knox College.

must resolve to place truth before that which is new. *Non nova, sed vera.* This should be the motto of every philosopher who is worthy of the name." Robinson added:

> If it be the business of philosophy to maintain the verdict of the centuries against the whims of the moment, it is certainly not the business of those who have the Word of the Eternal to be turned by every wind of doctrine. A book as irenic and tolerant as the new edition of Principal Paterson's "Rule of Faith," a book that we regard as much too broad in places, nevertheless, closes with this weighty word: "The mind is ever interested in novelties; but the heart ever seeks the permanent and unchangeable, and is assured that its quest is not in vain, according to the song of our pilgrimage, 'His truth at all times firmly stood and shall from age to age endure.'"[1]

Dr. Robinson wanted above all to be a *biblical* theologian, not forcing Scripture into an arbitrary system, but allowing the Word to speak its own message. He insisted that the Reformed faith means "Reformed by God's Word."[2] The two greatest expressions of theological truth formed and reformed by God's Word, Robinson believed, were the *Institutes* of John Calvin and the Westminster Confession of Faith.

Dr. Robinson said that his Columbia Seminary colleague Paul T. Fuhrmann told him, "After all, we are asked by God not to conform to the world but to be transformed after the ideal image of Christ. To be ourself, we need a great uplifting force. I have found it in Calvin."[3]

Robinson also found much to admire and emulate in Calvin's teachings and life. "By means of his concept of common grace," Robinson wrote, "Calvin was able to draw his mighty scheme of God's all-inclusive purpose compassing life, history, eternity ... This doctrine shows the multiformity of the great Reformer's thought. It enables one to do full justice to the good in unregenerate men and at the same time maintain the total depravity of fallen man."[4]

[1] WCR, *Christian Observer,* March 15, 1933, 9.
[2] WCR, *Christian Observer,* January 9, 1935, 7.
[3] Jacob T. Hoogstra, ed., *John Calvin: Contemporary Prophet* (Grand Rapids: Baker Book House, 1959), 49. Paul Fuhrman became a professor at Columbia Seminary in 1948. He edited Calvin's *Instruction in Faith* and Bucer's *Instruction in Love* and wrote *An Introduction to the Great Creeds of the Church* and *Extraordinary Christianity—The Life and Thought of Alexander Vinet.*
[4] WCR, *Evangelical Quarterly,* October 1930, 438.

For the book *John Calvin: Contemporary Prophet,* Robinson contributed a chapter "The Tolerance of Our Prophet or Calvin's Tolerance and Intolerance." Robinson claimed that "fundamentally, Calvin sought tolerance where it was a matter of detail and of human differences. He was intolerant where it seemed to him that the truth of God was at stake ... whether that came from papal additions to the Word, Libertine misuse of the doctrine of the Spirit, or rationalistic denials of the trinity." Calvin praised charity in Christian conduct, but insisted that truth was more important. He wrote: "So charity ought to be subservient to the purity of faith. It becomes us, indeed, to have regard to charity; but we must not offend God for the love of our neighbor."[1] Furthermore, while recognizing failures of his own, Calvin was intolerant of all forms of carelessness and wickedness.

Robinson believed that in the execution of Michael Servetus, Calvin went against his own earlier and better impulse. Indeed, he began his public life, wrote Robinson, as "an advocate of tolerance. His initial book was a commentary on Seneca's *De Clementia,* and the first edition of the *Institutes* declares that 'it is criminal to put heretics to death. To make an end of them by fire and sword is opposed to every principle of humanity.'" Robinson noted that the great Calvin scholar Emile Doumergue initiated the construction of "a monument of expiation" at Champel on the three hundred and fiftieth anniversary of the execution of Servetus. "Since this was one too many to burn for his erroneous convictions," Robinson wrote, "the disciple of Calvin stops at the monument ... and bows his head in shame for Calvin's mistake."[2]

While Robinson regretted Calvin's role in the execution of Servetus, he praised the Reformer's tolerance and generosity in other areas. Calvin was tolerant toward the people of Geneva who had expelled him, encouraging his supporters not to abandon the church of that city. He was willing to defend the Genevans by answering the letter of Cardinal Sadoleto. When invited he returned to Geneva and was careful to avoid criticism of his opponents there. "One of the most beautiful examples of Calvin's personal tolerance," Robinson wrote, "is seen in his treatment of Melanchthon's *Loci Communes.*"

[1] John Calvin, *Institutes of the Christian Religion,* III,xix,13.
[2] WCR, *John Calvin,* 39, 47, 49.

Despite differences between the two men, Calvin published a new edition of Melanchthon's book, with a warm introduction. "Calvin wanted France to love Melanchthon as much as he did, and to be converted to Christ through him." Robinson pointed to Calvin's tolerance in dealing with the Marian exiles in the years 1554-55 and his mild objections to the Book of Common Prayer and episcopacy of the English Church. Calvin longed for Protestant unity, writing to Archbishop Cranmer that he would "cross ten seas" if he could help in uniting "churches seated far apart." Finally, Calvin was tolerant, added Robinson, about certain features of Protestant views of the Lord's Supper that differed from his. Summing up, Robinson wrote:

> As one bows at Calvary in confession for past failures and present transgressions, may each acknowledge anew the lordship of Jesus, beseeching His more complete guidance that one may tread in a more acceptable manner the path of tolerance and intolerance—that the truth of the gospel may remain intact among us.[1]

Dr. Robinson was one of the speakers at the First American Calvinistic Conference in June 1939. His topic was "The Sovereignty of God and American Attitudes." He began with a description of the Reformed faith,

> ... the proclamation that the Lord God omnipotent reigneth, King of kings and Lord of lords. Calvinism is a vision of God in all His glory, of the King in His beauty, and a consequent sense of our own absolute dependence on Him. We depend upon Him for knowledge and recognize the sovereign authority of His revelation. We depend upon Him for life and history, believing that the almighty God governs the works of His hands and that in Christ He has supernaturally intervened for our salvation.[2]

In his *Reformation: A Rediscovery of Grace,* Robinson devoted a chapter to Calvin—"The Theologian of the Reformation."

"The Reformation was first and foremost a theological revival" (T. H. L. Parker, *Portrait of Calvin*, 12). Consequently, the Reformers

[1] WCR, *John Calvin*, 41, 42, 49.
[2] Jacob T. Hoogstra, ed., *The Sovereignty of God or the Proceedings of the First American Calvinistic Conference* (Grand Rapids: Zondervan Publishing House, 1940), 147-48.

are witnesses to theology, to a biblical theology, as the very life of the church. In October 1512, Luther received the degree of doctor of divinity and thereafter devoted himself to the establishment of a biblical in place of a scholastic theology. While he was in seclusion in the Wartburg, the glory of reviving theology was ascribed to Zwingli. It fell, however, to their two great successors, Philip Melanchthon and John Calvin, to build theological structures of the mighty stones which they quarried from the Word. For his friend Melanchthon, Calvin published in French the *Loci Communes,* describing this book as a summary in simplest terms and by a learned man of the things a Christian should know in the way of salvation. When Calvin worsted Dean Robert Mosham of Passau at the Second Disputation in Worms, he was acclaimed by Melanchthon as *the theologian.* Melanchthon's tribute, as well as the high intellectual standing which *The Institutes of the Christian Religion* gave Protestantism, justify the treatment of Calvin as *par excellence* the theologian of the Reformation.

As Luther and others re-established the crucial position that the Church must be a *listening* Church, not listening to its own interior monologue, but to the voice of God it hears in Scripture, so Calvin insisted that the believer is a disciple in the school of Christ, studying the Bible under the illumination of the Holy Spirit. He is ever "listening to the Word of God and again and again listening! Not as a system builder who already knows all things, but as a captive of that Word that marks the way through the brush of the world" (G. C. Berkouwer, *Contemporary Prophet*, 195).

Calvin, like his Reformation colleagues, is a biblical rather than a speculative theologian. He is an exegete of Holy Scripture, and he interprets it by no one organizing principle but in the light of the tremendous reality of Him whom it sets forth, that is, he is a biblical realist. Standing in mighty majesty and high holiness above our sinful race, God has graciously condescended to put His Word nigh us, in our mouths and in our hearts (Rom. 10:8), that it might be a lamp unto our feet and a light to our pathway (Ps. 119:105). Calvin spent his life studying this Word, and like an Old Testament prophet he proclaimed it both by his words and his actions.[1]

With five points Robinson summed up "the basic structure of the Christian faith", as Calvin found it in the Bible and wrote it in the *Institutes*:

[1] WCR, *The Reformation,* 96-98.

1. The revelation of the holy God strips the sinner of every ground of glorying and gives all the praise to the glory of God's grace.

2. The light of the knowledge of the glory of God shines in the face of Jesus Christ.

3. As Christ is the theme of Scripture, so the Holy Spirit is the internal Teacher whose illumination opens the eyes of our faith to understand, and the trust of our hearts to appropriate the promises of salvation.

4. By His Word and Spirit God speaks forgiveness to the sinner.

5. Calvin read and preached the Word with a profound sense of God's presence and a passionate devotion to His glory.

To his dismay Dr. Robinson found that Christians, even some Southern Presbyterians, were abandoning or weakening "Calvin's" doctrine of predestination. Dr. Robinson insisted that to reject predestination was a serious departure, not only from Reformed doctrine but also from the Bible's consistent message of God's free grace. In the book *Basic Christian Doctrines*, Robinson presented the doctrine of predestination, which he described as simply "a vision of the King in the glory of His grace."[1] In a review of Gordon Rupp's *The Righteousness of God: Luther Studies*, Robinson wrote that "it is certainly a pleasure to find these testimonies" in the Methodist scholar:

> A doctrine of predestination is in any case an integral part of both Protestant and Catholic divinity, as it must always be a part of any Gospel which gives God the glory, and which maintains the divine freedom and initiative in creation and redemption, and which acknowledges that the ultimate judgment is not our verdict upon God, but His upon us … I hope it can be seen why this treatise [Luther's *Bondage of the Will*] still lives and why it is, as Bishop Normann has it, "the finest and most powerful *Soli Deo Gloria* to be sung in the whole period of the Reformation."[2]

Robinson not only defended Calvin but also the Calvinism of later Reformed theologians against the liberals in his own church,

---

[1] Carl F. H. Henry, ed., *Basic Christian Doctrines* (New York: Holt, Rinehart and Winston, 1962). See Selected Writings 14.
[2] WCR, *Westminster Theological Journal*, May 1955, 212.

and at times against criticism from his fellow conservatives. In 1974
Aiken Taylor, the editor of *The Presbyterian Journal*, wrote an article,
"Calvin vs. the Calvinists," in which he argued that

> the concept "Reformed" does not root in the theology of Kuyper,
> Warfield, Hodge, or any of the other great latter-day Christian think-
> ers. It roots in John Calvin. One may be a disciple of the Dutch or
> the Princeton schools and wear the label "Reformed." But if one is a
> disciple of John Calvin's school of the Word, his mantle may reflect a
> slightly different color in the area of evangelism.[1]

Taylor described what he called "the heart of the matter" by asking
the question:

> Is the gospel message itself, in the hands of a Christian witness, in some
> sense "alive" with the power of the Holy Spirit, or is He only in the
> wings, as it were, waiting to work on the heart of the hearer when the
> gospel is preached?

Taylor answered that "some latter-day Calvinists have lost the view of
the Word as an energizer. It has rather become a body of truth which,
though infallible, is nevertheless merely language."[2]

In a letter to the *Presbyterian Journal*, Robinson wrote that he
wished to speak for himself on two of the issues raised by Taylor.

> First, in common with such Calvinists as Hodge, Kuyper and Warfield,
> I heartily reaffirm this statement of Dort: "Moreover, the promise of
> the Gospel is that whosoever believeth in Christ crucified shall not per-
> ish, but have everlasting life. Which promise ought to be announced
> and proclaimed promiscuously and indiscriminately to all nations and
> men, to whom God in His good pleasure hath sent the Gospel, with
> the command to repent and believe."
>
> Secondly, one chapter in my book *The Reformation, A Rediscov-
> ery of Grace*, sets forth the preached Word as the instrument used by
> the Spirit in reforming the Church. The Reformation returned to an
> understanding of the Holy Spirit as the dynamic presence of God in
> Jesus Christ, under the veil of the preached Word.
>
> According to Calvin, "the eternal Word is of no avail by itself unless
> animated by the power of the Spirit." Thus he teaches both the pres-
> ence of the Holy Spirit with the preaching of the Word, and also the

[1] *Presbyterian Journal*, March 6, 1974, 9.
[2] *Presbyterian Journal*, March 6, 1974, 23.

witness of the Holy Spirit in the heart of the believer. In efficaciously
calling the sinner to the Saviour, the Spirit acts both *per verbum* and
cum verbo.[1]

In other letters to Taylor, Robinson expressed more fully his concerns with the editor's article "Calvin vs. the Calvinists." He felt that
Taylor had not treated Hodge, Kuyper, and Warfield with "loving
understanding of their testimony" and reminded him that "those
who founded the journal that you now edit were men who derived
their Calvinism in considerable degree from Hodge, Kuyper and
Warfield." He faulted Taylor with two mistakes in his description
of what Presbyterians believe: in placing justification before calling
("Romans 8:30 does the opposite") and in setting forth reprobation
with no reference to human sin ("John Calvin said that reprobation
was in the plan of God but in such a way that the ground and cause
of their damnation was in themselves").

Robinson stated his view of what Calvinists believe: "We accept
the mystery of divine sovereignty and human responsibility to accept
the free offer of the gospel—we admit that we cannot fathom God's
purpose from beginning to end—we walk by faith not by sight—we
trust where we cannot fathom—for we know Him whom we have
believed—even our Lord and Saviour Jesus Christ."[2]

* * * * *

John Leith, one of Dr. Robinson's students and later Professor
of Church History at Union Theological Seminary in Richmond,
Virginia, described Robinson as

a conservative in the classical (17th century) Reformed tradition. He
never really allowed the Enlightenment and the 19th century to influence his theology. Hence, his work was not acceptable to either the
liberals or the critically orthodox who did take the Enlightenment
seriously. Yet, as a classical Reformed theologian he was never fully
intelligible to the fundamentalists or the revivalists.[3]

[1] WCR, *Presbyterian Journal,* April 24, 1974, 3.
[2] WCR, *Presbyterian Journal,* March 1, 1950, 7.
[3] *Presbyterian Outlook,* January 10, 1983, 15.

Columbia Seminary's president, J. McDowell Richards, wrote

> As an exponent and a champion of the Reformed faith [William Childs
> Robinson] has sought to sound again and again the vital affirmations
> of the Protestant Reformation. In doing this he has emphasized always
> the authority of the Word of God and the lordship of Jesus Christ. For
> him the fact of the sovereignty of God has been central, and he has
> constantly taught and preached the doctrine of justification by faith—
> "By grace are ye saved through faith; and that not of yourselves: it is
> the gift of God."[1]

During a conversation at Reformed Theological Seminary, William
Childs Robinson's name came up. One of the professors, Dr. Morton
Smith, with deep feeling and enthusiasm, exclaimed, "He's my idea
of a Reformed theologian!"[2]

[1] Richards, *Soli Deo Gloria,* 6.
[2] [Ellis], "Biographical Tribute," 5.

12. THE WESTMINSTER CONFESSION OF FAITH AND CATECHISMS

D r. Robinson loved the Westminster Confession of Faith and Catechisms. In a sermon he explained:

> The title "Confession of Faith" testifies to the intent of our articles. They are written as a confession of our faith in the God of all grace, and only as such are they a constitution of the Church, that is, they are worship, not legalism. The realization of this fact delivers us from the tyranny of logic and brings us into the freedom of faith.

In the same sermon, Robinson explained the system of subscription as held by the American Presbyterian Church.

> The Adopting Act of 1729 requires every minister to accept the West-minster Standards as being in all essential articles good forms of sound words and systems of Christian doctrine, and to adopt the same as the confession of his own faith. If a minister has scruples about a con-fessional statement, he is to present his difficulties to his presbytery which is to decide whether or not they concern doctrines necessary or essential to the faith.[1]

In an article "Has 'Unreserved Dedication' Taken the Place of Creedal Subscription?" Robinson wrote that the meaning of the Presbyterian ordination vows is "not determined by the man taking it but by the natural, historical force of the words and by the body imposing the vow."[2]

Robinson insisted on "the *con amore* acceptance of the Confession of Faith as containing the system of doctrine taught in the Holy

[1] WCR, unpublished sermon on "How to Hold Our Theological Heritage." Historical Center of the Presbyterian Church in America, St. Louis, Missouri.

[2] WCR, *Presbyterian Journal,* January 2, 1950, 5.

Scriptures."[1] He was happy with the strong subscription vow required of professors at Columbia Seminary that stated:

> In the presence of God and these witnesses I do solemnly subscribe the Confession of Faith, catechisms and other standards of government, discipline, and worship of the Presbyterian Church in the United States as a just summary of the doctrine contained in the Bible, and promise and engage not to teach, directly or indirectly, any doctrine contrary to the Scriptures as interpreted in those standards while I continue a professor in this seminary.

On one occasion Robinson strongly protested when the seminary board allowed a new professor to subscribe to the Westminster Standards without the words "as interpreted in those standards."

Robinson believed that the theological requirements for teachers at Columbia Seminary were sound, but asked people "to pray that God would give to us at Columbia of His grace that we might maintain these obligations in spirit and in letter. Only by the grace of the living Lord Jesus Christ, only by the power of the Holy Spirit, can these good forms of sound words be a living blessing among us."[2]

Dr. Robinson urged the seminary students to provide ample opportunities for the children of their congregations to learn the Shorter Catechism. It was during his ministry in Gettysburg that Robinson became convinced of the importance of catechetical study. Some years later he wrote:

> It belongs to the minister's office "to catechize the children and youth." Jesus' first command to Peter was not "discipline my sheep," not "feed my sheep," but "feed my lambs" (John 21:15). To meet this primary obligation of a pastor I found it necessary to put in a weekday hour of religious instruction in which, with the help of public school teachers, I taught the Bible, the Shorter Catechism, and great hymns to the children of my congregation. This weekday hour met such a need that it continued to be carried on even during pastoral interims. As a second step in meeting this pastoral responsibility, I attended the closing exercises of the Sabbath school and heard each class recite a catechism answer. One result of this intensive inculcation of the catechism was that after a long dearth of candidates from

[1] WCR, *Christian Observer,* November 1, 1944, 6.
[2] WCR, *Presbyterian Journal,* January 16, 1950, 4.

the congregation, several of the most promising young men decided to enter the gospel ministry.[1]

Robinson published a short article in the *Southern Presbyterian Journal* summarizing Principal John Macleod's words on "Catechising."

Now we take it that our fathers never meant to satisfy themselves when a mere rote acquaintance with such statements was attained. They aimed at the opening up of the form of sound words in which they set forth the truth of the gospel. And when what was committed to memory was opened up by loving teachers at the fireside or in the congregation, the good of having learned the letter of such statements, which were a valuable exhibition of the faith, came out. And, what was more, those who, in the immature years of childhood, had their minds stored with what at the time when they learned to repeat it might be beyond their reach, had, in later years, when their powers came to a measure of ripeness, the chance of working in their mind what they once had learned only by rote. They carried with them from childhood a treasure, the good of which they came to know when in after years they asked themselves the meaning of those words with the letter of which they had been long familiar. Often have those who have gone through a course of catechetic training in their early days come to discover how useful this teaching is to them now that in later days they have come to feel the power of the truth. They are like a mill with all its mechanics in order that waited for the turning on of the water that it might work.[2]

In an article in the *Christian Observer*, Robinson briefly outlined the prominent place given to catechizing in the establishment of early Christianity. He added:

Even a cursory examination of this outline will show that Calvin and the Westminster divines were but following the apostolic example in the placing of the catechism in such prominence in the church. The Westminster Catechisms follow with remarkable exactitude the lines of catechesis marked out by the primitive Christian Church. In teaching the Shorter Catechism parents and teachers are following directly in the footsteps of Paul and Mark and the host of unnamed

[1] WCR, *Christian Observer*, September 20, 1933, 7.
[2] WCR, *Presbyterian Journal*, April 1, 1950, 3.

teachers who brought victory to the Christian banner in the first four centuries.[1]

Dr. Robinson prepared, at the request of the session of the Pryor Street Presbyterian Church in Atlanta, an exposition of the doctrinal portions of the Shorter Catechism (questions 1 through 38 and 84-87), which he gave to full congregations on Sunday evenings. These studies were published in the *Southern Presbyterian Journal* and reprinted in a booklet, *The Christian Faith According to the Shorter Catechism*. He offered these studies to parents to help them teach their children the principles of the Christian faith—"according to their baptism vows." He sent it forth "with the prayer that God may use it to encourage us to obey from the heart that form of doctrine which was delivered unto us." He hoped that ministers might use his brief treatment of the Shorter Catechism to "prime the pump" for a series of evening sermons or prayer meeting talks and looked "forward to the time when these great doctrinal themes will again become the strong meat for our morning congregations."[2]

Robinson began his exposition of the Shorter Catechism with a brief historical introduction.

> The Shorter Catechism is the work of the Westminster Assembly of Divines which met at the call of Parliament in Westminster Abbey, London, on July 1, 1643, and continued in session for six years. The assembly was composed of about a hundred and fifty English ministers and lay assessors and eight Scottish ministers and elders. They met to bring the worship, the doctrine, the government, and the discipline of the churches of Great Britain into closer conformity with the Word of God.
>
> The Shorter Catechism is the final and finest work of that great assembly. The work on the catechism was undertaken early but in its final form was approved last. All the fine Lutheran and Reformed catechisms from the days of the Reformation were at hand to draw upon. In the assembly itself there were at least a dozen members who had written catechisms. Calvin's Catechism, one by Herbert Palmer, a member of the assembly, and a manual by Archbishop Ussher influenced the work. In addition to Palmer, "the best catechist in England," Dr. John

---

[1] WCR, *Christian Observer*, September 20, 1933, 7.
[2] WCR, *The Christian Faith According to the Shorter Catechism*, February 1, 1950.

Wallis, the mathematician, and Samuel Rutherford of Scotland seem to have shared in the preparation of this work. Our Shorter Catechism ranks with Luther's Catechism and the Heidelberg Catechism and is described as "one of the three typical catechisms of Protestantism which are likely to last to the end of time."

The purpose of the authors of the catechism was to frame the answer, not according to the model of the knowledge the child has, but according to what the child ought to have. Thus it is a pre-eminently instructive work. It places thoughts in the mind and heart of the child which grow with him, which indeed help the child to grow in wisdom and in grace. Thomas Carlyle, the great Scottish thinker, said: "The older I grow, and I now stand on the brink of eternity—the more comes back to me the first sentence in the catechism which I learned when a child, and the fuller and deeper its meaning becomes: 'What is the chief end of man? To glorify God and to enjoy Him forever.'"[1]

Dr. Robinson influenced several generations of Presbyterian ministers to use and teach the Westminster Standards. Robert Bruce Wills speaks for many of Robinson's students when he says, "We gained from him a deep appreciation of the Shorter Catechism and I have used it in worship services and communicant classes over the years."[2] Paul Settle writes,

Dr. Robbie loved the Westminster Standards, often quoted from them, and urged them upon us as containing the only system of truth found in the Scriptures. Out of his deep appreciation of the Larger Catechism he encouraged us all to use it as a remarkably full and satisfying guide for preaching and teaching.

Occasionally a student was bold enough to ask Dr. Robinson if he thought the Westminster Standards were perfect. He would reply, "No, but their exposition of faith is better than yours, and you can improve yours by studying theirs!"

In one of his articles for the *Presbyterian Journal* Robinson reviewed the decline of Presbyterianism in England, Scotland, and Ireland during "the age of reason," and stated that two things saved American Presbyterianism "from the downgrade to Unitarianism": sound doctrine and the Great Awakening. He argued that today we

[1] See Selected Writings 15 for Robinson's material on Questions 29-38 and 84-87.
[2] *Presbyterian Journal,* January 12, 1983, 2.

need "creedal subscription taken and kept in the fear of the LORD" and we need revival. He stated that the Presbyterian Church in England "closed its ears to the revival led by Whitefield and the Wesleys" and prayed that the Southern Presbyterian Church "may welcome a revival, may be blessed and edified by it—may not be split by it, but above all may not reject it."[1]

[1] WCR, *Presbyterian Journal,* April 1, 1950, 6.

13. "DR. ROBBIE"

William Childs Robinson was a challenging teacher. "If I have ever studied under a brilliant professor," writes Sam Cappel, "Dr. Robinson was the one." One day Robinson was lecturing and reading long sections from a book. After class Cappel went up to make sure of a quotation and discovered that the book was in German. Dr. Robinson's students often felt that he overestimated their ability. "At times some of us felt a bit lost," Paul Settle writes, "as 'Dr. Robbie' rapidly leaped from Ignatius to Augustine to Erasmus to Calvin to Beza to Savonarola to Warfield to Edwards to Billy Graham!" "One of Robinson's most disconcerting practices," Settle comments, "was to suddenly peer over his notes or whirl from the blackboard, fix his squinting eyes upon an unsuspecting student, cry out his name, and, in his rapid-fire delivery, blurt out a question."

Aiken Taylor wrote:

> Until you caught on to what he was trying to do with your lazy mind, he seemed acid in his comments and infuriating in his style … But he believed what he taught and when he finished with you, you believed it too … It took me about six months of my first class in church history to "catch on." "Dr. Robbie" did not waste time with pabulum; he started with strong meat. It was the strong meat of classical Reformed theology, laid over the fascinating story of the church.[1]

Robinson's seminary students were introduced to the primary sources and the best secondary works in church history. Those who went on to graduate study were well prepared. A wide reader, Dr. Robinson kept abreast of current developments in theology at home and abroad, and from the beginning of his career was a frequent

[1] *Presbyterian Journal,* February 9, 1983, 23.

contributor to religious papers and journals. John Leith, a noted theologian and church historian in the Southern Presbyterian Church, wrote that as a scholar William Childs Robinson had "no superior in his denomination."[1]

Julius Scott, professor at Wheaton College, says that throughout his teaching career in two colleges and a state university, pictures of his two academic mentors, William Childs Robinson and F. F. Bruce, stood on his desk. "Without the former," he wrote, "I would never have met the latter. In seminary Professor Robinson worked patiently with me, a weak, but determined student. It was from him that I learned the necessity and rigors of academic research, of critical thinking, and breadth of knowledge."

D. James Kennedy wrote:

> I have often said that Dr. William Childs Robinson was probably the greatest scholar I had the privilege of studying under. Some students considered him to be "dry" as a teacher, but I felt that the content of his classes was so extraordinarily valuable that I would not have cared if he was a monotone. I believe that I took every elective that he offered and would say that his theological influence on my thinking was greater than that of any other living teacher. I have quoted him more than probably all of my other professors combined.

Dr. Robinson was a church historian and theologian who was also a Bible scholar. He was more conversant with his Greek New Testament, his students claimed, than most preachers were with their English Bibles. The students marveled at how skillfully Dr. Robinson would bring forth some appropriate passage or striking point from the Greek text. They were impressed with how he would take a topic and trace it through the Bible from Genesis to Revelation, quoting the relevant scriptures. John Neville maintains that he found assurance of his salvation on one of those occasions. When Dr. Robinson reached the book of Psalms, Neville knew that he was "saved and secure"!

Thomas Ellis remembers "the doctor's 'flights' out of the sometimes long, cold corridors of history into some warm, majestic room within the house of God's truth." He writes:

[1] *Presbyterian Outlook,* January 10, 1983, 15.

I can never forget one such occasion when with eyes almost shut and animation of voice, if not of body, the topic became the "I am's" of Christ in John's Gospel. For perhaps ten minutes the class was carried by the professor beyond the lecture of the day into the very heart of our Lord's words: "I am the good shepherd"; "I am the light of the world," *etc.* "The expression in Greek is emphatic," he declared. " I *myself* am … I *and no other* am … I *and I only* am the bread."[1]

D. James Kennedy tells of the time when Dr. Robinson said in class that we have all violated—in word, thought, and deed; in omission and commission—all of the Ten Commandments every day. One student with an unusual amount of temerity, since Dr. Robinson "did not suffer fools gladly," raised his hand and said, "But professor, how do we break the fourth commandment on Tuesday?" Everyone thought that he had caught Dr. Robinson in a mistake. Robinson reached up and snatched off his glasses in a dramatic manner as the classroom became as silent as a tomb. He looked the student in the eye and said, "Six days shalt thou labor and do all thy work—thou sluggard, thou—and the seventh is the Sabbath of the Lord thy God. When you goof off and fail to do all your work on Tuesday, you are violating the fourth commandment." Apparently, Dr. Robinson repeated this assertion in every new class, and some student fell into the trap every time.

Once a student was asking many rapid-fire questions without giving the professor time to answer. Robinson laughingly took him by both ears and said, "Dear brother, the good Lord gave you two ears but only one mouth—now hush and listen!"

Dr. Robinson would ask, "Who is the head of the church?" If a student answered correctly, but softly, that "Jesus Christ is the only head of the church," the professor would stamp his foot on the floor and with a booming voice reply, "Don't *say* it, dear brother, *shout* it."

One of Robinson's "pet peeves" was the statement "Christ has no hands but your hands." A hymn he disliked was "Rise up, O men of God." He would exclaim, "To your knees, to your knees, O men of God." One day a student prefaced his question with another question, "Isn't God dependent upon man?" He did not finish because Dr. Robinson broke in with "God forbid!" He threw a piece of chalk he

---

[1] [Ellis], "Biographical Tribute," 2.

was holding against the wall, and spent the rest of the class answering such a shocking question. After the bell, another student picked up the shattered pieces of chalk and handed these to Dr. Robinson, saying, "I was not able to get the ink bottle that Luther threw at the devil, but I did get this piece of chalk."[1]

Dr. Robinson was very aware of the theological undercurrents at the seminary, which reflected the heated debates in the denomination. He sometimes answered questions in class with "clipped, passionate responses" that appeared to be "angry and defensive." The "liberal" students enjoyed "baiting" him; the "conservatives" prayed that "he would simply provide an irenic, well-reasoned and biblical answer, which," writes Paul Settle, "he was wonderfully equipped to do."

Dr. Robinson was "feared rather than loved by many of his students," remembers Paul Settle. "But he was loved by those who got to know him, who visited with him between classes, or walked with him in the halls of the classroom building or along the sidewalks beside Columbia Drive." He had "a sincere interest in the faith of his students," each of whom he addressed as "dear brother." He encouraged them in their prayer life, devotional reading, and practical ministry. When Paul Settle was serving as student preacher in two small Alabama country churches, he appreciated Dr. Robinson's interest and helpful suggestions, "given humbly, patiently and sympathetically."

Robinson wrote many letters in behalf of his students, recommending them for places of ministry but including candid comments. He described one student this way: "He is a steady, hardworking, believing student. He is not the most brilliant man in the class, but he will be liked and wear well with his people."[2] He closed his letters to former students and others with words like these—"May our gracious Father guide you. He knows better and sees further and always is right."[3]

Julius Scott says:

I learned far more than academics from Professor Robinson. Through his teaching and example I learned much about the nature and person

---

[1] Richards, *As I Remember It,* 44.

[2] WCR to O. M. Anderson, January 1, 1962. Historical Center of the Presbyterian Church in America, St. Louis, Missouri.

[3] WCR to Gregg Singer, July 19, 1957. Historical Center of the Presbyterian Church in America, St. Louis, Missouri.

of God, the ministry and work of Jesus Christ, the importance of the church. During my senior year I was sick in an Atlanta hospital. I was in considerable pain and had received less than encouraging news. Dr. Robbie entered the room and, for a while, listened to my complaints and questionings. Finally he put his hand over my mouth and said, "Hush, Julius, God is still on the throne!" At first I almost resented what I thought to be insensitivity. But through the following hours, weeks, years, and decades those words have rung in my ears. The truth of his statement has propelled me on, no matter what.

Robinson on occasion sought out students for conversation and even advice. One day, just before Christmas break, first-year student John Neville encountered Dr. Robinson in the dormitory looking for another student. Neville, who was in awe of the professor, told him that the student he sought had already left for home. "I need to talk with someone," said Dr. Robinson; "I'll talk with you." The two of them sat on a bed in one of the dorm rooms while the professor asked the terrified young man for his advice and counsel about a matter.

Charles McGowan recalls personal conversations with his teacher, especially stories about the seminary when it was still in Columbia, South Carolina, reflecting Dr. Robinson's enduring interest in the "Old Columbia Seminary."

McGowan remembers Dr. Robinson as "a gentle and gracious Southern gentleman." He had "a cute sense of humor," according to Kennedy Smart. When Smart introduced him to his wife, Mary, Dr. Robinson replied with a twinkle in his eye, "This is your second wife?"—implying that she was much younger-looking than her husband!

Mrs. Robinson, Mary McConkey Robinson, was "a colorful character," says Charles McGowan. "While being the consummate gracious Southern lady, she had a bold, no-nonsense manner about her." Mrs. Robinson was known to lose patience occasionally with the squirrels in the yard of their house, which was right across the street from the seminary, and go after them with a shotgun. Students hearing the sound of the gun would remark that another squirrel had "bit the dust." Mrs. Robinson "took good care" of her husband, driving him around Atlanta, and guarding his time. She would admit a student who came to see the professor to a little room in their house, go and get her husband, and come back later to be sure that the student left on time! Robinson accepted his wife's leadership in many areas, and was grateful for her love and care for him.

Robinson held a kindly conservative view about the role of women, believing that he was constrained to do so by Scripture. He wrote on one occasion:

> In Christ Jesus there is neither Jew nor Greek, neither bond nor free, neither male nor female, for ye are all one in Christ (Gal. 3:28). I understand this to mean that each one of us has direct access to God through faith in Jesus Christ. My standing before Him is no different from my wife's. I have no priority over her in the things of Christ and God. But the Apostle did not interpret this to mean that there was no difference in the ordering of the home (*Eph.* 5:22-23), or of order in the church (*1 Tim.* 2).[1]

Dr. Robinson dedicated his book *Our Lord: An Affirmation of the Deity of Christ* to Mary—"The wife of my youth, the mother of Billy and James, the light of the home, with whom 'the best is yet to be.'" Arguing for catechetical instruction against those who would say that children were not able to understand such theological statements, Dr. Robinson wrote in 1933: "After teaching theological students for six years, I can testify that my theological classes have brought me no more metaphysical questions than have been raised by two young minds in my own home."[2]

[1] WCR, *Presbyterian Journal*, August 17, 1955, 3.
[2] WCR, *Christian Observer*, September 20, 1933, 7.

14. PREACHER OF THE GOSPEL

D r. Robinson was a seminary professor who preached, or, as he probably would have preferred, he was a preacher who taught in a seminary. Thomas Ellis describes Dr. Robinson's preaching as "clear, logical, biblical-theological exegesis" combined with "memorable expressions of language to produce what is truly precious in preaching because it is so rare."[1] "Whenever I heard Dr. Robinson preach," writes Robert Bruce Wills, "the good doctor aimed at bringing his listeners to a decision for Christ, never ceasing to express the urgency and responsibility of giving a positive answer to the gospel call."[2] Dr. Robinson frequently told the seminary students that the first professor at Columbia Theological Seminary, Dr. Thomas Goulding, had said, "Let every sermon preached contain so much of the plan of salvation that, should a heathen come in who never heard the gospel before, and who should depart never to hear it again, he should learn enough to know what he must do to be saved."[3] Robinson told his students that "preaching becomes more effective when it calls men to behold God working for them than when it scolds them for not serving Him."[4] He also liked to tell them that "Calvin says that a preacher ought to be much in the third of Genesis, the third of John, and the third of Romans."[5]

[1] [Ellis], "Biographical Tribute," 1.
[2] *Presbyterian Journal,* January 12, 1983, 2.
[3] WCR, *Christ—The Bread of Life,* preface. See George Howe, "History of Columbia Theological Seminary," in *Memorial Volume of the Semi-Centennial of the Theological Seminary at Columbia, South Carolina* (Columbia: The Presbyterian Publishing House, 1884), 186.
[4] WCR, *Christian Faith and Modern Theology,* 391.
[5] WCR, *The Word of the Cross,* 71.

Again and again Robinson stressed the urgent need for ministers to preach the Bible and the Bible only. In one of his earliest books Dr. Robinson wrote:

> The time has come for the church to concentrate upon the gospel with the intensity of a Luther and the clarity of a Calvin. It is time to cease modifying the gospel to suit the fancies of an unbelieving world. The minister is called so to immerse himself in the scriptural statement of the gospel that he will preach a full-orbed evangel. When our preaching is molded by the Word of God written, that preaching will again become the Word of God proclaimed. Then with confidence we may pray that the Holy Spirit will make it the power of God unto salvation.[1]

Robinson wrote in 1935:

> The Presbyterian Church places the pulpit—not the altar—in the center of the church as a sign that the book which adorns the pulpit is ruling the church. Woe unto the Presbyterian minister who fails to hide himself behind that book! The pulpit means that the Word of God rules the church ... The church is true just in proportion as the Word of God is truly preached and wholeheartedly received as the unique, final and sufficient revelation of the whole counsel of God for His own glory and our salvation. God is speaking! Hear Him! Or as Thornwell would say, the church has a creed (what she believes God has revealed in His Word); she does not have opinions (what men are saying).[2]

In 1962 Robinson wrote a brief article about preaching with the title "Tell Us What God Said!" In it he set forth the views of the earlier Columbia Seminary professors about preaching. "This is part of the heritage of yesterday," he wrote, "that stands as a challenge for today." Henry Alexander White, Robinson recalled, told his students that "to preach was to take a passage of Scripture, expound it, and sit down." William M. McPheeters gave his life to teaching the Bible and left as his last message, "Oh! that our ministers would realize the utter reasonableness of doing what the apostles did—preach the Word and pray the Holy Spirit to bless it."[3]

In his *The Reformation: A Rediscovery of Grace*, Robinson wrote: "The Holy Spirit gathers the church through the proclamation of

---

[1] WCR, *The Certainties of the Gospel*, 33.
[2] WCR, *Christian Observer*, January 9, 1935, 8.
[3] WCR, *Christian Observer*, January 24, 1962, 6.

the gospel as He opens the Bible both to the understanding of the preacher and to the heart of the hearer, making the sermon a corporate action that links speaking and listening."

Robinson described how Christ sent his disciples to preach to all nations repentance and remission of sins. The apostles proclaimed the things of Christ with the Spirit sent down from heaven, so that believers were born again. As Paul preached, the gospel came to the Thessalonians in the Holy Spirit and worked with great effectiveness. The Galatians and the Corinthians received the Spirit by the word of the cross. For the Romans, faith came by hearing and hearing by the word of Christ. To the Ephesians, the word of truth was the gospel of salvation, the preached Word, the sword of the Spirit. That sword was handed on to the succeeding ministers with this commission: "Preach the Word."

Robinson showed how in the Reformation Luther "gave his life to preaching the gospel from the Word and to translating that Word into a language that the people could understand and appropriate." And John Calvin, he wrote, "found the sheep of the Lord scattered on a thousand hills, and he lifted a banner to gather them, not a new banner but the old banner of God's Word." In the Reformation the pulpit was given the focal center as a visible sign that the Word of God was ruling the church and as a reminder to the preacher that he was not there to air the philosophies or the opinions of men, but to serve as *Dei verbi minister*.

To the Reformers the Word was the sword of the Spirit. Robinson wrote:

> As the Word without the Spirit would not be the saving Word of God, so the Spirit without the Word would not be the revealing Spirit. The Word is thus the door or the window through which the Spirit comes to us, or the bridge or path on which He moves … Commenting on the action of God both by the voice and by the Spirit of God in Ezekiel 2:1-2, Calvin adds: "This work of the Spirit is, therefore, joined with the Word of God. But a distinction is made that we may know that the eternal Word is of no avail by itself, unless animated by the power of the Spirit."[1]

---

[1] WCR, *The Reformation*, 127-28.

"Thus in revealing God to us by His Word," Robinson wrote that

> the Spirit acts in a threefold way. He inspires the prophets and apostles in receiving and writing the Word. Again He accompanies the Word as it is preached, speaking by and with it, so that it becomes the Sword of the Spirit. Then the same Spirit penetrates into our hearts so that we believe the doctrine of the Scriptures as from the person of God speaking by the mouth of men. The blessed circle is complete, from the apostles through the preachers, into the hearts of the hearers. By this triple work of the Spirit with the Word we are drawn into the orbit of Christ and find ourselves no longer strangers but children in our Father's house, given a partnership in the covenant of grace.[1]

Illustrating the fact that the Word was understood by the Reformers as a powerful means of grace, Robinson wrote:

> John Witherspoon, the great evangelical divine of Scotland, accepted the second invitation from the struggling little college of Princeton. His entrance upon the pulpit that first Sunday was like a king ascending his throne. What would the great man have to say? Taking as his text "Paul may plant and Apollos may water, but only God gives the increase," Dr. Witherspoon declared that the success of the Gospel is wholly of God. Some years later he used the same sermon at the organization of the first American General Assembly. God heard that humble avowal and so blessed the Presbyterian family until, from those small beginnings, there are now millions in the Presbyterian and Reformed churches in this land, and their missionary testimony sounds to the ends of the world.[2]

Robinson began an article on "What Shall the Preacher Preach?" with these words:

> What finer boon for Christendom could there be than for every Church of England and Episcopal rector to trumpet "Justification" next Sunday in the incisive tones of their "judicious" Richard Hooker; or for every Church of Scotland and Presbyterian minister to unite with John Maclaurin in "Glorying in the Cross" or in James Denney's "The Death of Christ"; or for every Methodist to proclaim the gospel as clearly as John Wesley did in his sermon "The Lord Our

[1] WCR, *The Reformation*, 130.
[2] WCR, *The Reformation*, 134.

Righteousness"; or for every Baptist pastor to send forth the message in the urgent tones of Spurgeon's "Pardon and Justification."[1]

Robinson on occasion taught classes on preaching and was always present for the two student sermons on Tuesday evenings. He was known for his candid remarks. He once said that faculty criticism was the only honest criticism most ministers ever heard except in the *second* year of their married life! More than once he told the students, "When you are preaching and you say, 'I think,' I hope that some dear brother will stand up and say, 'I don't care what you think, tell us what the Word says.'"

John Leith wrote:

> The high point in the education of a seminarian for the pastorate fifty years ago at Columbia Theological Seminary was student preaching. Each student was required to preach before the entire student body and faculty and then submit to public criticism by the homiletics professor and briefer criticisms by all of the faculty in the presence of the student body ... In my own experience I have never preached three better-prepared sermons than those I preached before the faculty and student body at Columbia Theological Seminary.[2]

The Columbia professors taught their students how to preach as they did or as their famous predecessors preached—men like James Henley Thornwell, Benjamin Morgan Palmer, and John Lafayette Girardeau. They discovered, however, that Peter Marshall was unique. Catherine Marshall wrote:

> They might have discouraged or even killed the very thing in their young student that was to lift his preaching out of the mediocre. But the consecrated men on Columbia Seminary's faculty were too wise for that.
>
> Early they realized that Peter's instinctive approach to sermonizing was different from theirs—different from the method they taught ... Therefore, their conclusion was, "Do it your own way, Peter." Many years after Peter's graduation, he wrote to one of his beloved professors: "I shall never forget how you encouraged me to be a preacher; how you wisely insisted that I be myself, that I try to develop by God's help whatever talent He had given me ... It was you who saw to it that it

[1] WCR, *Christianity Today,* April 26, 1968, 10.
[2] Leith, *Crisis in the Church,* 108.

was Peter Marshall that graduated and not a student trying to imitate someone else."[1]

Peter Marshall remembered a statement made by one of the seminary professors—a statement that shaped all his sermons. "Gentlemen," the professor said, "in writing your sermons, I beg of you, use a sanctified imagination."[2] And that was what Peter Marshall did.[3]

Dr. Robinson used the book *The Relevance of Preaching* by the French Reformed pastor Pierre Marcel for his classes in preaching, first in its French edition and then in a mimeographed translation. He later wrote the introduction for the publication of *The Relevance of Preaching* in English translation, praising the book "for the manifold emphases which it places upon the Holy Spirit and His work in inspiring the Word, in directing the preacher both in preparing and in delivering the sermon, and in opening the hearts of the hearers. By His threefold ministry the circle is completed. The great and gracious acts of God in Christ are recorded in Scripture, proclaimed in the church, and given for our salvation."[4]

Dr. Robinson encouraged his students to use the church year, with its gospel and epistle lessons, and to preach through the books of the Bible. He told them to preach on the Apostles' Creed, the Ten Commandments, the Lord's Prayer, and the Westminster Catechism, so as to give "added variety and breadth" to their preaching and to "honor the whole counsel of God as set forth in His Word." He insisted that the students give a clear exposition of the plan of salvation, suggesting five points from the Bible and the Shorter Catechism: (1) Why do I need a Saviour? (2) What has Jesus done to save me? (3) What does

---

[1] Catherine Marshall, *A Man Called Peter*, 195. Catherine Marshall does not identify the professors, but William McPheeters, J. B. Green, and William Childs Robinson were all involved in teaching homiletics and offering sermon criticism during the time that Peter Marshall was a student at the seminary.

[2] Marshall, *A Man Called Peter*, 191.

[3] Marshall graduated from Columbia Seminary in 1931. He served pastorates in Covington and Atlanta, Georgia, before moving in 1937 to the 1,800-member New York Avenue Presbyterian Church in Washington, D.C. In 1947 he was elected Chaplain of the U.S. Senate, where he was known for his brief and memorable prayers. He died of a heart attack at the age of forty-six.

[4] WCR, Introduction to Pierre Ch. Marcel, *The Relevance of Preaching* (Grand Rapids: Baker Book House, 1963).

the Holy Spirit do to save me? (4) What does God the Father do to save me? (5) What does God ask of me to be saved?[1]

Robinson's own sermons always contained a clear and pointed presentation of the gospel. He ended his sermon "The Prayer of a Soldier" this way:

> Soldier, as you find in this text—"And what shall I say: Father, save me from this hour? But for this cause came I unto this hour: Father glorify Thy name" (John 12:27-28)—the perfect example for your prayer, look deeper and find here also the prayer that leads to your salvation. If Christ had turned His back upon His *via dolorosa*, if He had refused the cup of agony and the burden of the Cross, if His ultimate prayer had been "Father save me from this hour," our ultimate fate would have been damnation. "There was no other good enough to pay the debt of sin. He only could unlock the gate of heaven and let us in."
>
> Christ swapped places with us. He bore our sins in His own body on the tree. He who knew no sin was made sin for us that we might be made the righteousness of God in Him. Jesus Christ, Jesus Christ alone, is our righteousness in the presence of God now. As Anselm of Canterbury taught the men of old, we place the death of Christ between us and our sins, between us and the punishment we deserve, between us and the wrath of God. For in His great final prayer Christ willed to place Himself between us and the destruction we deserved, to take our burden upon His shoulders and to bear our punishment on His cross. And when as our representative up from the grave He arose, He became the Lord our Righteousness, the ground of our forgiveness living in Heaven to intercede for us. The same Christ who ultimately prayed for the cross on Calvary Hill, that on that cross He might die to save you and me, is today pleading on the basis of that cross for your salvation.[2]

Dr. Robinson saw his seminary classroom as an evangelistic opportunity. Writing on "Evangelism in the Classroom," Robinson said that there are theological students "who are having a life and death wrestle with doubt and temptation. They need to know that God has come down to us in Christ and that faith itself is the gift of the Holy Spirit."[3] More than one student has testified that he came to faith in Christ in Dr. Robinson's classes.

---

[1] WCR, *Presbyterian Journal,* March 1, 1947, 5.
[2] WCR, *Presbyterian Journal,* March 1944, 8-9.
[3] WCR, *Presbyterian Journal,* March 15, 1950, 3.

Robinson preached on special occasions in churches and assisted during times of pastoral transition. He served as interim pastor for at least ten churches during his busy years as a seminary professor.[1] Several times Dr. Robinson was stated supply at the Ingleside Presbyterian Church, a few miles from Columbia Seminary in an economically depressed community. Kennedy Smart, who was pastor of that church from 1952 to 1960, heard from the people how "Dr. Robbie," with galoshes on his feet, raincoat on his back, and a felt hat on his head, would slosh through mud and puddles in rain and snow to visit the congregation and call on prospective members. "A home-going pastor," Dr. Robinson told the students, "makes a church-going congregation." He recommended a visitation program utilizing the elders of the church so that they could "search for the fruit of the preached Word" among the people of the congregation.[2]

On Easter Sunday, April 1, 1945, Robinson preached on "God Incarnate for Suffering Men" in Warm Springs, Georgia.[3] Among the worshipers were seventy-five polio sufferers including President Franklin D. Roosevelt. The whole front of the chapel was free of pews so that the patients could be brought in on stretchers and in wheelchairs. Robinson described his sermon:

> The incarnation of God, the central Christian affirmation, was the theme of the Easter sermon. As the music was redolent with Christ's resurrection, so the sermon was steeped in His suffering and dying for our sins. And these two great events—Christ's death for our sins and His rising again the third day—are the Christian gospel. Or, to quote the sermon, "The Lord of Glory of His own will entered into our life of grief and suffering, and for love of men bore all and more than all that men may be called to bear."[4]

It was President Roosevelt's last Easter. The day before his death, April 12, 1945, he wrote to Robinson, "That was indeed a grand service and it was wonderful that you could participate." "It is not likely

[1] The Presbyterian Church in Covington, Georgia; First Presbyterian, Charlotte, North Carolina; Reid Memorial, Augusta; and West End, Pryor Street, Morningside, Westminster, Ingleside, North Avenue, and Capitol View, Atlanta.
[2] WCR, *Presbyterian Journal,* March 1, 1947, 4.
[3] See Selected Writings 16. Two other sermons, "The Joy of the Lord" and "Under His Wings," are Selected Writings 17 and 18.
[4] WCR, *Presbyterian Journal,* May 1945, 8.

that I shall ever again preach to a president of the United States," Dr. Robinson said, "but I may well remember that the King of kings is always in the audience and that I ought to preach Him as in His presence."[1]

Dr. Robinson preached at Westminster Chapel in London and in other major pulpits at home and overseas. He was a preacher at the World Conference of Evangelicals at Clarens, Switzerland. He was a popular speaker to college student groups. Robinson preached at several annual conventions of the League of Evangelical Students, and to students at Mississippi State College, Presbyterian College, Hope College, Agnes Scott College, Queens-Chicora College, Salem College, Belhaven College, and Berry College. Preaching the baccalaureate sermon at his alma mater, Roanoke College, he said:

> Preaching Jesus Christ means preeminently preaching Him as crucified. The church has never found the symbol of her faith anywhere but in His cross. Since the cross met Luther everywhere in the Scriptures, the reformer declared, "When I listen to Christ, there is sketched in my heart a picture of a man hanging on a cross, just as my countenance is sketched upon the water when I look therein." Calvin is certain that only by the preaching of the cross will any man ever find his way back to God as his Father. In their chorus, we unite:

> Our glory, only in the cross,
> Our only hope, the crucified.[2]

Robinson spoke at Bible conferences all over the South. In 1961, with Gregg Singer, he taught at the Pensacola Theological Institute. Dr. Robinson wrote to Donald Graham, the convener of the institute, proposing that he lecture on "The Faith of the Southern Presbyterian Worthies." "I hope that Dr. Singer and I can both get in a good 'plug' for the sole headship and kingship of Christ—the only lawgiver in Zion," he added. Robinson was greatly concerned about the content of his sermons, but he did not consider himself a great speaker. He wrote somewhat playfully to Gregg Singer that "neither of us has any reputation as an orator to uphold."[3]

[1] WCR, *Presbyterian Journal*, May 1945, 7, 9.

[2] WCR, *Christianity Today*, April 13, 1962, 8.

[3] Letters in the Historical Center of the Presbyterian Church in America, St. Louis, Missouri.

Dr. Robinson continued to insist on "the relevancy of preaching"—not just any kind of preaching, but true, biblical preaching. He wrote:

As the clouds on the horizon get more ominous, there is a rising cry for a sure word from God. The legacy of our fathers is found in the faithful exposition of the holy Scriptures at each service of worship. The increasing tensions of life summon us to answer this cry not less faithfully than they did.[1]

15. WORSHIPER OF GOD

One of William Childs Robinson's students says that "perhaps worship was the greatest contribution Dr. Robinson made to the church. He showed me (and I am sure others also) what it means to be a true worshiper of God." "Underlying all the work of a Christian," Dr. Robinson reminded us over and over, "there needs to be a devout, worshiping heart."

One day Robinson began the chapel service with the words, "Thus saith the high and lofty One that inhabiteth eternity, whose name is Holy; I dwell in the high and holy place, with him also that is of a contrite and humble spirit, to revive the spirit of the humble, and to revive the heart of the contrite ones" (*Isa.* 57:15). "There was something in the way those words were uttered," Thomas Ellis says, "to cause me to ask myself, 'Have I in my twenty-two years of life ever really worshiped the living God?' How solemn and yet joyful the speaker was—as if his face shone while he pronounced those words in such singular and impressive tones with his eyes not opened, yet hardly closed." As he left the chapel that day, Ellis repeated quietly to himself the words that Dr. Robinson had spoken, then aloud to a friend who was walking with him. The friend quickly responded, "You can't say them like Dr. Robbie." "No, nor could anyone else," Ellis thought.[1]

In Robinson's book *Our Lord—An Affirmation of the Deity of Christ,* there is an impressive chapter on "The Worship of Jesus." He wrote an article "The Lamb in the Midst of the Throne: The Focal Center of Christian Worship."[2] In 1956 Robinson presented a paper

---

[1] [Ellis], "Biographical Tribute," 1.
[2] WCR, *Presbyterian Journal,* January 1944, 5-6. See Selected Writings 19.

on "The Unitive and Divisive Elements in Christian Worship" to the American Theological Committee meeting in Philadelphia.[1] Robinson began:

> As the church is the place where God acts and man serves, Christian worship is primarily divine action. It moves from the Godward pole to the Godward pole. It is both inspired by God and directed toward God. It is directed toward God as He has revealed Himself to us in Christ Jesus as our gracious heavenly Father. It rises from hearts that have been regenerated by God the Holy Spirit and from mouths that He has opened in His own praise.

Robinson continued:

> Christian worship is the response of quickened hearts to God's revelation of Himself. God has never left Himself without witnesses, giving us sunshine and rain and fruitful seasons. He has spoken unto us in divers portions and manners through the prophets. Most of all He has manifested the light of the knowledge of His glory in the face of Jesus Christ. Accordingly we "richtly worship and imbrace him be trew faith in Christ Jesus, quha[2] is the only head of the same Kirk" (Scots Confession).

Robinson stated that Christian worship unites Christians when it is faithful to the directions God has given in his Word.

> The Son of Man walks in the midst of the churches, holding them like stars in His hand and governing them by the sword out of His mouth. By the messengers of the several churches the incarnate Word speaks His own Word to His people as they preach Christ from the Holy Scriptures.
>
> The ultimate condition for unity in and through Christian worship is the recognition that the primary ground, the primary content and the primary form of Christian worship is divine activity, and the continual effort to conform the secondary or human ground, content, and form of this worship to the action of God in Christ.
>
> Christian worship is unitive in proportion as it recognizes and proclaims the sole lordship of Christ in His body, the church, and in her worship. It is divisive in proportion as it deflects or divides this lordship, giving part thereof to preacher or to hierarch, to a naturalistic

[1] WCR, *Presbyterian Journal,* September 1946, 7-9.
[2] who

system which mutilates the gospel, or to an idealistic empiricism which has no essential place for the unique events of God's saving intervention, to a hue and cry for His body to yoke itself to the chariot in which Caesar rides, or to diversion of her energies into a humanistic program in lieu of His Great Commission.

Robinson asked the question:

Will the introduction of this or that ancient prayer or chant or creed or response into our worship draw us closer to our Lord or will this so-called aid to worship attract attention to itself and so deflect it from the true object of worship?

He answered:

Every proposed enrichment of the liturgy also properly comes under the test of the obedience of the Christian faith. There is a presupposition in favor of an act of worship that God's true people through the ages have found, bringing them closer to their Lord either in confession or in adoration. This testimony is not to be lightly esteemed. But it is to be tested to find out whether it is an act authorized by the Word for the church or merely introduced by man's ingenuity. The only true Christian unity is under the sole reign of Christ the King. Therefore, we must ever seek to tread the courts of His house in a worship that is of His ordering. And as we do so, we recognize that the risen Head of the Church is blessing other branches of the one vine as they worship the Triune God in forms not identical with ours.

The essential elements of worship, Robinson maintained, were the Word, the sacraments, and prayer or praise. Robinson wrote about the Lord's Supper:

I first cast anchor in Calvin when I went to the *Institutes* for a more adequate treatment of the Lord's Supper. Now, a third of a century later, I am convinced that this approach was providential and that the full sweep of Calvin's doctrine of the supper as a matter of faith and of the analogy of faith is yet to bear fruit in the Protestant world. The first thing we are to do, at the Table of the Lord, is to feed upon Christ who here presents Himself to us as the bread of life.[1]

---

[1] WCR, "The Tolerance of Our Prophet or Calvin's Tolerance and Intolerance," in *John Calvin: Contemporary Prophet,* ed. Jacob T. Hoogstra (Grand Rapids: Baker Book House, 1959), 43. For his course in church polity, nineteenth-century Columbia Seminary professor John Adger followed the advice of James Henley

He understood the relationship between the Word and the Lord's Supper as Calvin did.

> Only by a balanced emphasis on the Word and on the Sacraments can God be honoured as the One who both speaks and acts through the means of His own ordering. It is well known that the churches which look to the Reformation have said *the Word* and the Sacraments, while those which have called themselves Catholic have placed the order rather, *the Sacraments* and the Word. The Reformed tendency is to think of the Sacraments as confirming the Word; the Tridentine is to regard the Word as preparatory for the real infusion of grace by the Sacraments.[1]

"The Church rests upon the Word as its foundation," Robinson wrote, "with the sacraments as the supporting stays ... In the New Testament Church God makes Himself audible in the proclamation of His Word, and His acts become visible in the administration of the sacraments, as the Holy Spirit effectively uses these instruments. The sacrament is a visible Word and the Word is an audible sacrament."[2] "While the sacrament is being administered," Robinson wrote, "Christ is more active in giving Himself and His blessing to the believer than the minister is in distributing the bread and the cup to the communicants."[3]

In an article in the *Southern Presbyterian Journal* Robinson described the worship service of the Shenandoah Presbyterian Church of Miami, Florida, not "primarily to throw a bouquet to a fine body of loyal Christian people," he wrote, "but to encourage other churches." "The reading of the Bible in the sanctuary is introduced by this sentence: 'In this church we believe the Bible to be the Word of God and the only infallible rule of faith and practice. It is recommended that this Book be used in your homes daily.'" At Shenandoah, Robinson

---

Thornwell, who told him, "I should make the fourth book of Calvin's *Institutes* a textbook on the subject of church polity and the sacraments." Adger taught Calvin's sacramental doctrine at the seminary, the effect of which continued into Robinson's time as a student there. Not only was Book Four of the *Institutes* taught at Columbia, but since Thornwell's time the first three books as well. See Calhoun, *Our Southern Zion*, 140-41.

[1] WCR, *Evangelical Quarterly,* October-December 1955, 195-96.
[2] WCR, *The Reformation,* 135.
[3] WCR, *Christian Faith and Modern Theology,* 391.

explained, "The Word is always used in dependence upon and with appeal to the Holy Spirit who inspired it." Each morning service is closed with the singing of the short prayer written by the pastor, Daniel Iverson:

> Spirit of the Living God! Fall fresh on me!
> Spirit of the Living God! Fall fresh on me!
> Break me, melt me, mold me, fill me.
> Spirit of the Living God! Fall fresh on me!

"Thus God's program for keeping His people in covenant union with Himself, by His Spirit and His Word (Isaiah 59:21) is carried out," Robinson wrote.[1]

Robinson was interested in church architecture. He believed that church buildings could be beautiful and at the same time appropriate for Reformed worship. He wrote:

When the old cathedrals and abbeys became Protestant, the chancels [a part of the church reserved for the clergy separate from the nave in which the people gathered] were an embarrassment. In some of the old church buildings in Switzerland the Protestants have sealed off the chancel and made it a separate room. Those who are conscious of their New Testament heritage accept the priesthood of all believers, not a mediating priest caste known as clergy. A choir arranged in two rows facing each other is a fine setting for a service sung by said choir as one can testify from the magnificent singing in King's Chapel, Cambridge. But such an arrangement is not the best for leading a congregation of believers in the praise of God ... Architecture that is appropriate for Reformed worship can be beautiful, as may be seen in the sanctuaries of the First Presbyterian Church of Charlotte, the Independent Presbyterian Church of Savannah, the Shenandoah Presbyterian Church of Miami, the First Presbyterian Church of Marietta, Georgia, and the church in Fincastle, Virginia.[2]

---

[1] WCR, *Presbyterian Journal,* July 16, 1952, 4.
[2] WCR, *Presbyterian Journal,* January 23, 1957, 3-4. For a "theological tour" of the Independent Presbyterian Church of Savannah, Georgia, see Terry L. Johnson's "The Stones Cry Out" in David B. Calhoun, *The Splendor of Grace: The Independent Presbyterian Church of Savannah, Georgia, 1755-2005* (Greenville, SC: A Press Printing, 2005), 569-80.

16. SOUTHERN PRESBYTERIAN

In "The Root and Fruit of the Reformation," the last chapter of *The Reformation: A Rediscovery of Grace*, Robinson dealt with the Reformers' doctrine of the church. "The Ninety-five Theses were the protest of a pastor against a wolf that was playing havoc with his flock," wrote Robinson. "Congregations of believers, in which God freely justifies sinners through the redemption which is in Christ Jesus, grew out of the proclamation of the Word and the administration of the biblical sacraments." He added:

> In view of the predominant place given the Word when the Reformation was in power, it is appropriate to ask our evangelical congregations whether the Word has an equally significant place in our worship today? Or have we changed as men have changed the adage of Scotland's great city? The old adage ran, "Let Glasgow flourish by the preaching of the Word"; the new became, "Let Glasgow flourish."[1]
>
> Every Christian baptized and having God's Word is taught of God and anointed by Him to the priesthood (John 6:45), and it is his duty to confess, preach and spread the Word (2 Cor. 4:13; Ps. 51:13). Where there are many Christians, the individual is not to thrust himself forward, but is to permit himself to be called and drawn forth to preach and teach by the commission of the rest. This right of the whole congregation to judge all teachings and call a fellow Christian of gifts to conduct the rites of divine worship was exercised in St. Andrews Castle in the call of John Knox, and in the home of La Ferriere in Paris by that of La Riviere. If a single Christian find himself where there are no other Christians, he is bound in brotherly love to preach to the heathen. The church is the building of God, but in the construction thereof He uses people as His workmen (1 Cor. 3:5-9; Eph. 4:11). The

---

[1] WCR, *The Reformation*, 160.

Christian community has the right to withdraw from the authority of a bishop who opposes God and His Word and to select teachers and preachers of the Word.[1]

Robinson described the characteristics of the evangelical church as continuity, apostolicity, catholicity, unity, and holiness. Speaking about the continuity of the church, Robinson wrote:

> For the conservative Reformers, Christ is always actively continuing His ministry at the right hand of God, and since His is the one essential ministry there has never failed to be a church on the earth. As Luther finely put it, "It is not we who sustain the church, nor was it our forefathers, nor will it be our descendants." The church was preserved in the centuries past by the Christ who was the same yesterday, it is preserved by the Christ who is the same now, and in the ages to come it will be preserved by the identical Lord who is our help in trouble, "for vain is the help of man."[2]

Describing the apostolicity of the church, he wrote:

> The church is built upon the foundation of the apostles and prophets, that is, upon their proclamation of Jesus Christ as the chief cornerstone (Eph. 2:20). The apostles had companied with Jesus throughout His ministry and were eyewitnesses of His resurrection. By the apostolic *kerygma,* God brought those who had not seen Jesus into a like precious faith with the apostles. As they directly represent Christ and speak with the authority He confers, so there is no way to Him which detours around the apostolic witness to Christ. The recognition of the apostles means the acceptance of Him whose apostles they were. As indicated, in view of the nature of their function as eyewitnesses, the apostles can have no successors, nor does a foundation repeat itself in the superstructure. With the completion of the New Testament canon the norm of their authority was established in the apostolic Scriptures. The church which heeds their apostolic writings and holds on her heart their content—Jesus Christ and His grace—is the apostolic church.[3]

On the catholicity of the church, Robinson wrote that Calvin, in his commentary on the Great Commission, finds the successors to the apostles in those who devote their services to Christ in preaching

[1] WCR, *The Reformation,* 162-63.
[2] WCR, *The Reformation,* 167.
[3] WCR, *The Reformation,* 174.

the gospel in all the world. In his exposition of the Lord's Prayer, Calvin said that "it ought to be the object of our daily wishes that God would collect churches for himself, from all the countries of the earth, that he would enlarge their numbers, enrich them with all gifts, and establish a legitimate order among them." Calvin closed one of his sermons on Jeremiah with the prayer:

> May we strive to bring into the way of thy salvation those who seem to be now lost, so that thy mercy may extend far and wide. Thus may thy salvation obtained through Christ, thine only-begotten Son, be known and embraced among the nations.[1]

Treating the unity of the church, Robinson wrote:

> The vital headship of Christ makes the church; her mission is to testify to His living kingship. Over against all rulers, ecclesiastical and secular, who have sought to dominate her life, evangelical ministers have set forth the sole kingship of Christ over the church. His vital headship invites the effective recognition of the juridical kingship of Christ. He is head over all things to His church, and He who was publicly crucified as a malefactor is to come as the visible King of kings and Lord of lords. Until He does, the evangelical is to attest His sole reign in the church and to find in Him her true unity. A holy unity exists among us, when consenting in pure doctrine we are united to Christ alone.

He quoted William Farel:

> The church of Jesus Christ is the holy congregation of the faithful believers who through real faith are united and incorporated into Jesus Christ of whom they are members. And inasmuch as Jesus Christ is true Son of God, all his members are through him children of God (Eph. 4:4-16; 5:23-27). Jesus is the head; the true Christians are his body (Eph. 1:22-23; Col. 1:18). He is the bridegroom; the faithful believers are his bride (Song of Sol. 1:1-5) whom he has cleansed by his blood, giving health to her body. Jesus has freed his people from their sins (Matt. 1:21; Heb. 9:11-28).
>
> This church does not consist in diversity of degrees, laws, ordinances and orders given by the will of man, but in the true union of faith in our Lord Jesus, in hearing and believing his holy voice (John 10:27).[2]

---

[1] WCR, *The Reformation,* 178-79.
[2] WCR, *The Reformation,* 181; G. Farel, *Summary of What a Christian Ought To Believe,* pp. 15-25, ch. 16.

"The holiness of the evangelical fellowship," Robinson wrote,

is that of a humble, a contrite, a praying, a penitent people. It is the holiness of those who confess themselves sinners at the same time as faith affirms that they are holy when seen in Christ their head and surety. It is a holiness in which we need daily forgiveness and restoration from many lapses. It is a holiness in which we are taught ever anew that there is no merit or worthiness or strength to hold out in ourselves, but that all our merit and worthiness and preservation are in the Lord our righteousness.[1]

Ben Haden, long-time pastor of Chattanooga's First Presbyterian Church, said that "Dr. Robinson stood for what the Southern Presbyterian Church historically stood for." When the *Southern Presbyterian Journal* was established in 1942 to "wave the banners which our heroic fathers lifted in the name of God," Dr. Robinson wrote the feature article for the first issue. In "Our Southern Presbyterian Banners," he developed four great themes: "the blue banner of covenanted loyalty to Christ as the only King in Zion, the only head of His body the church; the banner of His holy Word; the banner of the Westminster Standards which testify to His saving grace and sovereign glory; the banner of missions as the mission of the church."[2] Robinson became a frequent contributor, almost a staff theologian, of the *Southern Presbyterian Journal*, providing a clear, biblical, competent voice to counter the theological liberalism in the Southern Presbyterian seminaries and church leadership.

During the Southern Presbyterian centennial in 1961, Robinson gave an address to the Synod of Alabama—"God of the Marching Centuries"—in which "we unite our witness," he wrote, "with the good confession our fathers have made to our great and gracious God."[3]

Dr. Robinson strongly denounced developments in the Northern Presbyterian Church, especially the prosecution (he called it "persecution") of J. Gresham Machen and other members of the Independent Board for Presbyterian Foreign Missions. Robinson noted that a Presbyterian professor at Union Seminary in New York who denied

[1] WCR, *The Reformation*, 186.
[2] WCR, *Presbyterian Journal*, May 1942. See Selected Writings 20.
[3] WCR, *Presbyterian Journal*, October 18, 1961, 5-6, 8, 18. See Selected Writings 21.

the virgin birth of Christ was not censured for his "offense against the doctrine of Scripture as interpreted by the Westminster Standards," whereas Machen was censured for his part in founding an independent mission board even though the first Presbyterian mission agency in the United States, the Western Foreign Missionary Society, was an "independent board."[1] When the Presbytery of New Brunswick indicted Dr. Machen for holding office in the Independent Board, Robinson wrote:

> In the eighteenth century Dr. John Witherspoon waged a vigorous fight in the Church of Scotland against liberalism in doctrine accompanied by autocracy in administration. In the nineteenth century Dr. Abraham Kuyper faced the same combination in Holland, liberalism in doctrine, autocracy in church government. The historian of the future will write the same verdict over the current events in the Northern Presbyterian Church, unless the only true head of the church, by the power of the Holy Spirit, turn this great church away from the heresies of the Auburn Affirmation to a Christian manifesto of faith in the miracles of the Bible and of the Apostles' Creed.[2]

When Machen died on January 1, 1937, Robinson wrote: "For his uncompromising testimony that 'liberalism' was radically different from Bible Christianity, Machen suffered. But the gracious God, to whom he had committed himself and his cause, saw to it that, when he had borne enough, he was exalted to the Church above. He gave up everything for his faith; but the God in whom he believed was faithful to him in life and in death."[3] In an address to the League of Evangelical Students meeting in Charlotte, North Carolina, a few weeks after Machen's death, Robinson spoke about his own father, and then added:

> As I speak of the faith of my father some of you gathered here are thinking of the last testimony of one who was your father in the faith, Dr. J. Gresham Machen. He forsook position, prestige, comforts,

---

[1] Robinson wrote in 1947, "One may well differ with Dr. Machen as to the wisdom of his course (I did and do), but it is not good Southern Presbyterianism to defend the condemnation of this defender of the faith for refusing to bow to man-made church law" (*Christian Observer*, May 21, 1947, 9).
[2] WCR, *Christianity Today*, March 1935, 249-50.
[3] WCR, *Presbyterian Guardian*, February 13, 1937, 188.

hallowed halls and associations under the impulse of mighty convictions. He gave up everything for his faith; but having faith he had everything needful for this life and for that which is to come, for faith is the link that unites one to the unchanging God. In his last words, Machen … spoke of the preciousness of faith: "Isn't our faith glorious! It is sufficient to the very end."[1]

Robinson was troubled by some of the new ideas that were coming into the Southern Presbyterian Church and Columbia Seminary. Many others were also. The session of Independent Presbyterian Church in Savannah, Georgia, wrote to Dr. J. McDowell Richards, the president of the seminary, stating that in their judgment, "the purity of the fountain must be preserved at all cost." Dr. Richards answered admitting that Professor Robinson had expressed disapproval of some of the statements in a book by one of his Columbia Seminary colleagues, but Richards defended the orthodoxy of his faculty and the seminary. When Charles Woodbridge became Independent's pastor, he was asked by the session to investigate the situation at Columbia Seminary further, especially the views of the Old Testament professor. Woodbridge, after three months of careful study, concluded that the professor did not "hold to the Presbyterian point of view of the inspiration of the Scriptures." The session decided to "withdraw financial support from Columbia Theological Seminary until the situation be remedied." Dr. Woodbridge asserted that the professor's book in question, *Conservative Introduction to the Old Testament*, was "more dangerous than an out-and-out liberal book, for it suggested repeatedly that a person may hold liberal views and still call himself a conservative. That is deadly," he said, "as well as untrue."[2]

The Southern Presbyterian Church debated confessional revision. In 1938, after tentative approval had been given by the previous General Assembly, a special committee brought in a lengthy report recommending changes in some eighteen paragraphs of the Westminster Confession of Faith, the omission of three paragraphs, and the addition of two chapters with the titles "Of the Holy Spirit" and "Of the Gospel." "Some of the changes," states Ernest Trice Thompson,

[1] WCR, *What is Christian Faith?*, 80.
[2] Calhoun, *The Splendor of Grace*, 387.

"were simply an attempt to modernize the language, others to avoid expressions that were needlessly offensive ... Others sought to soften or eliminate some of the more extreme Calvinistic positions."[1]

Dr. Robinson charged that the amendments reflected a liberal, rationalistic trend and a movement away from the essential Calvinism of the Southern Church. Robinson's colleague at Columbia Seminary, J. B. Green, defended the changes as biblical improvements to the Confession. For an entire year Robinson and Green, living side by side on the campus and teaching across the hall from one another, debated these issues in the journals and papers of the church.

The Robinsons' younger son, fourteen-year-old James, recalled years later that his father reported

> at the dinner table that the Chairman of the Board of Trustees and the President of the Seminary had called him in to tell him to desist from writing in church magazines, articles opposing the published positions of our nextdoor neighbor, who chaired a committee of our denomination to update the standards of the church, such as the Westminster Confession of Faith. My father replied that he had taken an ordination vow to defend these standards and would not desist from honoring his commitment—they would have to fire him (which of course they did not do). I was thoroughly impressed by his courage and integrity, without really being aware of or interested in the issues themselves.[2]

All eighteen proposed changes to the Confession were approved by overwhelming votes of the presbyteries, but the 1939 General Assembly declined to enact any of the more significant amendments. Dr. Robinson, who was present as a commissioner, spoke in opposition to the amendments; and because "there was no one of equal weight to uphold the affirmative," writes Ernest Trice Thompson, "the matter was decided practically without debate." The General Assembly also passed Dr. Robinson's motion that the church understands "the acceptance of the infallible truth and divine authority of the Scriptures and of Christ as very and eternal God, who became man by being born of a virgin, who offered up himself a sacrifice to satisfy divine justice and reconcile us to God, who rose from the dead with

---

[1] Thompson, *Presbyterians in the South,* 3:491.
[2] James M. Robinson, "Theological Autobiography," in Jon R. Stone, *The Craft of Religious Studies* (New York: St. Martin's Press, Inc., 1998), 117.

the same body with which he suffered, and who will return again to judge the world, as being involved in the ordination vows to which we subscribe."[1] "The high-water mark" of William Childs Robinson's influence, according to John Leith, "was the 1939 General Assembly, when he persuaded the assembly to vote down changes in the Confession of Faith which the assembly had endorsed the preceding year and which had been approved by the presbyteries. This was an achievement without precedent or equal."[2] Three years later, however, the General Assembly adopted the two additional chapters to the Confession of Faith, "Of the Holy Spirit" and "Of the Gospel," identical to the chapters added to the Confession by the Northern Presbyterians a generation earlier.

Despite some inroads of liberalism, the Southern Presbyterian Church was still largely a conservative and evangelical denomination in the 1930s, but liberal forces were at work within it. In 1941 the PCUS voted to re-enter the Federal Council, from which it had withdrawn ten years earlier, and shared in the formation of the National Council of the Churches of Christ in the United States of America in 1950. In his *Presbyterians in the South*, E. T. Thompson wrote:

> Prior to 1940 theological students in the Southern Presbyterian Church were carefully trained by professors of systematic theology in one system of theology only—old-line Calvinism. Since 1940 they have been made increasingly aware of the wider spectrum of theological thought … The old battles between Calvinism and Arminianism by this time had long since ceased. The so-called five points of Calvinism were seldom proclaimed from the pulpits; they had ceased to be matters on which theological students were examined by their presbyteries. Theological faculties and students and ministers in their exposition of the gospel were concerned with the more vital issues of their own day.[3]

A movement for union with the Northern Presbyterian Church (Presbyterian Church in the United States of America) began in the 1940s and slowly gathered momentum. Dr. Robinson wrote in 1946:

> We do not admit that there are many churches. There is only one head and therefore there is only one body, the church. This one church is

[1] Thompson, *Presbyterians in the South*, 3:492.
[2] *Presbyterian Outlook*, January 10, 1983, 15.
[3] Thompson, *Presbyterians in the South*, 3:494.

made up of the whole number of God's elect. Its center of unity is Jesus Christ, the minister of the true tabernacle in heaven. It is manifest wherever the Word is preached, heard, and believed, and the sacraments administered … Organizational unification is not essential to unity … The one essential of unity is union with our Lord Jesus Christ. That oneness is properly manifest among congregations and denominations by exchanges of pulpits and intercommunion, that is, by the Word and the sacraments.[1]

Robinson opposed union with the Northern Presbyterian Church for doctrinal reasons. He pointed to the Auburn Affirmation that had been signed by more than 1,000 ministers and elders of that denomination in the 1920s. "Shall we stand for the faith," Dr. Robinson asked, "or shall we surrender our corporate testimony by uniting with Auburn Affirmationists in a body that does not regard such matters as the virgin birth, the substitutionary atonement and the resurrection of Christ as essential to ministerial ordination?"[2] In 1949 Dr. Robinson wrote:

We deny that the ground of our opposition to the Plan of Union is that we have not become reconciled to our brethren with whom our grandfathers had an unpleasantness in the sixties of the last century. In three great wars since, we of the South have served under the flag under which the boys of the sixties served. The writer has served as preacher and pastor in the USA Presbyterian Church, has studied and lectured in their chief seminary, and recognizes the profit he has received from these fellowships and contacts … We have repeatedly stated that we oppose the proposed plan because it gives up specific safeguards protecting the faith of the Son of God now in the polity of the Presbyterian Church, U.S., and because it surrenders our testimony to the sole kingship of Christ over His Zion—our witness that He is the sole lawgiver in the church.[3]

The next year Robinson wrote:

Now we accept the doctrine of Calvin and of our own Confession and the Book of Church Order that there is one Christ and one church, the unity of which is not destroyed by our organization as denominations.

[1] WCR, *Presbyterian Journal,* December 16, 1946, 5.
[2] Thompson, *Presbyterians in the South,* 3:570.
[3] WCR, *Presbyterian Journal,* May 2, 1949, 2.

And we hold no brief for the status quo and have no objection to emphasis on this unity in Christ … We remember, however, that when the Reformed Reformation came to expression, it formulated its faith in the Theses of Berne, which began: "The Holy Catholic Church of which Christ is the only Head is born of the Word of God, lives of the Word of God and hears not the voice of strangers."[1]

Henry Lewis Smith, a student at Columbia Seminary, remembers the visit of a prominent Northern Presbyterian Church pastor, who spoke in the seminary chapel and urged the PCUS-PCUSA union. The preacher told the faculty and students, "I'm orthodox. I believe the creed—I believe in God the Father, and in Jesus Christ his Son, crucified and risen. He ascended into heaven." When the service was over Henry heard Dr. Robinson quietly introduce himself and ask the visiting preacher, "I noted that you omitted 'Born of the Virgin Mary.' Was that deliberate?" The preacher told some of the students about Robinson's question. They in turn told some of the seminary faculty who were known to be opposed to Robinson's views. These faculty members produced a written rebuke for "his uncharitable conduct to a guest" and delivered it to Robinson. Dr. Robinson's response was courteous and without any display of resentment. One of the seminary professors told Henry Smith that in a faculty meeting a few days later, Robinson was warm and cordial to one and all.

Dr. Robinson did not oppose organic union between denominations that were doctrinally agreed. Early in his ministry, when there were conversations between the Southern Presbyterian Church and the United Presbyterian Church, Robinson wrote: "Should a union be consummated on the principle of the sole headship of Christ in His church and the strictly spiritual character of the Church, such a union, by making the church national rather than Southern, would more adequately safeguard the outstanding principle of the Southern Church [that is, the spirituality of the church] from the danger inherent in a sectional institution."[2]

Dr. Robinson often warned his students, "Be careful what you do with Christ's church." In the final sentence of a sermon on "How to

[1] WCR, *Presbyterian Journal,* April 1, 1950, 5.
[2] WCR, *Columbia Theological Seminary,* 67.

Hold Our Historical Heritage," Robinson wrote: "Only the breath of the Almighty can keep our church from floundering on the shoals of doctrinal indifferentism, or splintering on the rocks of dispensational separatism. Only the Holy Spirit is able to hold us together in the faith of our fathers and in the fellowship of the future awaiting the coming of the Lord." He remained hopeful, however, resting in the truth of the words that he had written in one of his books: "The foundation of the church is this session of Christ at God's right hand, in the glory of the Father's throne interceding as the Lamb that hath been slain. We go into life believing that the time which lies before us, even as that which lies behind us, is in the nail-pierced hands of our Redeemer."[1]

Presbyterian Churchmen United was formed in 1969 to further the conservative cause in the Southern Presbyterian Church. Prayer groups were organized throughout the South to seek God's guidance. In a few months, over five hundred ministers had signed a Declaration of Commitment "continually to profess the Scriptures of the Old and New Testaments to be the Word of God written" and "to defend, support and teach the Reformed Faith as set forth in the Westminster Confession of Faith and Catechisms as the system of doctrine taught in Holy Scriptures." William Childs Robinson was a member of the Presbyterian Churchmen United, and was one of nine appointed to a "College of Scholars." In *Contact*, the PCU newsletter, Dr. Robinson explained the purpose of the organization. "No, the Presbyterian Churchmen United are not in rebellion," he wrote. Rather, "we are in love protesting those things which are being said and done in our Church contrary to the standards to which our ordination vows obligate us." He concluded the short article with a prayer:

> We humbly pray that the God and Father of our Lord Jesus Christ may use our imperfect selves and inadequate testimonies to bring our beloved church back from secular humanism to the faith which is in Christ Jesus and by His Spirit make her again a body bearing witness to Him.[2]

[1] WCR, *Christ—The Hope of Glory*, 40.
[2] John Edwards Richards, *The Historical Birth of the Presbyterian Church in America* (Liberty Hill, SC: The Liberty Press, 1986), 142-44.

A new Presbyterian denomination, made up largely of Southern Presbyterian pastors and churches, formed in 1973. Dr. Robinson's "life, teachings and influence," writes Paul Settle, "were used in God's providence to lay important and strong foundations for the Presbyterian Church in America." Robinson did not join the PCA, but it is easy to believe that his heart was with those who did. Nearly half of the founding pastors of the PCA were taught by William Childs Robinson at Columbia Seminary. Twenty-two of the thirty teaching elders on the Constitutional Documents Committee, charged with getting a Book of Church Order ready for approval by the first General Assembly, had studied under Dr. Robinson.

17. THE MISSION OF THE CHURCH

William Childs Robinson championed the doctrine of the spirituality of the church as taught by his professors and predecessors at Columbia Seminary.[1] He held that Christians should cooperate with proper efforts for social improvement because "we live in a world where men and women and little children are dying of hunger, shivering with the cold, unsheltered from the wintry blast, dislocated wanderers, lost sinners, sheep having no shepherd." He congratulated the Northern Presbyterian Church, which had inaugurated its greatest financial drive, 27 million dollars, not for local church building programs and projects, but to give to those

---

[1] See Calhoun, *Our Southern Zion,* 128-32 and 334-36. See also "Spirituality of the Church" by John H. Leith in *Encyclopedia of Religion in the South,* eds. Samuel S. Hill and Charles Lippy (Macon, Georgia: Mercer University Press, 1984), 731. Leith states that the doctrine of the spirituality of the church, a view that has a long history in Christianity, was the fundamental conviction of many Presbyterian theologians in the South, especially during the century from the 1830s to the Second World War. Its most powerful advocate was James Henley Thornwell, who argued that the church has a definite purpose as outlined in the Scripture "for the gathering and perfecting of saints." Social and political opinions and organizations outside the church's biblical charter may be supported by Christian people, but the church in its organized capacity "cannot identify ambiguous political and social causes with the will of God." Leith adds: "The doctrine of the spirituality of the church was corrupted by the pressures of racial and economic issues into an escape from social responsibility. This has kept it from receiving the attention it deserved as one way of relating church and culture." Mark Noll writes that the doctrine of the spirituality of the church "had great positive potential in an American landscape where varieties of civil religion so regularly dictated a political agenda for the churches." "Yet as Leith notes," Noll adds, "this doctrine was 'corrupted' when Southern leaders, with Presbyterians in the lead, used it to defend slavery in the antebellum church and tolerate segregationalist injustice after the Civil War." Mark Noll, "Theology, Presbyterian History, and the Civil War," in *Journal of Presbyterian History,* Spring/Summer, 2011, 12.

in need around the world.[1] But such efforts, Robinson maintained, "will never do more than make life tolerable." The greatest service the minister can offer society, he stated, is to preach Christ.[2]

Writing about a ministers' retreat in Macon, Georgia, led by Otto Piper, Robinson expressed his agreement with the Princeton Seminary professor's opinion that it is futile to seek "to secure Christian solutions from non-Christian society." It may be necessary for Christians to cooperate at times in various efforts in order to secure "a tolerable situation." But it is necessary that the Christian minister not give his strength and time to secular social reforms but to the preaching of the Word. When issues arise that demand Christian response, Robinson wrote:

> The body of Christ must come together in a spiritual atmosphere. We need to listen to one another, to accept the other's criticism in humility and prayer. We must wait upon the Lord until the Spirit gives us a basic conviction which we can express as our united confession. And we wait upon the Lord by returning to the Bible as the sole authority on which our conviction rests.[3]

Robinson believed that members of the church could and should be actively involved in appropriate social action. In his article for the first issue of the *Southern Presbyterian Journal*, Robinson noted

> that our three ministers who have done the most noteworthy social service have been men who most emphatically maintained that missions was the mission of the Church. While they were loyally preaching the Gospel in season and out of season, God gave to Hampden C. Dubose the added privilege of sharing largely in the suppression of the opium traffic, to J. Leighton Wilson to contribute the decisive article which stopped the African slave trade, and to B. M. Palmer to deliver the eloquent civic address which crushed the Louisiana lottery. As these fathers of the Southern Presbyterian Church administered in the church the task which the Founder laid upon the church, God gave them the added privilege of accomplishing noteworthy things as citizens. They did not confuse the two distinct spheres in which men ought to serve the one God.[4]

[1] WCR, *Presbyterian Journal*, November 1, 1946, 3.
[2] WCR, *Presbyterian Journal*, April 1, 1947, 6.
[3] WCR, *Presbyterian Journal*, April 1, 1947, 6.
[4] WCR, *Presbyterian Journal*, May 1942, 6.

Robinson was greatly concerned, however, that Southern Presbyterians remember that "missions is the mission of the church" and that the evangelization of the world remain primary in the church's work. Concerned that in the use of the denomination's funds, missions could be replaced by other demands, Robinson wrote:

> Let us manifest our care for the house of God in prayerful rather than precipitate, careful rather than rash, action in dealing with the sacred trust of Christian benevolences. The people of the Lord give to Him. The Lord Christ sits over against the treasury. He not only notes how we put into the treasury, but also how we use that which is put there. The eyes of Him, with whom we have to do, run to and fro in the earth, and to whom much is given from him shall much be required. By His grace may we each be able to give account of our stewardship with joy and not with pain.[1]

One of the last writings by Robinson was a short piece in the *Presbyterian Journal* entitled "Honoring the Prince of Peace." In it he expressed dismay that his denomination had approved donations of money to several groups in Africa known for revolutionary and violent activity. "What individual people care to do with their gifts is their own business," Robinson wrote, "but what the church gives in the name of Christ ought to be given to support the spread of the example and teaching of Him whom we rightly acclaim as the only Lord and head of His body, the church."[2]

Dr. Robinson promoted missions in the seminary and in the church. "At the beginning of the Junior Year," he wrote, "we start church history with the study of the history of Christian missions and with students contributing mission texts and leading in prayer for missions at the opening of the hour. With this beginning we have continued to use students to lead the opening devotions—each man is given a day and quotes or reads a text and offers the prayer." For a number of years Robinson taught a separate course in the history of missions. In *Our Lord—An Affirmation of the Deity of Christ* there is an impressive chapter called "A Solitary Throne." In the concluding part of that chapter, "The Place of Jesus Christ in Christian Faith,"

[1] WCR, *Presbyterian Journal,* October 15, 1946, 4.
[2] WCR, *Presbyterian Journal,* April 18, 1979, 14. This was perhaps the last writing of William Childs Robinson to be published.

Robinson surveyed briefly the mission of the church, especially the work of missions in Southern Presbyterian history.[1]

Robinson was often invited to preach at mission services in the churches. On May 5, 1955, the Independent Presbyterian Church of Savannah, Georgia, celebrated its bicentennial. In the evening service, Dr. Robinson spoke on "Two Centuries of Advance in World Missions." He said:

> As one sees the signs of God's blessing upon this two hundred years of life and progress, he is reminded of Calvin's testimony. The Reformer of Geneva said that he found the sheep of the Lord scattered upon a thousand hills and that he lifted a banner to gather them—not a new banner, but the old banner of God's Word. This goodly gathering of God's people to celebrate the two centuries of His work in and through this congregation assures us that *your* John Calvin [the pastor, Dr. Cousar] is lifting that same old banner of God's Word, and that the sheep are hearing the voice of the Good Shepherd through his faithful exposition of God's Word.[2]

* * * * *

When the president of the United States called for volunteers as America entered the Second World War, Robinson experienced "strong inward 'tugs' to help by serving as a chaplain," but providence, he wrote, "kept me at the task of training others as ministers and chaplains."[3] One of these was Eugene Daniel, a graduate of Georgia Tech and of Columbia Seminary. On one occasion Chaplain Daniel delivered New Testaments throughout the foxholes when the fighting was too fierce for a service. Then he stayed behind to care for the wounded German as well as American soldiers. He was taken prisoner, but was allowed to teach the Bible to the other prisoners. Dr. Robinson wrote to Chaplain Daniel, sending him a copy of his sermon "Sparrow, Soldier, Sailor: Not One Shall Fall Without Your Father." Daniel replied: "Thanks for the letter and sermon. Surely it

---

[1] WCR, *Our Lord—An Affirmation of the Deity of Christ*, 173-83. See Selected Writings 22.

[2] Calhoun, *The Splendor of Grace*, 423-24.

[3] WCR, *Presbyterian Journal*, May 1945, 7.

is good to know that God rules the affairs of men and loves all. As you know, He has saved and blessed me and has given me a great opportunity to minister to many men here. I have baptized three men in this camp."[1]

Robinson preached sermons of hope and courage during the dark years of the war. Preaching "The Prayer of a Soldier," he told the story of Dr. James Myers, who closed a half-century of foreign missionary service with six months in a Japanese jail. Myers wondered why God sent him so much suffering after so much service until these two texts came to comfort his heart: "All things work together for good to those who love the Lord," and "What I do thou knowest not now, but thou shalt know hereafter."[2]

In another sermon he ended with a story to illustrate his main theme and to have—as he told his students they should have in every sermon—a clear presentation of the gospel:

> In a small country church in Alabama a minister was preaching on that extra sparrow that the Jewish marketeer threw in to make the deal. The sparrow that the buyer demanded to seal the trade, that the seller didn't count, was remembered by God. In the back of the auditorium was a woman whose life had been soiled. She had become a mother without becoming a wife. She thought no one could care for her life. But if God remembers that extra sparrow, surely He thinks of me. And then like a great tidal wave the message of the Gospel of His Love enveloped her soul with the revelation of just how much more valuable she was than many sparrows. For her God had not spared His only begotten Son, but had freely offered Him up for her salvation. And the Father's seeking, saving love made her a daughter of the King that day.[3]

* * * * *

The troubling period of civil rights agitation created special tensions and tragedies in the South. Dr. Robinson encouraged Christians to do all they could to further justice in society. "Let us do whatever God leads us to do in the current campaign for the Negro work of

[1] WCR, *Presbyterian Journal*, May 1945, 7.
[2] WCR, *Presbyterian Journal*, March 1944, 8.
[3] WCR, *Presbyterian Journal*, June 1943, 12.

the Assembly," he wrote, "and whatever we can to ease the tensions caused by color among us." Robinson wrote in the August 15, 1946, issue of the *Southern Presbyterian Journal*: "The State of Georgia has been polluted by the killing of four Negroes, three of whom were wholly innocent, at the Apalachee River on July the twenty-sixth. And unless this shedding of innocent blood be properly punished we may expect the curse of God upon our State, visiting such punishments upon us as He sees fit." He continued:

> May the Angel of the Covenant intercede with God for His mercy upon those this loss touches most closely, upon the State whose name is thus shamed ... yes and upon those who did this deed. For unless these men meet God in His justice and in His mercy in this life; unless they repent, confess and find forgiveness now for Christ's sake—they shall receive the wrath and the curse of the Almighty in the life which is to come—when it is too late for repentance and for forgiveness.[1]

Robinson's anger about this evil act poured out in his denunciation of those who had done this terrible crime, but, characteristically, he included a brief word about salvation and a plea for the guilty men to turn to God in repentance.

Robinson was not convinced that "racial amalgamation" or "the abolition of all social segregation" would lead to "the promotion of justice toward the Negro." But he was confident "that God's hand will be laid upon His people of the white and Negro races as they labor together in Christ, that God's blessing will be upon souls and upon bodies, upon individuals and upon society, upon homes and upon churches—that our two races will be helped to walk together in peace and in contentment."[2]

While acknowledging Robinson's sincere desire for racial justice and equality, we wish that he had taken a more courageous and more biblical stance in promoting racial integration, as did his beloved professor at Princeton Seminary, B. B. Warfield.[3] Robinson mentions in one of his books that when an effort was being made to restore

[1] WCR, *Presbyterian Journal*, August 15, 1946, 2-3.
[2] WCR, *Presbyterian Journal*, January 15, 1947, 4.
[3] See Bradley J. Gundlach, "'Wicked Caste': Warfield, Biblical Authority, and Jim Crow," in *B. B. Warfield: Essays on His Life and Thought*, ed. Gary L. W. Johnson (Phillipsburg, N. J.: P & R Publishing, 2007).

the Ku Klux Klan in the 1920s, B. B. Warfield's brother, Ethelbert Warfield, speaking to the men of the Gettysburg Presbyterian Church, said:

> When I am asked to join a body organized against the Negro, the Roman Catholic, and the Jew, I cannot forget that I was nursed in infancy by an old Kentucky mammy, that the Christian faith was preserved through the middle ages by the medieval Catholic Church, and that my Saviour was, according to His flesh, a Jew.[1]

* * * * *

The Southern Presbyterian Church assigned to Dr. Robinson the task of preparing a paper on the relationship between church and state in the United States. He surveyed the history of the religious heritage of the "Anglo-American" state, from the Reformation through the Puritans and Scottish Presbyterians. He then presented various political theories that have built "a wall of separation between nature and grace and consequently between the state as allegedly built on natural law and the God of grace." This wall of separation, Robinson argued, "is issuing in a secular state and a pagan public school." "We are likely to see," Robinson wrote, "the distinction between church and state turned into a stone wall separating the covenant children of our homes in their major educational experience from the Word of the living God who has named them as his own in holy baptism."

Robinson deplored decisions of the Northern Presbyterian Church General Assemblies of 1962 and 1963 to surrender "our public schools to secularism by appeals to the pluralism of modern society." He appealed to Abraham Kuyper's Stone Lectures at Princeton, which showed that "Calvinism emancipates the state from the dominion of the church *but not from God.*" He appealed to Karl Barth's Barmen

---

[1] WCR, *The Reformation: A Rediscovery of Grace* (Grand Rapids: Eerdmans, 1962), 180-81. Ethelbert Warfield, Benjamin's younger brother, followed him to the College of New Jersey (Princeton College), then studied for a year at Oxford. He took a law degree at Columbia University and practiced law in Lexington, Kentucky, before moving through a succession of academic positions. He was a member of the Board of Directors of Princeton Seminary from 1894 to 1929 and served as president of the board from 1904 to 1915.

Declaration that read:

> In the decisions of the state, the church will always support the side
> which clarifies rather than obscures the Lordship of Jesus Christ over
> the whole world, which includes the political sphere outside the
> church. The church desires that the shape and reality of the state in
> this fleeting world should point toward the kingdom of God, not away
> from it.

He quoted the words of S. C. Guthrie in the *Bulletin of Columbia
Theological Seminary* (June 1963): "The first and last primary thing we
have to say about the world into which we are sent is that *it already
belongs to Jesus Christ!* There is no part of the world, however hostile
or merely indifferent, over which He is not already Lord."

Robinson's concluding summary of "the Reformed conception of
the living God in His relation to the state" is typically Robinsonian
in its clear statement of the gospel and call to worship:

> The living God is the Lord who confronts us in His biblical revelation;
> He is the Holy One of Israel before whom the world is so sinful, lost
> and hopeless that only God can help; in Jesus Christ, God is the Sav-
> iour of the world, whose arms are ever stretched out to fallen man in
> the words of the promise "… him who comes to me I will not cast out"
> (John 6:37); this God has established the state as truly as the church,
> the school as definitely as the home, and His sovereignty ought to be
> recognized in worship. For His might which made us, for his majesty
> which governs us, for His mercy which saves us, we worship God.[1]

Dr. Robinson's paper was one of four contrasting positions presented to the National Council of Churches for consideration at the
National Study on Church and State meeting on February 4, 1964.
Not surprisingly, Dr. Robinson's position did not prevail at the study
nor in his own denomination.

When the 1970 General Assembly of the Southern Presbyterian
Church voted to approve abortion on the grounds of "socio-economic
conditions of the family," Dr. Robinson strongly protested the action
as "condoning the murder of the unborn." In "God and Unborn
Children," Robinson defended his position with many scriptures

---

[1] WCR, "God and State: A Plea for Prayer in the Schools," Campbell Library,
Columbia Theological Seminary Library, Decatur, Georgia.

under three main points: (1) God is the creator of human life, made
in His own image. (2) The God of the Covenant is the God of our
seed, that is, they are His children in the covenant sense. (3) Even
prior to their birth God personally relates to unborn babies as persons, children, sons. Robinson noted that "the primitive church
condemned pagan abortions" (citing four documents prior to A.D.
200) and that "our Presbyterian catechisms protect the sanctity of
human life." He urged that people "consider any proposed abortion
coram Deo" in the light of Proverbs 3:5-6 and Psalm 119:105. And he
reminded those who had aborted babies that with God there is forgiveness, as seen in the Scriptures, such as Psalm 130, John 8:11, and
1 Corinthians 6:9-11.[1] Dr. Robinson's resolution opposing abortion
was defeated by a large majority of the 1970 General Assembly. The
Southern Church had changed, and Robinson's words seemed to
many to be a voice of the past.

---

[1] Richards, *The Historical Birth of the Presbyterian Church in America*, 144-46.

18. FACING DEATH

Dr. Robinson's longtime colleague J. B. Green died in September 1967 at the age of ninety-six. Green was born in a log cabin in Lexington, Alabama, on May 10, 1871. At his funeral service the president of the seminary, James McDowell Richards, said that Dr. Green was a real part of the nineteenth and twentieth centuries and that he was also "very much at home in the first century." Called from the pastorate of the First Presbyterian Church of Greenwood, South Carolina, Green was the last of the men who had taught at the seminary when it was in Columbia. He was known as an expository preacher who had few peers "and perhaps no superiors." Green taught Systematic Theology, his principal field, as well as Homiletics, Ethics, and English Bible. During his later years he led the students in a study of the book of Psalms. He was the author of two books, *Studies in the Holy Spirit* and *A Harmony of the Presbyterian Standards.* He was elected moderator of the Presbyterian Church in the United States in 1946. When he learned that he was going to be nominated, he was disturbed. A student found him walking behind his house on the campus, obviously in distress. When asked why he was so upset, he replied, "I have just learned that I am to be nominated as moderator of the General Assembly, and I am not worthy of the office."[1] Dr. Green taught at the seminary until he retired in 1951, when he was eighty years old.

In 1967 Dr. Robinson retired, after teaching at Columbia Seminary for forty-one years. In response to the many words of praise and esteem that he received at his retirement, he said that he

> could not help but recall the old story that comes from the time when it was customary to eulogize the departed. A widow listened as the

[1] *Bulletin: Columbia Theological Seminary,* December 1967.

parson waxed eloquent over the virtues of her departed husband until she could stand it no longer. Pulling her son closer, she whispered to him, "Johnny, you go open that lid and see if the man in that box is your Pa."

"The apostle reminds us," Dr. Robinson said, "that we have this treasure in earthen vessels. Compared with the pricelessness of the divine treasure the earthiness of the human vessel overwhelms one."

Robinson told the friends who had gathered to honor him at his retirement that from early years he had "lived in the shadow of Columbia Theological Seminary" [in Columbia and Decatur]. "And through the kindness of this institution's president," he said, "I own the unused part of a lot in Elmwood Cemetery in Columbia around which there is a small coping stone with the words COLUMBIA SEMINARY cut into it. So I hope, in due time, to sleep beneath the shade of Columbia."[1]

For his seventieth birthday Dr. Robinson was honored with the publication of a festschrift—*Soli Deo Gloria: New Testament Studies in Honor of William Childs Robinson*—with chapters by scholars from England, Scotland, Germany, and Switzerland, as well as the United States.[2] The list of contributors is impressive—Oscar Cullman, F. F. Bruce, Bo Reicke, George Eldon Ladd, Joachim Jeremias, John H. Leith, T. F. Torrance, and Dr. Robinson's two sons, William Childs Robinson Jr., Professor of New Testament at Perkins School of Theology, Southern Methodist University, and James McConkey Robinson, Professor of Religion at Claremont Graduate School. William Childs Robinson was grateful for this book, especially its title, *Soli Deo Gloria*, words, he said, that are "precious to every Christian's heart."[3]

J. McDowell Richards wrote in his foreword to the festschrift a tribute that is especially meaningful coming from one who was more inclined to the progressive members of the faculty:

As a teacher and as a churchman, Dr. Robinson has not sought for popularity. A diligent scholar himself, he has expected hard work of his

[1] *Bulletin: Columbia Theological Seminary*, December 1967.
[2] J. McDowell Richards, *Soli Deo Gloria: New Testament Studies in Honor of William Childs Robinson* (Richmond, Virginia: John Knox Press, 1968).
[3] *Bulletin: Columbia Theological Seminary*, vol. 60, December 1967, no. 5.

students, in some of whom at least he has inspired a new concept of and devotion to scholarship. A man of deep conviction concerning the centralities of the Christian faith, he has steadfastly sought to oppose error as he saw it, and to bear witness to the truth as revealed in Scripture and in Jesus Christ. Such teaching has not always been received with enthusiasm by his hearers.

Richards closed his introduction with these words: "It is not likely that Dr. Robinson, or any other reader, will agree with all that is contained in this book. Of one thing, however, we may be sure. He will approve of its title, for this represents the witness of his life—the goal of his endeavor as a minister, a scholar, a writer, and a teacher. *Soli Deo Gloria*—To God alone be the glory."[1]

Dr. Robinson certainly did not agree with everything in the book. His greatest disappointments were, no doubt, the contributions of his two sons, especially that of James.

William Childs Robinson Jr., New Testament professor at the Perkins School of Theology at Southern Methodist University, wrote on "Word and Power," an exegetical study of 1 Corinthians 1:17-2:5. This topic was, of course, of great interest to Dr. Robinson, one of whose books was titled *The Word of the Cross*. His son's treatment contained much that Robinson could accept, but at least one sentence would have caused him great concern. Bill, as he was called, wrote that the Apostle Paul, in asserting the historicity of the earthly life of Christ, "was interested, as Bultmann rightly observed, 'only in the *fact* that Jesus became man and lived on earth. *How* he was born or lived interested him only to the extent of knowing that Jesus was a definite, concrete man.'"[2]

William Childs Robinson Jr. studied at Davidson College, Columbia Seminary, and the University of Basel. He was ordained in the Southern Presbyterian Church and served as a pastor in Raleigh, North Carolina, for four years. He became professor at King College, then at Perkins School of Theology, and in 1970 at Andover Newton Seminary.

If Dr. Robinson was disappointed by some of the statements in Bill's chapter, he would have been greatly troubled by what James

[1] Richards, *Soli Deo Gloria*, 6.
[2] Richards, *Soli Deo Gloria*, 81.

wrote—"World in Modern Theology and in New Testament Theology." In a paper, read originally at Colgate Rochester Divinity School,
James surveyed modern theology from Schleiermacher to Bultmann
and New Testament theology from apocalypticism to gnosticism. He
summed up his long and complex chapter with these words—"At
the opening of this essay it was suggested that the new theology may
well be cast primarily in terms of world, and the essay has concluded
with the suggestion that New Testament theology could be so recast
as well."[1]

James M. Robinson was Professor of Religion at Claremont
Graduate University and Director of the Institute for Antiquity and
Christianity. He became the most prominent Q and Nag Hammadi
scholar of the twentieth century. He was a leading member of the
Jesus Seminar movement, seeking to determine the authentic words
and deeds of Jesus by critically examining the canonical Gospels and
the other New Testament-era literature.

In his "Theological Autobiography," James Robinson described
his path from his father's orthodox Calvinism to his own very liberal form of Christianity. James graduated from Davidson College
and attended Columbia Seminary, where he made a good grade in
the required course in Calvinist theology, but did not, he wrote,
"really get involved" in it. He preferred reading Kierkegaard, who
seemed to him to have "a more relevant way" of coming "to grips
with the human dilemma." After seminary James taught Bible for a
year at Davidson, his classes made up mostly of returning veterans.
"Whether or not they actually believed anything I said," he wrote,
"by the end of the year I no longer did." James earned a doctorate
in theology from the University of Basel (Karl Barth was his super-
visor) and another doctorate (in New Testament) from Princeton.
He taught at Emory University from 1952 to 1958 and at Claremont
School of Theology from 1958 to 1999.

James wrote that his "theological trajectory over half a century …
moved step by step from right to left," from Barth to Bultmann and
beyond. He criticized "the godly Christianity" in which he grew up
for not catching sight of "racial segregation, militarism, or the plight
of sharecroppers, as problems to be addressed." James believed that if

[1] Richards, *Soli Deo Gloria*, 110.

he had followed a career other than Bible study he would "no doubt have abandoned Christianity completely as hopelessly outdated and irrelevant." His faith now rested, he claimed, in a more authentic Jesus, not a savior but an example—"a real idealist, a committed radical, in any case a profound person who had come up with a solution to the human dilemma that is at least worth listening to." "Christological creeds," James claimed, "may be no more than pious dodges to avoid this unavoidable condition of discipleship: Actually do what he said to do!"[1]

One of the seminary students, walking with Dr. Robinson across the campus, remarked on the many academic accomplishments of his sons. Robinson quietly and sadly replied, "Pray for my boys."[2]

* * * * *

Dr. and Mrs. Robinson continued to live in Decatur for a time, in a lovely house near the seminary. Later they moved to a Methodist retirement home in California, near their son James. The theological gap between James and his father was wide and getting wider. The home went bankrupt and the Robinsons lost much of their retirement savings. They came back to the South and lived for a short time in Augusta, Georgia, and then moved to Clinton, South Carolina. Robinson had said at his retirement that he intended to spend his last days in the Presbyterian Home in Clinton.

Dr. Robinson defended the faith he loved by writing short articles for the *Presbyterian Journal.* He wrote on historic Presbyterian church polity, insisting that the "headship and lordship of Christ over His body" commits the church to faithful interpretation and application of His words as given in the Bible. As he had done so often in his career, he defended the virgin birth and the deity of Christ. He criticized the "cliché of Paul Tillich that 'God accepts us as we are'" in the light of Scripture and the Reformed faith. "In one sense,"

[1] James M. Robinson, "Theological Autobiography," in Stone, *The Craft of Religious Studies,* 117, 121, 145, 146, 148.
[2] Dr. Robinson dedicated *The Word of the Cross* to his son James McConkey Robinson, "with his father's prayer that if God open his mouth in the Evangel, he will be true to the Word of the Cross."

Robinson wrote, "it is true that God accepts us as we are, but only after He has done something about how we are."[1] Robinson found much to praise in John A. Mackay's *The Presbyterian Way of Life* but was disappointed that the book "does not give a clear answer as to how the church is to safeguard the faith once delivered to the saints."[2]

Dr. Robinson closed his response to the alumni who honored him at his retirement with the words:

> Augustine declared that Christianity was his faith because it was the catholic faith. Then he advised the Augustinian reader not to love him more than the catholic faith, and warned his critic not to love himself more than the catholic truth. "To the one, I say be unwilling to yield to my writings as to the canonical scriptures ... Likewise I say to my critic: Be unwilling to change my writings by your own opinion, but correct them only from the divine text or by unanswerable reason."[3]

In what was perhaps his last sermon, "How to Hold Our Historical Heritage," Dr. Robinson took Paul's words to Timothy as his text—"Hold fast as a pattern the sound words which you have heard of me in the faith and love which is in Christ Jesus. This good deposit guard through the Holy Spirit who dwells in us" (2 Timothy 1:13-14).[4] It was, Robinson wrote, the apostle's "swan song." It also may be considered Dr. Robinson's "swan song." He urged Southern Presbyterians—the church's officers especially—to hold fast the truth they had received from the Bible, the Westminster Standards, and their founders and leaders—holding it in faith and in love and guarding it by the Holy Spirit.

"We are to hold fast our historical heritage in the faith, which rests on Christ Jesus and lives and feeds upon His faithfulness," Dr. Robinson wrote. "The title 'Confession of Faith' testifies to the intent of our articles. They are written as a confession of our faith in the God of all grace, and only as such are they a constitution of the church—that is, they are worship, not legalism." Robinson added:

[1] WCR, *Presbyterian Journal*, August 2, 1978, 12-13; September 13, 1978, 10-11; October 18, 1978, 14; and November 22, 1978, 14-15.
[2] WCR, *Christianity Today*, February 27, 1961, 44.
[3] WCR, *Bulletin: Columbia Theological Seminary*, December 1967, 8-9.
[4] The sermon was not preached or published, as far as I know, but was "mimeographed" and sent to a number of Robinson's friends. Historical Center of the Presbyterian Church in America, St. Louis, Missouri.

Propositions are good in their place. But we rejoice that our Westminster Standards call us to entrust ourselves ultimately not to a *that* but to a *Him*, and to do so in the first person. *We* receive and rest upon *Him*, Jesus Christ alone, for salvation. Faith looks away from self—even away from one's own faith—and glows and grows as it focuses upon Christ Jesus who is the object of faith.

"Likewise," Robinson wrote:

We are bidden to hold fast the sound words of the apostle in the love which is in Christ Jesus. At this point there is a bit of difficulty in translating the text. Shall we render it in good English—"in the faith and love which are in Christ Jesus"? Or shall we give a more literal rendering of the Greek—"in the faith and love which *is* in Christ Jesus"? In any case the singular relative indicates how closely the apostle keeps together faith and love.

Robinson concluded:

The text bids us to guard this deposit of truth by the Holy Spirit who dwells in us. Only the Spirit can take the things of Christ and make them ours. Only He brings and keeps us in the faith and love which is in Christ Jesus.

* * * * *

Dr. Robinson was confined to his bed for several years after a stroke. Many friends and former students came to see him. A visitor who prayed with him was rebuked by Mary for not praying for her husband's health and brought back to his bedside to pray again! Dr. Richards, the president of Columbia Seminary, visited him just before his death and reported that "Dr. Robbie" was not as clear in his thoughts as he had been—but that he was still crystal clear on justification by faith. Not long before he died, Robinson wrote to a Christian magazine called *Present Truth* stating that it "was doing a significant service in calling the attention of the church to that objective righteousness which is the meritorious ground of justification." He offered some suggestions for themes or seed thoughts for a series of sermons on justification. It is fitting that one of the earliest

writings by William Childs Robinson was on the Reformation doctrine of justification by faith, as was one of the last letters he wrote.

In *Christ—The Hope of Glory* Dr. Robinson asked: How then
shall we face death? What comforts are there for the fatal hour? He
answered:

> In Jesus Christ, God's everlasting arms are beneath this transitory life;
> behind death is the Prince of Life; beyond the grave is the Resurrec-
> tion. "For," says the Apostle Paul, "whether we live, we live unto the
> Lord, or whether we die, we die unto the Lord. Whether, therefore,
> we live or die, we are the Lord's. For to this end Christ died and lived,
> that He might be Lord of both the dead and the living" (Rom. 14:8-9).
> In these words the Apostle states the very heart of the Christian faith:
> namely, that *we are the Lord's* and He is our Lord whether we live or
> die. Because God has made Himself our God and made us His people,
> therefore, there is comfort and forgiveness, life has a purpose and a
> meaning, and there is a light in the valley of the shadow.[1]

Describing "The Sleep of Death" in *Christ—The Hope of Glory*,
Robinson asked, "How then shall one interpret the frequent descrip-
tions of the dead, especially of the departed believers, as a sleep?"
He answered, "The New Testament describes the dead in Christ as
having fallen asleep in Jesus with the connotation that they will wake
to a blessed resurrection." In the meantime "Christ is present with
the souls of the pious and receives them into paradise where they
enjoy consolation." "The imagery of sleep," wrote Robinson, "carries
a special sense of tenderness reminiscent of the ordinary act of putting a child to bed with a loving hand." He quoted Elizabeth Barrett
Browning:

> And, friends, dear friends—when it shall be
> That this low breath is gone from me,
> And round my bier ye come to weep,
> Let one, most loving of you all,
> Say "Not a tear must o'er her fall!
> He giveth His beloved, sleep."

Dr. Robinson also quoted a poem written by a missionary to China
as a testimony of the dying Christian's faith and hope.

[1] WCR, *Christ—The Hope of Glory,* 110, 118-19.

Afraid? Of what?
To feel the spirit's glad release?
To pass from pain to perfect peace,
The strife and strain of life to cease?
Afraid — of that?

Afraid? Of what?
Afraid to see the Saviour's face,
To hear His welcome, and to trace
The glory gleam from wounds of grace?
Afraid — of that?

Afraid? Of what?
A flash—a crash—a pierced heart;
Darkness—light—O Heaven's art!
A wound of His a counterpart!
Afraid—of that?[1]

In one of his first books Robinson described "the exceedingly appropriate burial service" of the Rev. William L. Smith, "an excellent man who entered the ministry late in life and served mission churches in West Virginia and Pennsylvania." Smith found that the bare committal, "ashes to ashes, dust to dust," accompanied by the falling of clods of earth, or even of rose petals, was depressing. Instead his words at the grave of a departed believer were those great summaries of the hereafter found in our catechisms and confession:

The souls of believers are at their death made perfect in holiness and do immediately pass into glory. There they behold the face of our Father which is in heaven in light and blessedness. Their bodies being still united to Christ do rest in their graves until the Resurrection. At the Resurrection believers shall be raised up in glory and openly acknowledged and acquitted in the day of judgment and made perfectly happy in the enjoyment of God to all eternity.

Robinson added:

What a mass of comfort and encouragement there is in these blessed certainties. Even if I wait beside the silent sea, I know "I cannot drift beyond His love and care." For He hath made me certain that neither

[1] WCR, *Christ—The Hope of Glory*, 138-43.

life nor death nor any other creature shall be able to separate me from His love which is in Christ Jesus, our Lord.[1]

* * * * *

Dr. Robinson died on November 21, 1982, in Clinton, South Carolina. His body was brought the fifty miles to Columbia and buried in Elmwood Cemetery in the Columbia Seminary lot. Nearby are the graves of James Henley Thornwell, John Lafayette Girardeau and others of the old Columbia Seminary. Robinson said at his retirement in 1967 that he was glad to think that in due time he would "sleep beneath the shade of Columbia."[2] His tombstone reflects his long connection with Columbia Theological Seminary:

Wm Childs Robinson

Student 1917–1920

Professor 1926–1968

1897–1982

After the death of her husband, Mary McConkey Robinson continued to live in the Presbyterian Home in Clinton. She died on February 1, 1993, and is buried in the Columbia Seminary lot at Elmwood next to her husband.

At the Robinsons' gravesite there is an obelisk engraved with the words CHRIST IS OUR RIGHTEOUSNESS.[3] These words summed up their faith and "the Reformation vision" that Dr. Robinson preached and taught his whole life. In *The Reformation: A Rediscovery of Grace* Robinson wrote:

> When there was no room in England for William Tyndale to carry on his work of translating the Bible, the English evangelical fled to Luther at Wittenberg. There he interested John Bugenhagen in the progress of the Reformation in England. Bugenhagen's *Letter to the English* is the first tract in behalf of the Reformation written to the English people. In it the author says:

[1] WCR, *The Certainties of the Gospel*, 136-37.
[2] *Bulletin: Columbia Theological Seminary*, vol. 60, December 1967, no. 5.
[3] See Selected Writings 23.

We could not but rejoice, dear brethren, when we heard that in England also the gospel of the grace of God has had a good report. But we are informed also that many have turned away from it because of slanderous stories against us and our way of living. We shall not stop to answer these calumnies. Know, therefore, that whatsoever ye may have heard, and however simply minds may be puzzled and confused by the flood of controversy, we have only one doctrine: *Christ is our righteousness.*[1]

* * * * *

"When news of Dr. Robbie's death … began to spread throughout the church," Editor Aiken Taylor wrote in the *Presbyterian Journal,* "something unprecedented in this office began to happen. For the first time since I have been at this desk, testimonial letters began coming in from former students who wanted to express their love and appreciation for their beloved professor."[2] One of those former students, John Leith, spoke for many when he wrote, "The death of William Childs Robinson is a great sorrow to all those who cherish the history of the Presbyterian Church in the United States." Dr. Robinson, Leith wrote,

> lived in the presence of the living God. He honored his convictions against the pressures of the time and the lure of career ambitions … Even though his work was against the times, this very fact is perhaps the best reason for taking his work seriously. It is likely that his work as a churchman and teacher of ministers was more lasting than can now be estimated. In any case, the final judgment, as he knew so well, belongs to God. Few of Robinson's critics have been able to match his brilliance, his diligent churchmanship and scholarship, his commitment to the faith and to participation in the organized life of the church.[3]

Dr. Robinson was the last of "the Old Columbians." Charles McGowan writes that when Dr. Robinson, Dr. Gutzke, and several other professors retired, the integrity of Columbia Seminary was essentially lost. "By 1970," he states, "all of the conservatives had

[1] WCR, *The Reformation,* 79.
[2] *Presbyterian Journal,* February 9, 1983, 23.
[3] *Presbyterian Outlook,* January 10, 1983, 15.

retired or 'graduated' to heaven." McGowan expresses his debt to Dr. Robinson "for the part he played in shaping [his] theological commitments and philosophy of ministry." Paul Settle pays heartfelt tribute to his teacher.

> He was one of the last in a line of Southern Presbyterian worthies, extending from Thornwell, Dabney, Palmer, Girardeau, and others, to the present, who proclaimed and lived the whole counsel of God. His many articles that graced the pages of the *Southern Presbyterian Journal* for almost forty years gave honor to Christ, challenged the Church to orthodoxy and passionate service for the Kingdom, and ably expressed the agenda and shredded the false teachings of liberal churchmen. He was one of the few "establishment" professors and churchmen who fearlessly stood for the faith once delivered to the saints.

Settle speaks for many of Robinson's students when he says, "I probably could not overestimate his influence on my life and ministry."

Julius Scott says that he "learned far more than academics" from Dr. Robinson. "In both precept and example I learned much about God, the person and work of Jesus Christ, and the importance of the church. Robinson demonstrated that the essence of Christianity is more than intellectual; it is a personal relationship with God through Christ."

William O. Harris, minister in the Presbyterian Church (USA) and Archivist at Princeton Theological Seminary, met Dr. Robinson during the summer of 1950 at Montreat, North Carolina, where the young Davidson College student had a summer job as a bellboy. Harris wrote:

> When Dr. Robinson discovered that I was struggling to find a personal faith, he gave what seems like an unlimited amount of time and counsel. He made the distinction between faith and theology clear to me and gave me a freedom to believe. Conservative theologian he was, but much more to the point, he was a man of lively personal faith who took the time to share it in kindness and good humor with a bellboy.[1]

Lowell B. Sykes, pastor emeritus of the Rivermont Presbyterian Church in Lynchburg, Virginia, writes that Dr. Robinson, "my most beloved professor," was "the last in the line [of the Columbia Seminary

[1] *Presbyterian Outlook,* January 31, 1983, 2.

faculty] to love, proclaim, promote, defend, and demonstrate the classical Reformed faith."

Thomas Ellis explains why he uses the word "beloved" to describe Dr. Robinson: "beloved especially because he so profoundly loved our Lord and Savior, Jesus Christ, and understood so clearly and fully the Word of Life." Ellis says that few on either side of the "fundamentalist" controversy understood or appreciated Dr. Robinson because "he was so out of step with the times." Ellis ended his "Biographical Tribute to William Childs Robinson" with the words I use at the end of this summary of Dr. Robinson's life …

Faithful ministers are the gift of Christ.
To Him be all the praise,
and let the memory of the past lead us all to pray:
"Turn us again, O Lord, God of hosts,
cause Thy face to shine;
and we shall be saved"
(Psalm 80:19).

SELECTED WRITINGS OF
WILLIAM CHILDS ROBINSON

The following *Selected Writings* are described in the *Life of William Childs Robinson* where their inclusion here is indicated. These selections have in some cases been abridged. The footnotes that accompany these writings are those given by Dr. Robinson.

1. THE THEOLOGICAL EMPHASES OF
THE OLD COLUMBIA SEMINARY[1]

Justification

As a student seeking the way of salvation, James Henley Thorn-well stumbled upon the Westminster Confession of Faith and "cast anchor" in its chapter on Justification.[2] Small wonder then that he found here the center of gravity.

[For Dr. Thornwell] the great question of revealed religion is "How shall a sinner be just with God?" (*Collected Writings,* 1:581). The solution of this question, consonant with the essential principles of moral government, necessitate all the provisions of the covenant of grace—the incarnation, the person of the Saviour, His humiliation, His death, His resurrection, and ascension, and His coming at the last day to judge the world. "All the facts of His history and media-tion depend upon God's purpose to justify the ungodly" (*Collected Writings,* 1:580-81).

In setting forth this principle Dr. Thornwell was following the earliest Columbia tradition. Hon. J. H. Lumpkin, Chief Justice of Georgia, was a member of Dr. Thomas Goulding's Session. Of Dr. Goulding's preaching, Mr. Lumpkin says: "The doctrine of justifica-tion by faith he regarded as the epitome of the Christian system, and … (it) formed the favorite theme of his ministrations."[3]

---

[1] WCR, *Columbia Theological Seminary and the Southern Presbyterian Church, 1831-1931,* 213-28.
[2] *Life of B. M. Palmer,* by T. C. Johnson, p. 272.
[3] *Memorial Volume of the Semi-Centennial of the Theological Seminary at Columbia,* p. 185.

The Life of Dr. Archibald Alexander indicates that the doctrine also had a primary place in the thinking of the first professor in the Theological Seminary of the Presbyterian Church at Princeton.

The Federal Theology

Perhaps nothing shows more clearly that Dr. John Lafayette Girardeau, while a disciple of Thornwell, was an independent thinker, than his proclamation that the federal or representative principle is of first import and regulative influence in the Reformed theology. (If further proof be sought it can be found in the marginal notes in his own copy of *Thornwell's Collected Writings*—these show many sharp differences in details of exposition.)

Dr. Girardeau's Semi-Centennial Address is entitled *The Federal Theology; Its Import and Regulative Influence*.[1]

The principle of representation was involved as an essential element in the covenant of redeeming grace. This covenant *to Christ* was a covenant of works requiring of Him perceptive and penal obedience. As the head and representative of His elect seed, He secured justification for Himself and His seed in Him. Christ Himself was justified in the sense that His imputed guilt was removed by God's justifying sentence—and His justification involved the justification of His elect seed. The elect were in mass justified *in foro Dei* in the justification of Christ as their federal head and representative; and they are severally justified *in foro conscientiae* when, in the period of their earthly history, they actually exercise faith in Christ. On the basis of their *representative* or *virtual* justification the elect are invested in the court of heaven with a right and title to eternal life; and on this basis, at God's appointed time, their Advocate and Intercessor sues out for them the gift of the Holy Spirit, who regenerates and "enables them to exercise that faith which conditions their conscious and actual union with Jesus," and hence their *conscious* or *actual* justification.

The regulative influence of the federal theology is shown in affording "the only tolerable solution" of the mysteries which hang over the moral history of the race. It shows that "our inability is not original; it is penal." It shows that the only dealings of God with the race

[1] *Semi-Centennial of the Theological Seminary,* p. 96 ff.

are covenant dealings; and salvation is only through the covenant of grace.

In the field of Supernatural Religion the representative principle has the solution of the question of the relations of justification and regeneration and offers the following *ordo salutis*—forensic justification (or implicit justification); intercession, suing out the grace of the Holy Spirit for the sinner (implicitly justified); regeneration, uniting the sinner vitally and spiritually to his federal head; faith and actual justification. On this principle the electing decree is found to be utterly unconditioned; atonement, particular; vocation, efficacious and irresistible; perseverance, certain; the enthronement of Grace, secure.

Adoption

Still another key-note in the Columbia Theology is the doctrine of Adoption, a subject not indexed in Hodge's *Systematic Theology*. Discussing Dr. Thornwell as a theologian, Dr. Thornton Whaling said:

> The most valuable work of our master Theologian was accomplished in the Theology of Redemption by the supreme and regulative place he assigned *Adoption*. In fact the organic and unifying principle in Thornwell's theology is found in his doctrine of Adoption. The question proposed, both in natural religion and in supernatural religion, was the same, viz: how may a servant, through adoption, become a son. In the Covenant of Works the question relates to a righteous servant; in the Covenant of Grace to an unholy and condemned servant: but the end proposed in each case is the same, the change from the status of a servant to that of a son through adoption. From this point of view, Election is election "into the adoption of sons." Justification is a means devised by which the standing of the servant may be so assured that adoption of sonship shall certainly follow; Federal Headship, again, is a sublime means which the adoptive decree utilizes, in order that the one who is represented shall receive this gracious benefit of the change from the status of a servant to that of a son; Regeneration is the effective way in which the spirit of sonship is made real in those who have secured the adoption of sons. No other system of theology has assigned so large a place to this ruling conception which occupies so supreme a position in the Scriptures and in religious experience. And in making

Adoption central, Dr. Thornwell is at once the more scriptural and the more philosophic. This is his chief achievement as a Theologian, making a distinct advance upon the Reformed Soteriology and that of all subsequent thinkers, by giving Adoption the regal position assigned to it in revelation, and belonging to it in Christian experience, and which theology ought to recognize in its systematic construction of Scripture and experience by giving Adoption the same influential and regulative place in the doctrinal system.[1]

All the powers of Dr. Girardeau's eloquence are called into play to magnify the blessedness of adoption. The adopted are heirs of God and joint heirs with Christ with an indefeasible title to an inheritance which is "all that can be conceived or believed as embraced in the paternal favor and love of God"—here and hereafter, "the riches of grace and the riches of glory." It signifies "Home!"; "ineffable communion," immunity from slavish obedience or fears; boldness of access; liberty of communion as children; the wholesome, loving, saving discipline of children in God's family; the enjoyment of all conceivable good in God as the portion of the soul.[2]

But if the primary sense of theology, as the word of God, or the revelation of God, is to have a genuine place in determining its central or unifying principle, some principle must be sought which bespeaks the nature, being, or self-revelation of God in Himself—and not only a great principle in His relationships with His creatures. A study of Dr. Thornwell's *Collected Writings* presents two principles for such consideration—spirituality and holiness.

The Spirituality of God

The only conception of God's being which can seriously be considered as disputing with His holiness the central place in the Thornwellian system is the spirituality of God. God in Himself is indefinable. Man's finite conceptions of Him can be expressed. The expression of these concepts should begin with the recognition that, as, to His genus, God is Personal Spirit. No believer in God as immaterial reality can desire more emphasis than Thornwell placed upon this doctrine. He

[1] Thornwell, *Centennial Address*, pp. 28-29.
[2] Girardeau, "The Doctrine of Adoption" in *Discussions of Theological Questions*, p. 428 ff.

said, "The spirituality of God is the foundation of all religious worship—it is the foundation of all the Divine attributes."

The central place of the spirituality of the Church—an inference
from a high conception of the spirituality of God—has been elsewhere treated. Another effect of this principle has been the simplicity
and spirituality of worship. As Dr. Girardeau led the worship, there
was no reading in concert, no repeating of creeds and prayers; "but
only the simple, old time Presbyterian worship—consisting of solemn, earnest prayers led by the minister, plain congregational singing,
the impressive reading of the Scripture," the exposition of the Word,
and an offering. In this plain bill of spiritual fare, instrumental music
and, generally, trained choirs were never allowed, being regarded as
without New Testament warrant.[1]

The Holiness of God

The most distinctive and most vital doctrine of the Columbia
Theology as revealed by the present study is that of the *holiness of
God*. This principle stands out as determining the formulation of and
space given to many of the themes discussed in Thornwell's *Collected
Writings*. Whether or not it is the logical center, it is the vital center
of the Thornwellian Theology.

The Reformed Theology has been characterized as the vision of
God in His majesty, of the King in His beauty.[2] Dr. Thornwell laid
hold of the beauty of holiness, the supreme vision of God, to bow
souls in adoration, humility, and absolute dependence upon Him.
In emphasizing this element as the very life of God, Dr. Thornwell is
standing in the line between Charnock[3] and B. B. Warfield, both of
whom make God's holiness His crown and His glory. More generally,
this element has found a large place in P. T. Forsyth's *The Cruciality
of the Cross*; in Harris E. Kirk's *The Consuming Fire*; and is a vital element in Edward Thurneysen's *Das Wesen der Reformation*.

One can not define terms that are in their very nature indefinable.

[1] T. H. Law, *The Life Work of J. L. G.*, pp. 141, 142. See J. L. Girardeau, *Instrumental Music in the Church.*
[2] C. W. Hodge, "The Significance of the Reformed Theology Today" in *Addresses at his Inauguration*, p. 19.
[3] *Discourses upon the Existence and Attributes of God*, p. 469.

It is impossible to scale the inaccessible heights of the Divine Holiness with a definition. In this Alpine effort, Dr. B. B. Warfield was compelled to fall back upon a negative or apophatic method: according to its Hebrew etymology the central thought is found to be division,

> specifically separation from the world conceived as a sinful world. When we call God holy, then, the central idea in our minds concerns His absolute and complete separation from sin and uncleanness. Not that the idea has this negative form as it lies in our minds. There is no idea so positive as that of holiness; it is the very climax of positiveness. But it is hard to express this positiveness in a definite way, simply because this idea is above the ideas expressed by its synonyms. It is more than sinlessness, though it, of course, includes the idea of sinlessness. It is more than righteousness, although again it includes the idea of righteousness. It is more than wholeness, complete soundness and integrity and rightness, though, of course, again it includes these ideas. It is more than simpleness, high simplicity and guilelessness, though it includes this too. It is more than purity, though, of course, it includes this too. Holiness includes all these and more. It is God's whole, entire, absolute, inconceivable and, therefore, inexpressible completeness and perfection of separation from and opposition to and ineffable revulsion from all that is in any sense or degree, however small, evil. We fall back at last on this negative description of it just because language has no positive word which can reach up to the unscalable heights of this one highest word, holiness. It is the crown of God, as mercy is His treasure; as grace is His riches, this is His glory. Who is like unto God, glorious in holiness?[1]

Thornwell followed Charnock in making holiness the glory of all of God's other perfections.[2] But he seems to have gone beyond Charnock in making the holiness of God almost the synonym for the nature of God; and in the nature of God as thus conceived, rather than in the will of God, he laid the ultimate foundation for his theological structure. He declares:

> As moral character in man depends upon dispositions and principles back of his volitions, must there not be something analogous in God, something in the very nature and grounds of His being which

---

[1] Warfield, B. B., *Faith and Life,* pp. 443, 444.
[2] Charnock, p. 469.

determines His will to command and forbid what it does? Unquestionably there is; it is the holiness of the Divine nature, that essential rectitude of His being, which constitutes His glory and without which we could not conceive Him to be an object of worship or reverential trust. Holiness is represented in the Scriptures as the very life of God. In all other beings it is an accident separable from the essence; in God it is His very self. It pervades all His other attributes and perfections and makes them to be preeminently Divine. His infinite knowledge, tempered by His holiness, becomes wisdom. His infinite power, wielded by that same holiness, becomes the guardian of justice, truth and innocence. His infinite will, impregnated with holiness, becomes the perfect standard of rights and duty. This perfection is God's crown and glory (*Collected Writings* 1:357).

Dr. Whaling has mentioned, as first and foremost "among the striking instances of Thornwell's originality," the large place and novel treatment which he gives to Christian Ethics as a section of Systematic Theology. Concluding his first discussions on Truth, Dr. Thornwell says, "I have now completed what I had to say upon the ethical system of the Bible. The true light in which redemption should be habitually contemplated is that of a Divine institute of holiness" (*Collected Writings* 2:474). One ground of his objection to the Roman Catholic system is that "her doctrine of venial sins ... is utterly incompatible with those awful impressions of the malignity of the least departure from rectitude which the holiness of God imparts" (*Collected Writings* 2:372).

Thornwell finds that sin, objectively considered, is non-conformity with the law. But the moral law is the expression of God's will. And God's will is not arbitrary or capricious; it is grounded in the very nature and being of God. It is determined by "the holiness of the Divine nature, that essential rectitude of His being, which constitutes His glory and without which we could not conceive Him to be an object of worship or reverential trust" (*Collected Writings* 2:357). Sin, therefore, is "the transgression of the law, disobedience to God and contradiction to His holiness" (*Collected Writings* 2:361).

Sin in its subjective determination is traced back to "the want of holiness." A subjective consideration of sin shows that "supreme devotion constitutes the moral condition of the soul indispensable to holiness" (*Collected Writings* 2:358); that this devotion is expressed in love; and that a negation of the feeling of devotion and dependence (i.e. independence, estrangement from God, self-affirmation) is the root thought in sin. "As love to the creature in a state of holiness is determined by its relations to the purpose of God, so, in a state of sin that love is determined by relations to our own views and selfish purposes" (*Collected Writings* 2:260).

Sin, then, is nothing but the contrast of holiness—enmity toward God. It is rebellion against God—opposition to God and opposition even to Him in the height of His glory, His holiness. It is the denial of the creature's fundamental relation of dependence and the putting up of self as the rival and enemy of God. "Sin stands revealed in awful malignity as a profane attempt to dethrone the Most High and to exalt ourselves to His glory and sovereignty."

According to Thornwell, holiness comprehends the righteousness of God—righteousness is what holiness affirms. And the justice of God is His holiness acting in His power. And when sin stands before this manifestation of the holiness of God, it is seen in its blackness of guilt. Conscience, the echo of the holiness of God, brings the soul into the depths of agony with her solemn declaration that sin ought to be punished and that sin will be punished. The moral law as the expression of the very nature of God is ineradicable.

The flaming glory of the holiness of God is revealed for Thornwell in the consideration of the sacrifice of Christ as that of a holy priest. This theme is presented in two of Thornwell's Addresses preserved in Volume 2 of his *Collected Writings*: "The Priesthood of Christ" and "The Sacrifice of Christ, the Type and Model of Missionary Effort." Here Thornwell presents the glory of God not only in the saving work which is done, not only even in the Lord of glory who does it, but in the sublime way in which it is done, the work of a priest. "That our substitute, ransom and surety should be a priest is grace on top of grace—the exuberance of grace." More recently, Dr. P. T. Forsyth in *The Person and Place of Jesus Christ* has declared, "New Testament religion is a priestly religion or it is nothing. It gathers around a priestly cross on earth and a Great High Priest in the heavens—it means the priesthood of each believer—and the collective priesthood of the Church as one." The same writer makes the fundamental action of Christ's death a prime regard for the holiness of God.

Thornwell represents the soul of the Lord Jesus as burning with a holy adoration of God, as He sees the Father in the radiant glory of His holiness. And from this vision he gathers the unescapable argument for the necessity of the atonement:

> When I consider His soul as a pious offering, and then reflect that He celebrates the grace and the condescension of God in accepting the gift; when I consider the extent and severity of His sufferings, and then remember that all were to express to the universe His sense of the Divine holiness, I ask no more: I am satisfied that thus it must be—that without the shedding of blood there could be no remission. So intense was His conviction that His death was indispensable to the righteous pardon of the guilty, that He seems to have coveted the cross, and to have been straitened for His baptism of blood. He could not brook the thought that man should be saved at the peril of the Divine Glory, and whatever His Father's honour demanded He was prepared to render at any cost of self-denial to Himself (*Collected Writings* 2:420).

But more than the need of the atonement, Thornwell teaches here the beauty of the atonement. In the priestly work is seen, not a price demanded, but a sacrifice freely offered, a heart of adoration and worship under the falling darkness and sacrifice, a heart so full of the sense of the glory of holiness that it rejoices to glorify that holiness even at such a cost to itself. "The whole transaction is an august and glorious act of worship." The sacrifice of the Great High Priest is the most glorious litany ever chanted, the grandest doxology ever sung—worship of the glory of holiness at its highest and noblest. "We feel that God is glorious, that the law is glorious, for Christ glorifies them." We "enter into the awful reverence for God which invests the cross with the sanctities of worship and converts its shame into glory. The beauty of holiness gilds its terrors." The atonement is defined, as, "guilt expiated by an act of worship."

Instead of a feeling of the harshness of God which sometimes comes from exclusively contemplating the legal aspects of the cross, Thornwell's vision of Calvary focuses the eye on the light of the holiness of God and ravishes the heart with the glory of the Triune. It is with the free, voluntary, spontaneous, self-devotion of the priest that the offering is made. It is made with His heart full of mingled adoration and zeal for the Divine glory, and sympathy and love for those He represents. Our happiness was not purchased at the expense of the rights of another; "and though there was an immense cost of suffering and blood, it was never for a moment begrudged, never for a moment sustained with reluctance. We have no occasion for regrets that the blessings which we enjoy have been put into our hands by cruelty, injustice or overharshness and severity to others. They are the free gifts of that sublimest of all spirits—the spirit of the priest." Entering into the scene and into the workings and emotions of the Saviour's heart, it is maintained that nothing less than the Divine nature could be the dwelling place of such holy zeal and such ineffable love. At one and the same time, adoration of the glory of holiness and the energy of that same holiness are manifest; the Father is reflected in the Son. "The piety of the Priest flows from a fountain of inexhaustible fullness"—the holiness of God. In His own unspot-ted holiness He confesses the guilt of His brethren and adores the justice which dooms Him to woe as their substitute. With profound adoration of the Divine character, He, in His own spontaneous act, lays His life upon the altar, virtually saying; "Take it, it ought to be taken; let the fire of justice consume it; better ten thousand times better, that this should be than that the throne of the Eternal should be tarnished with an effeminate pity!" The grandest hymn of praise, of worship, of adoration of the Lord glorious in holiness, arose when the High Priest of our Profession offered up Himself a voluntary sac-rifice to express the love of God, to satisfy the justice of God, to magnify the holiness of God.

Justification, the Federal Theology, Adoption, have all found prominent places in the Columbia Theology. But the supreme theme in God's self-revelation is "the idea of the holy." That theology is the vision of the Lord glorious in holiness; the vision of sin as the con-tradiction of His holiness; the vision of redemption as an institute of holiness; the vision of the saving Cross which the Fourth Gospel presents as Jesus' own, "Holy Father, Glorify Thy Name!"

2. THE COLUMBIA TRADITION[1]

The Sons of Columbia are intensely interested in her! That was the delightful conviction the writer received from a few hours happily spent among them at Montreat. Men like Dr. W. M. Hunter, North Carolina Synod's Secretary of Education; Dr. S. L. Morris, the greatly loved Secretary of Home Missions; Dr. C. R. Hemphill of Louisville, bespoke a deep interest, a true filial love. As the dean of our Southern Presbyterian theological professors gave his blessing to the youngest member of that group he spoke touchingly of his farewell visit to the old grounds in Columbia, S. C.

And the Presbyterian Church in the United States is intensely interested in Columbia Seminary, as well she may be. For she was cradled in the Columbia tradition. Those who presided at the momentous occasion of her birth were Columbia men: Dr. B. M. Palmer, Dr. J. H. Thornwell, Drs. J. Leighton and Joseph R. Wilson. The great architectonic principles of our Church were laid down by James Henley Thornwell; while Dr. Adger supervised the writing of the Book of Church Order along the lines of these constitutive principles. Those who love most this Southern Zion are concerned that the Columbia tradition live, in order that this tradition may keep the Presbyterian Church in the U. S. true to her own fundamental ideals.

But wherein does the Columbia tradition lie? In the walls and buildings in Columbia in which these words are penned, or in the great, abiding, rock principles of truth according to the Word—principles like the sole Headship and Kingship of Christ in His Body, the Church? Just at this moment we are witnessing a great effort to transform a sister seminary—Princeton—from a citadel of orthodoxy into

[1] WCR, *Bulletin: Columbia Theological Seminary,* January 1928.

a different tradition. The plan there seems to be to preserve the old landmarks, the same buildings, towers, turrets, and grounds; but to make them symbols of something different. Instead of standing as symbols of the granite-like, consistent, Old School Calvinism of Charles Hodge's "Three Volumes," or of B. B. Warfield's scholarly defense of the supernatural character of the Christian origins, these towers are to be made the symbols of a conglomerate, hodge-podge known as "the inclusive church." A seminary with which the writer is familiar in another denomination seems to have swung from the conservative position to the liberal position in the space of a few months by the replacing of old professors by new ones. In the last few years many have expressed grave doubts as to whether the name, the place, or the blood of the great Dwight L. Moody have been sufficient to hold his loved Northfield true to the testimony he bore. A school, in which the teachers chafe under the bonds of orthodoxy, instead of glorying that they are set for the defense of the faith, will lose the very life of its tradition and will turn out men untrue to the name of that school. The point to these comparisons is that the Columbia tradition is a matter of heart, of principle, of love, of loyalty to a great heritage; not of location, nor of buildings. The soundness of the heart is the question; not the cut of the clothes!

Is it time for any lover of Columbia Seminary to bid goodbye to this great Southern Presbyterian tradition as the school moves to Atlanta? When the writer entered Columbia Theological Seminary in Columbia, ten years ago, there were in the faculty two men (out of six) who were alumni of the school. These two men had put in a total of five years as students in Columbia Seminary. Those who enter Columbia Seminary this year will have (in a faculty of seven) four men who have had a total of twelve years in the classroom study in Columbia Seminary. And, if a personal allusion may be pardoned, of these four, two are Columbia men who have been reared in the very shadow of the Seminary and imbibed its theology not for three years each—but for twenty. Dr. Clark grew up as the son of a leading director, and a son of Columbia First Church, the Church whose life has ever been most closely entwined with the life of the Seminary. The writer has known the Seminary influence from a father who is a director, from a mission Sunday school of which Dr. R. C. Reed was superintendent, from Arsenal Hill Church where Girardeau's theology was faithfully reproduced by his son-in-law, Dr. Geo. A. Blackburn, from Woodrow Memorial Church where most of the preaching was done by Columbia Seminary professors. The name of our president has been the synonym of true blue Presbyterianism since the days of the Westminster Assembly, and every student of Columbia's history knows the place that the "Gillespie Clan" had in giving to the Southern Church her greatest mind—Thornwell.

The other members of our faculty are men whose training in great kindred traditions has fitted them to take up and bear onward the Columbia tradition. Indeed among those who bear to us the nobility of the Richmond tradition, the name of Dr. Wm. M. McPheeters has in the last half century become so closely interwoven with that of Columbia that to mention the one is inevitably to think of the other. While still in the old Columbia atmosphere, Dr. J. B. Green has closely devoted himself to the study of the Columbia theology. As a result of this study of our two great traditions it is hard to find Dr. Green's peer, either in the pulpit proclamation, or in the classroom exposition of Southern Presbyterian Theology.

Moreover, these are men who have earned and enjoy and bring to the new "home Synod" (Georgia), the highest confidence, love, and esteem of the old "home Synod" (South Carolina). And we rejoice in the approaching coming of another representative of the great Princeton traditions—Dr. H. B. Blakely. Two other members of our faculty have taken post-graduate work at Princeton. All have studied carefully the books and articles there produced. If our great Northern sister denomination does not care for the Princeton heritage, we, in Columbia, will do our best to perpetuate the matchless defense of Christian beginnings worked out by Princeton's great Southern triumvirate, Benjamin Breckenridge Warfield of Kentucky, J. Gresham Machen of Georgia and Baltimore, Wm. Park Armstrong of Alabama. An exposure to the contrary viewpoint has taught some of us to appreciate anew the value of this great line of defense. We believe that these two additional traditions will make the new Columbia a mighty cord woven of three noble strands for the preservation and proclamation of those truths on which our souls depend.

Perhaps a word as to our attitude toward this Columbia tradition may not be out of order—for this is the crux of the matter. What is our purpose and aim on the new foundations? We purpose to keep the old landmarks—not of buildings, but of truths; not of location, but of vocation; not of method, but of meat and matter. We are set for the defense of the Gospel in our day and time as were our fathers in theirs—the same Gospel they preached, the same Christ—'The Lord of Glory"—the same Cross and gloriously emptied tomb. We have girded our loins to take care that the Columbia tradition is re-embodied in new foundations. The controlling Synods have decided that Atlanta gives us a larger pulpit to reach a greater audience with the Columbia tradition. Atlanta enables us to follow those of South-eastern lineage and of Columbia theology who have moved westward toward the Mississippi — and the New Orleans of Palmer. In Atlanta we promise the Church our best endeavors to exalt the Columbia tradition.

But just because the Columbia tradition is a Scriptural tradition, a spiritual tradition, our human efforts are not sufficient to guarantee its perpetuation. We earnestly ask the prayer support of every one who loves this great heritage. In this year of removal we ask the prayers of those who have so faithfully held the lines and proven the bulwark of support for the Seminary. One of the Seminary's most devoted supporters recently suggested that the attention of its friends be called to the gracious promise recorded in Isaiah 40:31. Will every lover of the Seminary lay to heart this year our spiritual need and plead to God His promise, "They that wait on the Lord shall renew their strength"? Will you ask Him to renew Columbia Seminary this year in the great tradition of loyalty to Himself? Will you ask for her a regirding with strength by the Lord for service in His vineyard? In this crucial moment we earnestly appeal to you, who are "the Lord's remembrancers," to make mention of Columbia in prayer: that the Lord may renew His heritage, revive His work, regenerate with a rich baptism of redeeming grace every soul that comes in any way into contact with the Seminary you own and love.

3. THE MEANING OF GRACE[1]

"The love of God shed abroad in our hearts by the Holy Ghost."—Rom. 5:5.

The Gospel is the word of grace, the most gracious word this world has ever heard. It is the word of love and peace for a world marred by war and cursed with hate; the word of life for a world in death; the word of forgiveness and of beginning again for a world that awaited God's righteous wrath.

In order to keep the blessed truth of grace clearly before us we will seek to clarify its meaning. Let us compare grace to a beam of white light. When this beam is passed through a prism it breaks up into all the colors of the rainbow. Even so grace yields all the manifold hues of God's goodness dealing with sinful men. In particular grace means at least three things. Grace means love; grace means the gratuitousness or the freeness of that love; and grace means power.

Grace means Love—*"God commendeth His love toward us."*

Grace is the love of God even for a wicked world. Grace declares that when we were hateful and hating one another even then the kindness and love of God toward men appeared saving us according to His mercy. Grace teaches that God sent not His Son into the world to execute the awful judgment the world deserved; but that God so loved the world as to give His only begotten Son that through Him the world might be saved. Grace does not deny the dreadful character

[1] WCR, *The Certainties of the Gospel*, 88-98.

of sin or the infinitude of guilt. Grace proclaims a God whose love is mightier than sin. Grace is "the revelation of the incredible goodness of God" (W. Lowrie).

In the second chapter of Ephesians Paul ransacks his vocabulary to find terms to describe God's love actions. "God who is rich in mercy, for His great love wherewith He loved us—by grace are ye saved—that in the ages to come He might show the exceeding riches of His grace in kindness toward us." Mercy, love, grace, kindness—all mirror His benignity. Mercy means His concern for and interest in the wretched, "the Divine pitifulness toward feeble, suffering men akin to the compassions of God." Mercy is the psalmist's favorite note. Even the thunders of Sinai did not hide the blessed fact that Jehovah was a God full of compassion and gracious, plenteous in mercy and truth. Among men kindness is the touch of a father's hand, the accent of his voice, the breath of his generous spirit. In the ages to come the heavenly Father will draw us closer and we shall know the fatherly kindness of the Most High.

> So the all-Great were the all-Loving, too
> So through the thunder comes a human voice
> Saying, O heart I made, a heart beats here!
> Face, my hands fashioned, see it in myself.

In moments of great stress, such as separation or death, we come face to face with the intensity of human emotion. When the deeps are broken up what a mighty thing is human love. In grace Paul sees the intensity of God's love. Perhaps we ought to dwell more on the *heart* of the Eternal. "His love looks mighty but is mightier than it seems." The greatest human love pales before "His great love wherewith He loved us."

Grace expands the measure of our apprehension of God's immeasurable love. In order that we may contemplate the length of His love it reveals the vistas of eternity in which He elected a people for His own possession. Luther used to say that if we only realized that God loved us before He made the universe, how it would inflame our love for Him in return. Grace uncovers the heights of divine holiness revealing God's love as His delight in His own perfections and His purpose to stamp those perfections on His creatures until above the sea of glass rises the throne of grace. Grace sounds the depths of a love that reached to the Cross of deepest woe to snatch sinners from the jaws of Hell. Grace expands the heart to include an innumerable host, those who have washed their robes and made them white in the blood of the Lamb.

Grace tells of "The love that tops the might, the Christ in God." Grace reveals God's last best name, for "God is love." Grace is the supreme teacher of life's great lesson.

> For life, with all it yields of joy and woe,
> And hope and fear—believe the aged friend—
> Is just our chance o' the prize of learning love,
> How love might be, hath been indeed, and is;
> And that we hold henceforth to the uttermost
> Such prize despite the envy of the world,
> And, having gained truth, keep truth: that is all.
>
> *A Death in the Desert.*

There are so many reasons for believing the Christian Gospel. Grace says even if there were only the revelation of redeeming love

> Men should, for love's sake, in love's strength, believe.
> Let the heart stand up and answer "I have felt."

for oft

> The heart hath her reasons which the mind may not know.

In this was manifested the love of God toward us, because that God sent His only begotten Son into the world, that we might live through Him. Yea Jesus Christ is love incarnate, "self-forgetting love made visible." John writes, "grace and truth came by Jesus Christ"; Luke tells us that they wondered at the words of grace that fell from His lips; Matthew lets us hear Him from the Mount speaking the great word of grace, "Blessed"; the psalmist sings of the grace that is poured upon His lips. "The life of Jesus presents in shapes of loveliness and symmetry the else invisible music of Divine love. He lets us see the music of the Father's heart" (Maclaren).

> And so the Word had breath, and wrought
> With human hands the creed of creeds

> In loveliness of perfect deeds,
>> More strong than all poetic thought.

In Memoriam.

The love of God reached all the way to the Cross. There are only two things that a holy God can do in the face of sin: execute the penalty for sin, or accept the penalty for sin. "God commendeth His love toward us in that while we were yet sinners Christ died for us." "Herein is love, not that we loved God; but that He loved us and sent His Son to be the propitiation for our sins." The greatest love that our Lord Jesus knew was the love of the Father for Himself, John 15:9. And yet the Triune God so loved a sinful world that for us men and for our salvation the Father spared not His own Son, but delivered Him up to be made sin for us and to endure for us the penalty of the wrath and averted face of God. Greater love hath none than this! Grace means love, the love of the Father.

Grace means Gratuitousness—"Being justified freely by His grace."

Grace means God's love to the undeserving, to the ill-deserving, yes God's love to the Hell-deserving. God loved us though we had naught of our own His love to merit. Grace means that we are indebted to God and that He is not indebted to us. God owes no man. We are by nature as well as by grace pensioners of His bounty. God is not dependent for His being upon any creature. Every creature is wholly dependent upon the Creator for his existence and continuance in existence. Thus grace accords with the everlasting fitness of things. "My goodness extendeth not to Thee."

> For merit lives from man to man
>> And not from man, O Lord, to thee.

Or, as Robert Louis Stevenson places on the lips of Attwater in *The Ebb-Tide,* "Why not Grace? Why not the grace of your Maker and Redeemer, He who died for you, He who upholds you, He whom you daily crucify afresh? There is nothing but God's grace. We walk upon it, we breathe it; we live and die by it; it makes the nails and axles of the universe; and a puppy in pyjamas prefers self-conceit!"

No merits of ours deserve God's love; no works of ours can earn life eternal. Pile up all your prayers, your charities, your churchliness, your social service and you have only erected another tower of Babel. "If it is by grace, it is no more of works; otherwise grace is no more grace." Or otherwise expressed, grace believes in a God who "justifieth the *ungodly.*" Grace is the love of God that imputeth righteousness apart from works.

> No offering of my own I have
> Nor works my faith to prove;
> I can but give the gifts He gave
> And plead His love for love.
>
> Whittier

In the great grace chapters of Ephesians Paul over and over makes it clear that grace is wholly gratuitous. It is God's free, unbought, unmerited favor. Even before we were, before the foundations of the world, God, in His eternal love, predestinated us unto the adoption of sons by Jesus Christ. If we but take time to consider that He purposed to bestow this love upon us ages before we were, we will realize that it is of grace—not of debt.

Further the grace chapter certifies that salvation is wholly to the praise of His grace because grace was bestowed upon us in the Beloved. We are not acceptable to God in ourselves; we are accepted in our Saviour. The ground of our acceptance is not what we have done; not what we are doing; not what we will do. It is what Christ hath done for us. Our righteousness is the finished work of Christ. Nineteen hundred years ago He paid the utmost farthing of our debt. He finished transgression. He made reconciliation for iniquity. In Him we have redemption through His blood. Verily salvation is free, gratuitous. The sinner is saved on the ground of a righteousness not his own—the righteousness of God, our Saviour, settled, fixed, accepted, shining resplendent in the heavens. On the ground of the perfect righteousness of Christ imputed to the sinner and received by faith alone God graciously receives the sinner. He accepts us in the Beloved. "There is therefore now no condemnation to them that are in Christ Jesus." "Justification by Christ's imputed righteousness is the center arch of that bridge by which we pass out of time

147

into a blissful eternity." Of the gracious God, Christ is made unto us wisdom, righteousness, sanctification and redemption; that he that glorieth may glory in the Lord.

Luther wrote to Spentein, an Augustinian monk, "O, my dear brother, learn to know Jesus Christ and Him crucified. Beware of pretending to such purity as no longer to confess thyself the chief of sinners." Patrick Hamilton, the Scottish martyr for the Reformation, urges, "press not to the inheritance of heaven through the presumption of thy good works." A friend brought to John Newton a letter from one of the worst men in Brighton. Newton remarked that the letter showed concern and hope for the writer's salvation. The fellow minister replied that if God saved that fellow he would never despair of the salvation of anyone. The writer of "Amazing grace how sweet the sound that saved a wretch like me," answered, "I have never despaired of the salvation of anyone since God saved me." This is the gospel of the grace of God: After me anyone. God who saved me can save the last and the least and the lowest. For grace is free; grace is the free gift of the King. Therefore,

> Ho, everyone that thirsteth, come ye to the waters.
> And he that hath no money; come ye, buy and eat—
> without money and without price.

Grace Means Power—"The power that worketh in us."

Grace is "the love energy of the Holy God." Grace is God's saving power. Grace is the personal action of the Divine Paraclete. "It simply means the Holy Spirit at work in the soul. God does not (merely) bestow something on us: He works it in us." Grace is the love of God shed abroad in our hearts by the Holy Ghost. Grace is God's personal action making alive hearts that were dead in trespasses and sins.

God alone is good. He alone can create goodness. Having fallen into sin, man can never originate goodness. God made us alive together with Christ. He shined into our hearts to give the light of the knowledge of His glory in the face of Jesus Christ. He translated us from darkness into the kingdom of the Son of His love. He takes away the stony heart and gives instead a heart of flesh. The psalmist yearned for this action of God's grace, "Create in me a clean heart,

O God, and renew a right spirit within me." The prophet foretold a covenant under which God would write His law in the inward parts of man. The Christian is a new man, that after God hath been created in righteousness and true holiness. Grace is God's power that quickeneth us from spiritual death to spiritual life.

> Twas the same love that spread the feast
>   That sweetly forced me in,
> Else I had still refused to taste
>   And perished in my sin.

And day by day grace inspires us to work out our salvation knowing that it is God who worketh in us to will and to do of His good pleasure.

> Grace first contrived a way
>   To save a rebellious man,
> And all the steps that grace display
>   Which drew the wondrous plan.

Rowland Hill has a good illustration of the way of grace. An aged minister received from an unnamed friend a five pound note enclosed in a letter with these words, "More to follow." Some days later a similar note and still another and another, always with the same words "More to follow." So with each gift of His grace God writes His promises, "More to follow."

The same Saviour who spake those tender words of grace to Nazareth is with us today. In the power of His Word and the fullness of His Spirit He is present to preach the Gospel to the poor, to bind up the brokenhearted, to comfort those that mourn, to enlighten darkened eyes, to deliver sin's captives. By His Spirit Christ transfuses His life into His people. His holiness is available to undergird our wavering consciousness; His courage to encourage our discouragements; His ideals to exalt our paltry ambitions; His holy passion to extinguish the fires of our debased passion; His wondrous forgiving grace is able to sweeten even the bitternesses of our experiences; His love can transform our hate.

> When, sin-strickened, burdened, and weary,
>   From bondage I longed to be free,

There came to my heart the sweet message:
  My grace is sufficient for thee.

Though tempted and sadly discouraged,
  My soul to this refuge will flee,
And rest in the blessed assurance:
  My grace is sufficient for thee.

O Lord, I would press on with courage,
  Though rugged the pathway may be,
Sustained and upheld by the promise:
  My grace is sufficient for thee.

Soon, soon will the warfare be over,
  My Lord face to face I shall see,
And prove, as I dwell in His presence:
  His grace was sufficient for me.

The Saviour's arms are still extended and heaven's arches still echo His words of grace: "Come unto me all ye that labor and are heavy laden and ye shall find rest for your souls." Lay hold of that grace by which God has laid hold of men. The word of His grace is able to build you up and give you an inheritance among the saints. By the supply of the Spirit, the Lord Jesus Christ may be magnified even in our bodies. For grace means the power of the Creator Spirit.

Let us then unite in the Apostle's prayer, that the Father of our Lord Jesus Christ would grant us, according to the riches of His glory, to be strengthened with might by His Spirit in the inner man, that Christ may dwell in our hearts by faith; that we, being rooted and grounded in love, may be able to apprehend with all saints the length and the breadth, and the depth and the height of the love of Christ, which passeth knowledge; and be filled with the fullness of God.

4. THE TRINITY: GOD IN ACTION[1]

The Church's interpretation of the Trinity, wrote Bethune-Baker of Cambridge in *Early History of Christian Doctrine,* "is that of one God existing permanently and eternally in three spheres of consciousness and activity, three modes, three forms, three persons: in the inner relations of the divine life as well as in the outer relations of the Godhead to the world and to men."

In his current book, *The Triune God,* E. J. Fortman concludes that God is not dead. "God is, was and always will be the Triune God who has revealed Himself by His inhabitational presence."

These words emphasize that we must look to God Himself and His acts to keep our beloved Church in the Trinitarian faith; we must not permit the Church to be devoured by a unitarianism such as that which captured so many English Presbyterian and New England Congregational churches. Trinitarian experiences led Horace Bushnell to answer Unitarianism thus: "But my heart needs the Father, my heart needs the Son, and my heart needs the Holy Spirit, and the one as much as the other."

God is the living God, and as such He may be expected to reveal Himself primarily in action, not formula. This He has done in the incarnation of God the Son and in the outpouring of God the Holy Spirit.

The Old Testament is the preparation for this revelation, the New Testament the product of the revelation—spoken and lived by the Son and brought to believers by the Holy Spirit.

The climax of this record is found in many places: the farewell discourses in the book of John; the high priestly prayer of the Lord

[1] *Presbyterian Journal,* August 6, 1975, 9, 17.

Jesus; the Gethsemane prayer; the Gospel of the forty days before the ascension, with the Christian name of God given by the resurrected Lord in His Great Commission; the account of Pentecost and the acts of the Holy Spirit in the book of Acts and in the epistles.

Mindful that much of God's self-revelation has come through divine-human encounters—Abraham, Jacob, Moses, Isaiah, Paul— we agree with Frederick Gogarten that "faith is the concrete meeting with the triune God." We also agree with Rahner that "the immanent Trinity as such confronts us in the experience of faith, a constitutive component of which is the word of Scripture itself."

Through revelation man perceives revelation. "In His light we see light." By being in God the Holy Spirit, we behold the light of the knowledge of the glory of God in the face of Jesus Christ.

God's self-revelation as the Trinity is no impersonal system of hypostases in an essence. As Hodgson wrote, "It is the living, loving communion of Father, Son and Spirit into which we have been adopted in Christ." That is, we have been adopted to share in the "family life of God."

God the Holy Spirit bears witness with our spirits that God the Father has accepted us as His children and bids us call upon Him as "Abba," our dear Father, because of the merits of God the Son. The Trinity represents the concept of God involved in the Christian life, and the Christian shares by adoption in the sonship of Christ. Thus the Christian looks out upon the world from within the divine social life of the Trinity.

We are brought into this life by the threefold actions of God in the riches of His grace. God is before all and above all that He has created, and He has given to and for us His only begotten Son, the unspeakable gift of His love, for love came to earth in the incarnation of Jesus Christ.

This Son, of His own will, came not to be ministered unto but to minister and to give His life a ransom for many. His kind lips rang with the gracious invitation, "Come unto me all ye that labor and are heavy laden," with the reassuring promise that "him who comes to me I will in nowise cast out."

We accept the Father's gift and the Son's invitation. We come to Christ and we cast ourselves upon Him; we entrust ourselves to Him.

Yet we do this only as we are drawn by the Father, persuaded and enabled by the effectual calling of the Spirit. It is in the tripersonal experience of the presence of the Father, and of the presence of the Son, and of the presence of the Holy Spirit that God reveals the glory of His grace in saving us sinners.

The Anglican scholar, Bishop K. E. Kirk of Oxford, has said this: "The doctrine of the divine personality of the Spirit emphasizes what has been called the *prevenience* of God in the aspirations of the human heart, just as that of the divinity of the Son emphasizes that same *prevenience* in the work of human redemption, and that of the divinity of the Father—which is the doctrine of the existence of God—His *prevenience* over all the forces and powers in the creation and sustenance of the universe."

Professor Claude Welch put the truth this way in his book, *In This Name*: "God is present to us in a threefold self-differentiation. He makes Himself known as the one who stands above and apart, the one to whom Jesus points as His Father and therefore our Father. At the same time, He is the one who confronts man in Jesus Christ as the objective content of revelation, *i.e.*, the Son. And He is the one who seizes and possesses man so that he is able to receive and participate in revelation, new life, salvation, viz., the Holy Spirit."

It may be that the religious experiences of some denominations or congregations focus more upon one person of the Trinity than another. Certainly it is true that a person will find peculiar satisfaction in the contemplation of one person on one occasion and another in a different situation. But in the course of a normal life span, each Christian avails himself of the complete revelation of the holy Trinity.

As our propitious heavenly Father, the creator, who has life in Himself and gives life to all His creatures, has graciously revealed Himself in the gift and mediation of His only begotten Son. He bids us call upon Him as the Jewish toddler cried out to his parent, "Abba," dear father. In hours of stress, uncertainty, anxiety and loneliness, we draw close to the everlasting arms and nestle nearer to the heart of Him who makes all things work together for good to those who love Him, those whom He has called into His family.

The guilty soul finds the answer to the most poignant question life ever poses in Him, who is the eternal reason, the light of the understanding, and the source of all knowledge. "The work of Christ in relation to sin," wrote J. Denney, "is the culminating point in revelation; not the insoluble problem, but the solution of all problems." We do have an advocate with the Father; He is Jesus Christ, the righteous, the propitiation for our sins.

When the meanness, the wickedness, the littleness—the sin that does so easily beset us—threaten to engulf the soul in the lusts of the flesh, the pride of life, and the machinations of Satan, we then cling to the Holy Spirit, the author of all goodness, wisdom, love, mercy and purity that bless this sin-cursed world. In the words of Jonathan Edwards, "Holiness is entirely the work of God's Spirit."

The living God dispenses the riches of His grace in this three-fold way not just in our daily living; He also has "dying grace" for His people, for the triune God is sufficient for Himself and for His people. In their last hours God is present with those who are His, so that each is enabled to say with confidence, "Yea, though I walk through the valley of the shadow of death, I will fear no evil. For thou art with me." Our gracious God refreshes our memory with the promises of the many mansions in our Father's house, echoing back the final words of the Saviour Himself: "Father, into thy hands I commit my spirit."

5. THE BLESSINGS OF WORSHIPING JESUS[1]

According to the teachings of Scripture this question of the worship of Jesus is anything but a mere academic discussion. The import of the matter may be brought out by directing the attention to the following practical propositions:

First, the worship of Jesus Christ is the way to salvation.

According to the earliest sermons and summations of the Gospel the primitive Church was primarily occupied in presenting a Saviour to sinful men. Peter and the Apostles declare that God hath exalted Jesus at His right hand to be a Prince and a Saviour to give repentance to Israel and remission of sins (*Acts* 5:31). In other words Jesus Christ is the one completely equipped to meet the needs of sinners, "and in none other is there salvation." The sinner needs a new heart; Christ is a Prince to give repentance. The sinner needs forgiveness; Jesus is a Saviour to grant remission of sins. Paul has the same Gospel. The ex-persecutor's faith focuses on the risen, ascended Christ; but a Christ equipped by His expiatory death to forgive sinners, and by the quickening Spirit to make dead hearts alive. Therefore, both the original apostles and Paul exhort and beseech men to cry to Jesus Christ to save them. The New Testament message to the sinner is: "Whosoever shall call upon the name of the Lord shall be saved" (*Acts* 2:21; *Rom.* 10:13). And the confession unto salvation is the sinner's avowal that he has called upon the risen Jesus and does confess that Jesus is Lord (*Rom.* 10:8-10; *1 Cor.* 12:3; *Acts* 2:38). From the story of Pentecost, as well as the situation in the Church at Corinth (*1 Cor.* 12:3), we learn that it is by the regenerating grace of the Holy Spirit that faith is

[1] WCR, *Our Lord—An Affirmation of the Deity of Christ*, 146-52.

worked in the hearts of sinners enabling them to call upon the Lord Jesus Christ for salvation, and confess Him before men.

There is truly a peril in a mere lip worship of Jesus. Those who say unto Him, "Lord, Lord," without doing His will in their lives shall not enter into the kingdom of heaven (*Matt.* 7:21; *Luke* 6:46). But there is an even greater peril in not worshiping Jesus. Neither this text, nor any other in the New Testament offers salvation to those who refuse to worship Jesus. The way of salvation is to call upon the Name of the Lord Jesus Christ with heart as well as voice, to worship Him with our lives as well as with our lips. "The Father hath committed all judgment to the Son in order that all men should honor the Son as they honor the Father. He that honoreth not the Son honoreth not the Father who sent Him" (*John* 5:22-23).

Secondly, the worship of Jesus Christ is the way to Christlikeness.

Some of the attributes of God, such as His infinity, eternity, omnipresence, are described as the metaphysical or incommunicable attributes. God does not impart these characteristics to men. However, He has other attributes such as holiness, love, wisdom, justice, truth, which are communicable or moral attributes. God wills to make us like Himself in these blessed virtues. In order to accomplish this great objective He has manifested these traits in sublimest action on the plane of the analogical, that is, in a historical life. The eternal Son of God took human nature in order that here where we live and act He might show the moral sublimity of the Divine Nature. As He unfolds the height of moral perfection in the great act of worship by which He expiated the sins of His creatures, our Lord is the object of the especial delight of the Father, "Therefore doth the Father love me, because I lay down my life that I may take it again" (*John* 10:17). In that zeal for the glory of God and that love for sinners which motivated our Lord's will when He offered Himself in our place is revealed the moral beauty which is God's delight, the angels' desire (*1 Peter* 1:12), and the image to which the elect shall be conformed (*Rom.* 8:29). God's method of making us like unto His Son is to allow us with unveiled faces to behold as in a mirror the glory of the Lord (*2 Cor.* 3:18).

Religion is the concentration of the entire personality under the idea of God. In religious worship our otherwise multiple interests find their unity. Therefore, the most important thing about any man is his idea of God. Abraham Kuyper has rightly shown that one's doctrine of God issues in distinctive world and life views and distinctive civilizations. As the personality of a sinner is focused upon the Lord Jesus Christ in this most uplifting, unifying, and soul-moving act—the act of worship—the Holy Spirit who comes from the Lord transforms the worshiper into the same image from glory to glory (*2 Cor.* 3:18). Here is the heart of Christian adoration, the concrete theme of the Church's worship.

At the present time the old story of the Stone Face is frequently repeated in the service clubs of our cities. By gazing at noble lineaments in stone a man may come to have some of those same lines in himself. Victor Hugo has given an unforgettable portrait of an inspector who worshiped the attribute of justice until he incarnated it and was undone thereby. We call men not to worship a discarnate principle, as Javert worshiped justice; but the Incarnate God, our Saviour, who carried every virtue to its sublimest expression and that on the field of our own history, where we can see unveiled the clouds of Divine glory. Read the record of the ages. Those who have shown most Christlikeness have been the worshipers of Jesus. And however short the present worshiper of Christ may be of the likeness of his Lord, yet each one testifies that looking to Jesus has wrought all the goodness which has ever shown in his soul. This is God's method of making us like Himself.

> By looking to Jesus
>   Like Him thou shalt be,
> Thy friends in thy conduct
>   His likeness shall see.

Then,

> Fix your eye upon Jesus,
>   Look full in His wonderful face,
> And the things of earth will grow strangely dim
>   In the light of His glory and grace.

Thirdly, the worship of Jesus Christ is the way to new power and grace.

The New Testament repeatedly declares that our Lord Jesus Christ is the precious cornerstone, the sure foundation spoken of by Isaiah (*Isa.* 8:14; 28:16; *1 Peter* 2:6 ff.; *Rom.* 9:33; 10:11; *1 Cor.* 3:11; cf. *Psa.* 118:22; *Mark* 12:10). Now according to Isaiah and the New Testament this tried stone is a sanctuary in which those who believe may take refuge and not be put to shame; but it is also a stone of stumbling and a rock of offense, a gin and a snare to both the houses of Israel. "The stone which the builders rejected, the same was made the head of the corner." If our day follows in the footsteps of those who stumbled at the word being disobedient and rejected the worship of Jesus Christ, again the Lord of the vineyard will take the vineyard from the husbandmen. On the other hand, if the Son of man remains to us the sanctuary, up which our prayer, aspiration, and adoration ascend and down which descend the angels of His grace and peace and power, if Jesus Christ is still precious to us who believe, the Church of our day shall rise "in power, in energy, in appeal, in victory." The Church which worshiped Jesus turned the world upside down. Through the faith, love, martyrdoms of those who worshiped Him the Galilean conquered the empire of the Caesars in three centuries. Indeed, every missionary conquest of the Church has been accomplished through the testimony of the worshipers of Jesus Christ. As Dr. James L. Fowle of Chattanooga recently declared, those who call on us to give up the worship of Jesus, His Virgin Birth, bodily Resurrection, Atonement, eternal Deity, are like Rehoboam who surrendered the shields of gold which Solomon his wise father had made and put in their stead shields of brass. Those who pray to Jesus have their petitions answered by Jesus in grace and peace for their congregations. Those who fail to pray to Him fail to receive from Him the power of His resurrection.

Fourthly, the worship of Jesus Christ is the way to enthrone the principles of Christ.

As a matter of history Jesus did not send word to the High Priest and the Sanhedrin, the group which had denounced Him as a blasphemer, or give them commission to teach His principles. But by those who worshiped Him (*Matt.* 28:9-10), Jesus sent word to His brethren to meet Him in Galilee; and when they had come and worshiped Him, He commissioned them to teach all things whatsoever He had commanded (*Matt.* 28:17-20).

Moreover, this is an entirely logical position. Those who worship Jesus do so because they believe that He is the unchanging Lord and God (*John* 20:28; *Heb.* 1:12; 13:8). Hence, His principles and His power to sustain them will never be out of date. Moreover, He made all things (*John* 1:3), the invisible principles as well as the visible creation (*Col.* 1:16). As God, He is the author of the eternal principles of truth, goodness, beauty, justice, and love. His principles are not like those of even the wisest of men, constantly needing revision. Rather, they are the eternal foundation of Jehovah's throne and the moral fabric of the universe. From the worshipers of Jesus come those who dedicate themselves to the preaching and the teaching of His words both in the home land and in the foreign mission fields.

On the other hand those who think that Jesus is not worthy of worship do not hesitate to modify, change, and at times diametrically oppose Jesus' teachings. In reading "liberal" books and hearing their lectures, the writer has found them differing with Jesus on providence, demon possession, the necessity of a new birth, the Old Testament, petitionary prayer for physical things, the Second Coming, pacifism, sexual purity, divorce, the parable of the ninety and nine, *etc.* To put the matter bluntly a Galilean peasant is not an authority for a university professor.

Easton has aptly said that it took the Gospel about Jesus to make the Gospel of Jesus canonical. By this cryptic phrase the Episcopal scholar meant that it took a preaching of Jesus as Saviour and Lord to develop a body of believers interested in discovering, preserving, and inculcating the things Jesus taught. In this section of America no man is more highly honored or gratefully remembered for his services to the men who worked for him and the body politic than the late John J. Eagan, for many years an elder in the Central Presbyterian Church of Atlanta—a church which worships Jesus Christ. After the death of this great public benefactor, his widow opened John's Bible at the Sermon on the Mount, only to discover that he had worn out these precious words of his Lord by constant usage. Those who worship Jesus are most concerned to do what He said. One may properly supplement Easton's statement by adding that it takes the Gospel about Jesus, and the worship of Jesus, to keep the Gospel of Jesus canonical.

One finds a fitting close for this chapter in the great hymn which the Church of the Ages has built upon the chorus of the angels:

> Glory be to God on high, and on earth peace,
>> good-will toward men.
>
> We praise Thee, we bless Thee, we worship Thee,
>> we glorify Thee,
>> we give thanks to Thee for Thy great Glory.
>
> O Lord God, heavenly King, God the Father Almighty,
> O Lord, the only-begotten Son Jesus Christ:
>> O Lord God,
>> Lamb of God,
>> Son of the Father.
>
> Thou that takest away the sins of the world,
>> have mercy upon us.
>
> Thou that takest away the sins of the world,
>> have mercy upon us.
>
> Thou that takest away the sins of the world,
>> receive our prayer.
>
> Thou that sittest at the right hand of God, the Father,
>> have mercy upon us.
>
> For Thou art holy; Thou only art the Lord.
> Thou only, O Christ, with the Holy Ghost,
>> art the most high
>> in the glory of God the Father.

6. THE CROSS IN CHURCH HISTORY[1]

When we come to study the history of the Christian faith, we find that the cross has maintained its centrality in all branches of the Church, in spite of efforts made by sundry human philosophies to supplant it. The tendency of neo-Platonism was to deflect Greek Christianity toward a mystical eternalisation or deification of man; the deflection of the mediaeval Church was toward the Aristotelian hierarchial principle; in the modern age, Humanism, the Enlightenment, and Kant have magnified the sufficiency of man. But with every departure from the preaching of the cross there has resulted such a decadence in the life, love, loyalty and faith of the Church, that Christians have ever returned with new insistence upon the centrality of "that green hill without the city wall where the dear Lord was crucified, who died to save us all."

The Early Church.

The faith of the early Church is indicated by the Apostles' Creed and the writings and the worship of the Fathers. The point of view of the most ancient Christian symbol is that Christ was born to die and enter into His glory. Every event in the life of Jesus after His birth is either passed over or else concentrated in His death. But the Creed does not pass over His death, rather it devotes three statements in its scant twelve articles to that fact. With mighty blows the Creed thrice rings the changes on the cross: *suffered ... crucified ... dead.*[2] Thus the cross condenses all the meaning of Christ's life and mission.

[1] WCR, *The Word of the Cross,* 12-30.
[2] Referring to this section of the Creed, Hilary writes: "The cross, death and hell are our life."

The Apostolic Fathers commend the Church which "rejoices in the Passion of our Lord,"[1] and bid us "fix our gaze on the blood of Christ, and know that it is precious to His Father, because it was poured out for our salvation."[2] "On account of the love which He had for us did our Lord Jesus Christ, by the will of God, give His blood for us, His flesh for our flesh, His life for our lives."[3]

Polycarp alludes to his Christian predecessors "who loved not the present world, but Him who died for us, and was raised again by God for us," and exhorts his readers to "hold stedfastly to Him who is our hope and the earnest of our righteousness, who is Jesus Christ, who bore our sins in His own body on the tree; who did no sin, neither was guile found in His mouth, but suffered all for us that we might live through Him."[4] The Letter of the Church of Smyrna referring to his heroic martyrdom comments thus: "Not considering that neither will it be possible for us ever to forsake Christ, who suffered for the salvation of the saved of the whole world, or to worship any other" (xvii).

In the light of such testimony Smeaton concluded that:

> From the first, the doctrine of the atonement by the death of God's Son was a central article never impugned. The whole worship was based upon it. The first Christians, as is well known, commemorated the Lord's death in the Holy Supper every Lord's Day; and from the peculiar theory which made the worship culminate in the Supper, the atonement was constantly before the mind of the worshippers. This gave colour to primitive theology. The atoning death was central and fundamental. This accounts for the fact that the atonement never was a subject of discussion among the early Christians, and consequently never came within those currents or controversies which gave precise symbolical expression to other topics. The doctrine was so fully recognised that heresy durst not assail it.[5]

The faith which the cross nourished in the hearts of the ante-Nicene Christians is eloquently presented in the *Epistle to Diognetus:*

[1] Ignatius to the Church in Philadelphia.
[2] I Clement, VII. 4
[3] I Clement, XLIX. 6.
[4] Polycarp, *Letter to the Philippians,* viii, ix.
[5] Smeaton, George, *The Apostles' Doctrine of the Atonement,* p. 480.

O the excellence of the kindness and the love of God! He did not hate us nor reject us, nor remember us for evil, but was longsuffering, endured us, Himself in pity bore our sins, Himself gave His own Son as ransom for us, the holy for the wicked, the innocent for the guilty, the just for the unjust, the incorruptible for the corruptible, the immortal for the mortal. For what else could cover our sins but His righteousness? In whom was it possible for us, in our wickedness and impiety, to be justified except in the Son of God alone? O the sweet exchange, O the marvelous work, O the unexpected kindnesses, that the wickedness of the many should be covered in the righteous One, and the righteousness of One should justify many wicked! Having convinced us, then, of the disability of our nature to attain life in time past, and now having shown the Saviour who is able to save even the disabled natures; it was His will for both reasons that we should believe on His goodness and regard Him as nourisher, father, teacher, counsellor, physician, mind, light, honour, glory, strength and life, and to have no care for clothing and food.

After recording other representations of Christ's work, Bavinck concludes: "Finally from the beginning this thought is also in the foreground, that God hath offered Christ in His sufferings and death for us and in our place, in order to obtain for us reconciliation, forgiveness, sanctification, and entire salvation."[1]

In his presentation of Christ as the victorious Redeemer, Irenaeus says that by transgressing God's commandment "we became His enemies. And therefore in the last times the Lord has restored us into friendship through His Incarnation, having become the Mediator between God and men; indeed, propitiating for us the Father, against whom we had sinned, and cancelling our disobedience by His own obedience; conferring upon us the gift of communion with, and subjection to, our Maker."[2] Tertullian teaches that "the death of Christ is the whole weight and fruit of Christianity."[3]

The moral heroism of these early preachers of the cross has been too little appreciated. Indeed, theirs was a courage which falls short only of that which carried their Lord to the cross. To the Greeks who worshipped beauty they preached One who had no form nor

---

[1] *Gereformeerde Dogmatiek,* III. 315.
[2] Irenaeus, *Against Heresies,* V. xii. 1; v. 1.
[3] Against Marcion, III. 8.

comeliness, who was marred more than any man, so that when we see Him there is no beauty that we should desire Him (*Isa.* 53). To Stoics who demanded one with such control and apathy as evidences no emotion, they preached "a Man of sorrows and acquainted with grief." To Jews who demanded miraculous signs in the heavens above and in the earth beneath, they preached the sign of a curse, for Moses had said, "Cursed is every one that hangeth upon a tree" (*Gal.* 3:13). Cicero declared that the cross ought to be for ever absent not only from the back but even from the mind of a Roman. And yet so mightily did the Holy Spirit honour that which was foolishness to the Greek and a stumbling-block to the Jew, that in less than three centuries the cross had conquered the Empire.

The Testimony of the Post-Nicene Fathers.

Athanasius presented the cross as "the sum of our faith"[1] and the satisfaction of the divine veracity. Eusebius of Caesarea, the scholar of the ancient Church, held that "the law of Christianity is the holy cross of Christ," that the Lamb of God offered Himself a penal substitute for our sins. Chrysostom teaches that "Christ saved us from death by delivering Himself to death … We were under sin and punishment; He by suffering punishment did away with sin and punishment. He was punished on the cross." Cyril adds, "We have paid in Christ Himself the penalties of the sins with which we are charged … Jesus Christ, the only Son of God, has redeemed us, by laying down His life for us, offering Himself to the Father as a sacrifice without blemish, giving His blood in exchange for the life of all, for He was worth more than the world."[2]

Augustine says: "All my hope is in the death of my Lord. His death is my merit, my refuge, my salvation, my life, and my resurrection … the certainty of our whole confidence consists in the blood of Christ." According to Gregory the Great, "an adequate penalty must be paid for every sin." Hence, "the Redeemer is represented as the sacrifice offered to God in satisfaction for the sins of man. The sinless One paid the penalty of the sinner, so that at once the law of God's

[1] Cited by Franks, R. S., *A History of the Doctrine of the Work of Christ*, I. 67.
[2] Cited by Grensted, L. W., *The Atonement in History and in Life*, p. 191.

justice was vindicated, and the sinner was released from the penalty that was his due."[1]

John of Damascus summarizes:

> The whole activity and wonder-working of Christ is most great and divine and wonderful; but His precious cross is the most wonderful of all. For by nothing else was death destroyed, the sin of our first parents atoned for, hell despoiled, resurrection bestowed, power given us to disdain things present and death itself, the restoration of original blessedness accomplished, the gates of paradise opened, our nature seated at the right hand of God, we made children of God and heirs of heaven—but through the cross of our Lord Jesus Christ. For through the cross have all things been set right.[2]

At the base of the teaching of the Fathers we find "a fundamental principle, a truth of faith deeply rooted in the Christian conscience—that salvation has come to us by the cross of the Son of God. For them all the death of Jesus Christ is something else than an example; it has had outside ourselves, according to the divine plan, a real and mysterious operation, it possesses an objective and distinctive value. Two general facts express this supernatural efficacy—the Saviour's death appeases for us the divine wrath; and it is a penalty, the penalty of our sins, voluntarily undergone by the Lord in our place."[3]

The Cross in the Mediaeval Church.

The Church of the Middle Ages had its Anselm, whose *Cur Deus Homo?* with its exalted conception of God, its serious view of the infinite demerit of sin, and the absolute necessity for a vicarious satisfaction, was pronounced by Denney "the greatest and truest book on the atonement that has ever been written."[4] Peter Lombard, the Master of the Sentences, reminds the mediaeval ecclesiastic of "the penalty paid by Christ, who absolves us." Hugo of St. Victor teaches that Christ expiates the guilt of man by His death, "that one such

[1] Dudden, F. H., *Gregory the Great*, II.341, citing Mor. ix.46; xvii.46; iii.27; *Hom. in Ev.* 33, par. 8.

[2] John of Damascus, *De Fide Orthodoxa*, iv. 11.

[3] Riviere, *Le Dogma de la Redemption*, quoted by H. Smith, *The Atonement in History and in Life*, pp. 196-7.

[4] Denney, J., *The Atonment and the Modern Mind*, p. 116.

man, who was guilty of no punishment, assumed the punishment for men."[1] Thomas Aquinas avers that "it is a convenient mode of satisfying for another when anyone subjects himself to the punishment which another merited," and that "the obligation of punishment is lifted by the exhibition of a sufficient satisfaction." Thus, "according to Thomas, the satisfaction wrought by the suffering of Christ is the proper ground for the release of the obligation of punishment."[2] Bernard of Clairvaux, sometimes designated the oracle of Western Europe, writes: "Three principal things I perceive in this work of our salvation: the pattern of humility in which God emptied Himself; the measure of love, which He stretched even unto death, and that the death of the cross; the mystery of redemption, in which He underwent the death which He bore. The two former of these without the last are like a picture on the void."[3] In the later Middle Ages many mystics adopted the motto of John Gerson, *"Spes mea crux Christi."*[4] John Wyclif reasoned: "It is to speak lightly to say that God might of His mere power forgive this sin, without the atonement which was made for it, since the justice of God would not suffer this, which requires that every trespass be punished either in earth or hell. God may not accept a person to forgive him his sin without an atonement, else He must give free licence to sin, both in angels and men; and then were sin no more sin, and our God were no God." "Except He keep His righteousness ... how may He judge the world?"[5] Following Anselm, the mediaeval Church taught dying men that their hope was to place the death of Christ between themselves and their sins, between themselves and the wrath of God, between themselves and the punishment they deserved.

That the unreformed Church of Western Christendom has scholars today who cling to the cross is shown in these weighty words of Karl Adam: "Christianity is nothing else than the Gospel of our redemption by the cross of Christ, by the death of Jesus for our salvation, by Christ's expiatory blood."[6]

[1] Cited by Seeberg, R., *Lehrbuch der Dogmengeschichte,* III, 1930, p. 245.

[2] Cited by Seeberg, *ibid.,* p. 437.

[3] Cited by Franks, *ibid.,* p. 199.

[4] 'The cross of Christ is my hope'. Schaff, P., *A History of the Christian Church,* VII, p. 109.

[5] Vaughan, Robert, *John de Wycliffe,* pp. 394-5.

[6] Adam, Karl, *The Son of God,* p. 277.

If one turns to the Orthodox Church which is rising from the ashes of Russian persecution, Arseniev writes:

> His death is and remains fundamental and decisive: "Ye proclaim the Lord's death till He come." "This is My body which is given for you." "This is My blood of the New Covenant which is shed for many"— that is decisive for the Oriental Church. His death, His sacrifice on the cross, is contacted as a heart-shaking, ever-present, ever-living reality. The whole Christian philosophy of salvation is concentrated here as in a focus.[1]

The Cross in Protestantism.

That this thought is not less precious to the heart of the Reformed may be conveniently seen in the words of John Knox in the Scots Confession, in the works of William S. Plumer, one of the most influential of the American Presbyterian theologians, in the recent writings of President J. Oliver Buswell.

In the very nature of the case the cross must have and does have for the Protestant Reformation a more central place and import than in the Roman or Oriental Churches. The implication of justification by faith alone is that the whole and sufficient work for our forgiveness and justification was completed on the cross. Faith alone is sufficient only because Christ's atoning work for us is sufficient. In His active and passive work which culminated at Calvary, Christ became the end of the law for the justification of the believer. When He died crying, "It is finished," the work of objective soteriology was accomplished. He was delivered for our offences, and raised for our justification; so that everyone who is led to trust in the satisfaction and merit of that death is forgiven and accepted as righteous. Hence, Luther insisted that present Christian theology is a theology of the cross, rather than a theology of glory; and that there is enough of the revelation of God in the cross of Christ to last a man all his days.

> Therefore this text—*He bore our sins*—must be understood particularly thoroughly, as the foundation upon which stands the whole of the New Testament or the Gospel, as that which alone distinguishes us and

[1] Arseniev, N., *We Beheld His Glory,* pp. 131-2.

our religion from all other religions. For Christians alone believe this text. Therefore, whosoever believes this article of faith is secure against all errors, and the Holy Ghost is necessarily for him.

Zwingli tells us how Thomas Wyttenbach taught him that the death of Christ was the sole price of the remission of sins, and that faith is the key which unlocks to the soul the treasury of remission.[1] Accordingly, a British scholar, who personally differs widely from the Reformation, rightly recognizes that Luther presented the death of Christ as the sole and adequate penalty for our sins, and that "the Reformers agree in accepting the penal view of the cross as being the sole and sufficient cause of reconciliation between God and man."[2] Sin deserves punishment, but our whole punishment has been transferred to Christ. Hence one is entirely free from its penalty apart from priestly absolution or good works if by grace he has been enabled to receive the atonement. Or, to return to Luther, Christ assumed our guilt in order to confer His blessing upon us. Thus, whereas Modernism does not rest on Calvary, and Romanism has only one foot there (the other resting on ecclesiastical works and penances), the Protestant Reformation stands with both feet, all its weight, resting upon the cross.

From the Reformation onward the cross has been the heart of evangelical preaching, and it is a misnomer to call any other preaching evangelical. The Protestant faith began in Scotland with Patrick Hamilton's declaration: "Christ is our Saviour. Christ died for us. Christ bare our sins upon His back, Christ bought us with His blood. Christ washed us with His blood ... Christ was the price that was given for us and for our sins." Knox adds that "He was wounded and plagued for our transgressions; He being the clean and innocent Lamb of God, was damned in the presence of an earthly judge, that we might be absolved before the tribunal of God."[3] The saintly M'Cheyne insisted: "Live within sight of Calvary, and you will live within sight of glory." Turretin writes that the cross is, at the same time, the altar of the Priest, in which He offers Himself in sacrifice to God; the school of the Prophet, in which He teaches us the mystery

---

[1] Lindsay, *A History of the Reformation,* II. 27.
[2] Brook, V. J. K., *Atonement in History and in Life,* pp. 214, 235.
[3] Knox, John, *The Scots Confession of 1560.*

of our salvation; and the trophy of the King, in which He triumphs over principalities and powers.[1] In the words of John Owen, representative Puritanism found in the death of Christ the death of death. The evangelical movement in Scotland a century ago centred in the cross, Candlish going so far as to say that John Maclaurin's *Glorying in the Cross of Christ* was the greatest sermon ever preached.

The Moravian revival with its magnificent missionary emphasis began with the contemplation of the thorn-crowned head, and never forsook the wounds of Christ. Augustus Montague Toplady and Charles Wesley vie with one another in seeing which can make the cross more central in their great hymns, "Rock of Ages" and "Jesu, Lover of my Soul." In my own communion, Dabney, Thornwell, Plumer, Palmer, Stuart Robinson, Strickler, and Baker have ploughed the cross deep into our hearts and lives. The position of the last named is well seen in his letters to his son, a young minister:

> My son, whilst others make a parade of learning, and boast of their knowledge of German literature, be it your praise that in scriptural language, and with simplicity and power, you preach Christ and Him crucified, as the world's last and only hope … Remember, my son, this saying of your father, that the sermon that does not distinctly present Christ in the beauty and glory of His mediatorial character, is no better than a cloud without water, a casket without a jewel, a shadow without the substance, or the body without the soul. You ask why my preaching is so much blessed. If it will throw any light upon the subject, I will tell you that my plan is incessantly to preach Christ and Him crucified.[2]

As the first rays of the morning presaged the near approach of the 20th century one of the outstanding scholars and statesmen of this and of the last century heralded the new day with the declaration that "history is not so much an aphoristic spectacle of cruel passions as a coherent process with the cross as its centre."[3] The present century has produced able and scholarly defenders of the central import of the cross of our blessed Lord, J. Denney, P. T. Forsyth, A. Whyte, D. Lamont, E. K. Simpson, H. Bavinck, A. T. Robertson, A. H. Strong, B. B. Warfield, J. Gresham Machen, S. M. Zwemer, C. E. Macartney,

[1] Locus xiv. quaest. v. 13.
[2] Cited by Wells, J. M., *Southern Presbyterian Worthies,* p. 99.
[3] Kuyper, A., *Calvinism,* 1931 edition, p. 192.

W. Elert, K. L. Schmidt, K. Heim, K. Adam, K. Schilder and, not least, Louis Berkhof. Introducing a series of sermons on the cross by Professor Heim, Professor J. Schmidt rightly insists that "the strength of Christianity is in the cross."[1] Heim declares that he can be helped only by the imputed righteousness of Christ *(aliena justitia Christi)* of which Luther speaks, and further magnifies the cross by endorsing these words of Pamdita Ramabai: "I looked upon the holy Son of God, who was lifted up on the cross, and who there suffered death in my stead, that I might be freed from the bondage of sin and the fear of death, and might receive life. O what love to me, the lost sinner, this inexpressible love of the Father, who gave His only-begotten Son to die for me! I did not deserve such love, but just for that reason He showed it to me."[2]

In view of the central place of the cross in the New Testament, in view of the way in which the cross has kept its place or returned to its saving centre in the life of the Christian Church, it were, indeed, an audacious man who would set himself against the consensus of the apostles, the fathers, the martyrs, the Reformers, the true evangelicals—the Church of the ages—and maintain that this verdict of the primitive community and Christian centuries is wrong. The writer is entirely convinced that the faith of the ages is right in the fundamental place which it gives to the cross.

[1] Schmidt, J., in Preface to Heim, K., *The Gospel of the Cross.*
[2] Ramabai, Pamdita, quoted by Heim, K., *The Church and the Problems of the Day,* pp. 92-3.

7. THE LAMB OF GOD ENTHRONED[1]

"Behold the Lamb of God, which taketh away the sin of the world." In John's mouth the meaning of the words was, the Lamb who taketh upon Himself the sins of the world. But in view of the One who did so take, we may well be assured that He would not stop until He had entirely removed that curse; and the New Testament record shows that our Lord did carry our sins to the tree and take away the accusations that were against us by nailing them to the cross. Hence, the Church has been essentially correct in reading this text in the light of the whole New Testament as it is translated in the Authorized Version.

This representation of the Saviour's work immediately struck the heart of His disciples, and has, perhaps, been more widely used than any other statement of the atonement. The Old Testament sacrificial system had prepared the way for an easy apprehension of this truth. Isaiah 53 guided the thought of our Lord as well as that of His apostles. Peter assured the believing Jews that they were redeemed with the precious blood of Christ, as of a lamb without spot or blemish. Hebrews rings the changes on Christ as both the priest and the sacrifice, offering Himself once for all to obtain for us an eternal redemption. As He yielded up His spirit a sacrifice to God, the veil of the temple was rent in twain, God thus signifying that the true sacrifice for sin had been made, guilt expiated, and the way of access into the holy of holies opened, never to be closed again. Any penitent sinner, every believing sinner may at any time or place enter into the very presence of God through the new and living way which Christ hath opened for us by the sacrifice of Himself. Sacred places, priestly

[1] WCR, *The Word of the Cross,* 163-68.

mediators are not necessary. Every Christian may equally be a true priest of the Most High God, and every place where one prays in Spirit and in truth may be a Bethel with angels of God ascending and descending to us through the sole mediation of the Son of man, the heavenly high priest of our profession. Christ has been openly set forth in His own blood as the propitiatory mercy seat (*Rom.* 3:25). John takes up the thought and presents Christ some thirty times as the Lamb. As long as the Apocalypse is read the Christian must remember that the heavenly Church clusters around the Lamb, yea, that the midst of God's own throne is reserved for the Lamb standing as it had been slain. With Hebrews and Revelation before us, Christian imagination visualizes the high priest of our profession pleading in glory the merit of His atoning sacrifice, and suing out for those whom the Father hath given Him gifts of saving and sanctifying grace.

Hence, the Church on earth, which is only properly a Church as she seeks to conform to the Church above and to reflect on earth the light of heaven, has also centred her thought in the Lamb for sinners slain. Several liturgical pieces widely used throughout Christendom are redolent with this thought. One seems to have formed part of an early Oriental hymn which was united with the *Gloria in Excelsis,* and now forms part of a chant which is found in the liturgies and hymnals of many Christian communions. This ancient canticle as given in the Anglican *Book of Common Prayer*, one of the documents of the Reformation, contains the petitions: "O Lord God, Lamb of God, Son of the Father, that taketh away the sins of the world, have mercy upon us. Thou that takest away the sins of the world, have mercy upon us. Thou that takest away the sins of the world, receive our prayer."

The *Common Service Book of the Lutheran Church* provides that the congregation shall sing at the celebration of the Lord's Supper: "O Christ, Thou Lamb of God, that takest away the sin of the world, have mercy upon us. O Christ, Thou Lamb of God, that takest away the sin of the world, grant us Thy peace. Amen." Elsewhere in the same liturgy occur the words: "He is the very Paschal Lamb which was offered for us, and hath taken away the sin of the world."

A well-known hymn by Horatius Bonar contains the stanza:

> Glory be to Him who loved us,
>> Washed us from each spot and stain!
> Glory be to Him who bought us,
>> Made us kings with Him to reign!
>> Glory, glory,
>> To the Lamb that once was slain!

The time-honoured Scottish piety of the psalms and paraphrases, of morning and evening worship, of thanks after as before meals, the heart piety that traces God's way in every season of reviving grace, glories in this Gospel.

> It welcomes His Word and rests in its witness, being satisfied as to its truth and its authority: and when that Word speaks of Him as the sacrificial Lamb and the enthroned Priest, the faith to which the Gospel summons us, hastens to take shelter under the covert of His sacrifice and the shield of His intercession … In coming to Him as priest, His people take shelter under the shadow of His one sacrifice once for all offered as the Lamb of God; and they put their case in His hand as their advocate, that He may plead their cause and perfect what concerneth them.[1]

Charlotte Elliott's much loved hymn is sung throughout the English-speaking world:

> Just as I am, without one plea,
>> But that Thy blood was shed for me,
> And that Thou bidst me come to Thee,
>> O Lamb of God, I come!

The lamb was a favourite pictorial representation of Christ in the catacombs. Arseniev assures us that, for the Oriental Church, Christ's "death, His sacrifice on the cross, is contacted as a heart-shaking, ever-present reality," that "the whole Christian philosophy of salvation is concentrated here as in a focus," that "we are lifted up into the presence of His eternal sacrifice" as we direct our minds to the vision presented in Revelation.[2]

It is a wise observation that no sermon is worth while which does not leave the hearer in the presence of the throne of God and of the

---

[1] Macleod, Principal J., *The Gospel Call in Peace and Truth*, XX. 73, pp. 22, 26.
[2] Arseniev, N., *We Beheld His Glory*, pp. 131-132.

Lamb. John beheld in the midst of the throne and of the four living ones and of the four and twenty elders, a Lamb standing as it had been slain. He saw the dignitaries of the Holy City falling down before the slain Lamb, offering Him the prayers of the saints in golden incense bowls, chanting His praises. The presbyters of the General Assembly and Church of the Firstborn in heaven, the myriads of angels, yea, all creatures in the universe, praise the Lamb because He was slain and did redeem for God with His blood men of every nation and kindred and tribe (*Rev.* 5).

And that part of the flock which treads earth's dusty way catches the notes of the heavenly worship and antiphonally echoes back the chorus:

> Crown Him with many crowns,
>   The Lamb upon His throne;
> Hark! how the heav'nly anthem drowns
>   All music but its own;
> Awake, my soul, and sing
>   Of Him who died for thee,
> And hail Him as thy matchless King
>   Through all eternity.
>
> Crown Him the Lord of love;
>   Behold His hands and side,
> Rich wounds, yet visible above
>   In beauty glorified:
> No angel in the sky
>   Can fully bear that sight,
> But downward bends his wond'ring eye
>   At mysteries so bright.

There is a fountain opened for sin and uncleanness; there is a river whose streams make glad the city of God, and on whose banks grow the trees, the leaves of which are for the healing of the nations. But this stream rises not from the systems of human philosophy; the ideologies of men are broken cisterns that can hold no water. The water of life, the crystal stream casting up its silver spray, the beautiful river at which the saints do gather, flows from the throne of God and of the Lamb.

And the city watered by this stream has "no need of the sun, neither of the moon to shine in it: for the glory of God did lighten it, and the Lamb is the light thereof" (*Rev.* 21:23). "The Lamb is all the glory of Immanuel's land." Or in simpler prose, "comprehensively, incarnation and expiation are accomplished for this purpose: that God might again be recognized and honoured by His creatures as God. Sin was erroneous knowledge of God and of all His virtues, and an approach to and adoration of the creature. But in Christ God has again revealed Himself, established His sovereignty, justified all His virtues, glorified His name, maintained His Godhead."[1] In the expiatory cross of Christ, the moral grandeur of the Triune Jehovah is revealed as nowhere else. "There never was witnessed such a scene in the universe before—the infinite holiness and goodness of God sounded to their depths, the whole moral energy of the Godhead in action." "Never was there such a doxology as when Jesus died, and the whole work of redemption is a grand litany which has no parallel in the history of the universe."[2] Since nowhere else was the divine worth so worshiped, naught else makes the glory of God so luminous; therefore, the cross is the focal point and kernel of the Gospel.

---

[1] Bavinck, III, 344, 377.
[2] Thornwell, II, 424, 419.

8. JUSTIFICATION BY FAITH[1]

One of my college classmates said, in my hearing, "Well, I have thought through the doctrine of justification by faith." It is the conviction of the writer that one cause for so much of our present loose theological thinking and for the diminution of the vitality and power of present Christianity is that too few of us have thought out just what this cardinal doctrine of the Reformation is. We have not the courage of our convictions, the transforming force in our lives, the faith that mocks the flames, which the Reformers had, because we have not felt the graciousness and blessedness of their doctrine of justification by faith.

We have gotten in the habit of using this term as a phrase to conjure with, a shibboleth, a form of words instead of taking the time to grasp its real meaning. And of all terms, this one, when used as a phrase only, is the one most capable of misinterpretation. This false interpretation can come either from loose thinking (or lack of thinking), or from the studied effort to deceive. The English words, "justification by faith," can be easily used to mean the direct opposite of the Reformation doctrine of justification. This is because of the indefiniteness of that preposition "by." A speaker or writer can use that "by" as meaning, "by the power of," "by the virtue of," "by the grace of," as easily as another can use it to mean, "by means of" or "by the instrumentality of." Even historians of the Reformation, in discussing Luther's heart acceptance of the doctrine of justification by faith, show a woeful misapprehension of the meaning of the term.

Many today are using the term, "justification by faith," to express their belief that we are justified on the ground of faith. That is, that

[1] WCR, *The Presbyterian,* 12 February 1925, 6-7, 30.

176

faith itself, and our own faith, is accepted by God as the ethical basis or meritorious ground on which He declares us righteous. Faith, then, is a substitute for obedience. Faith is taken to mean religious heroism—it is the seed of the new life which God is pleased to accept in place of the perfect life which formerly He demanded. Faith is made the basis of our judgment. According to this interpretation, the apostle of modernism says that God deals with a man, not on the basis of what he has done, or even what he is, but on the basis of the thing the man has set his heart upon, the direction of his life, the ideal which masters him. In accord with this interpretation, the eyes of men are turned in on themselves toward the examination of their own faith—be sure that you have faith in God like Jesus had. Scrutinize, perfect your faith, develop your faith, for your faith as the sum of your hopes and ideals and vital principle and life direction, is to be the ground of your justification. This form of reasoning makes the basis and ground of our justification to inhere in us—it is our faith (as the sum of our hopes, *etc.*) which is accepted by God as the equivalent of righteousness. We save ourselves if only we can get the right kind of faith, the right amount of it; Jesus' rebuke of this attitude with the words that if ye have faith as a grain of mustard seed you can remove mountains is forgotten. Furthermore, this meaning, read into the apostolic doctrine of justification by faith, is the opposite of what that term was used by the Reformers to mean.

The real meaning of justification by faith, as that term was used by the Protestants in the Reformation, and the real meaning of that doctrine as expounded in Scripture, and expressed in Protestant Confessions, can be made clear by noticing the real biblical attitude of faith, the ethical basis of justification, and the graciousness of the entire process.

The biblical attitude of faith, negatively, is a denial that man by his works or anything in himself contributes to his justification. Justification is "to him that worketh not"; that is, to him who does not want to work, does not intend to work, who acknowledges that he and his works are sinful and unrighteous. Faith, as Paul uses it, is the algebraic formula for not working—negatively, it is equivalent to saying that man contributes nothing to his justification. The attitude of justifying faith is seeking to be found in Him, not having one's own righteousness which is of the law. It is a recognition that we are saved, not of ourselves and not of our works, for by the works of the law shall no flesh be justified—in himself every man stands guilty before God. And every atom of human sufficiency and pride and boasting is excluded. "Merit lives from man to man, but not, O God, from man to thee."

Positively, the attitude of justifying faith is magnifying God, it is God-centered. Dr. Geerhardus Vos, whose careful thought the writer has freely used in this discussion, defines the attitude of faith as the unlimited willingness to let God do all the saving, a recognition of divine monergism. The attitude of faith is not looking at itself as though it were a new virtue substituted for the old, but it is looking to the object of faith. Justifying faith is faith towards or into Jesus Christ. It is resting on Him as the limpet clings to the rock. It is being found in Him. Faith denies all hope and trust in the man himself, or in the substance of the faith in itself, and rests men on the unchanging grace and character of God. Faith is the attitude of giving all the glory to God.

Again, as to the ethical basis of justification—the ground on account of which God declares a man righteous—Protestant justification by faith offers not itself. Our Westminster Confession of Faith for three hundred years has been denying this "modernist" idea that God imputes faith itself, the act of believing, or any other evangelical obedience to men as their righteousness. If we take the time to investigate justification according to the Aristotelian causes, it will save us many upsets. According to this analysis, faith is the instrumental cause—the means, the instrument, the human condition—of justification. But faith is not the efficient cause—for that is the righteousness of God; it is not the material cause—for that is the obedience and suffering of Jesus Christ; it is not the formal cause—for that is the righteousness of another (in distinction from one's own righteousness); it is not the final cause—which is the salvation of souls and the glory of God. Faith is taking Jesus Christ with the *naked* hand of the heart. Faith is the human condition, the receiving, but that which it receives is the meritorious ground of justification. And this ground or basis is the righteousness of God which is built up of the material furnished by the entire humiliation of

Christ—His satisfaction of the precepts and penalties of the law of God, by His human life, obedience, suffering and death. Protestant faith is receiving and resting on Christ and His righteousness; and Protestant justification by faith is God, on the occasion of man's act of faith, imputing to that man Christ's obedience and satisfaction as his righteousness, and so receiving the believer as righteous in His sight. The saving virtue is not faith as a new virtue, but the virtues and sufferings of Christ, our Substitute. Modernistic justification rests on what the believer is or aspires to be; Protestant justification rests on what Christ is and what He has done for the believer.

Finally, justification by faith, as far as the sinner is concerned, is entirely gratuitous. "We are justified freely by His grace." It is gratuitous because even faith, the instrumental cause, is the free gift of God. Faith is our coming to Christ, but no man cometh save as the Father draws him. We only call Jesus Lord by the Holy Spirit. We come to recognize Jesus as the Christ, the Son of God, but flesh and blood reveals it not unto us, that is done by the Father in heaven. We know the Son only as He willeth to reveal Himself. It is given unto us to believe on Him, and our total salvation, even with reference to faith, is the gift of God. Further, while the process of salvation has been so worked out by the wisdom of the Trinity that God is justified in that process, and it is just to Christ to accept as righteous those who are in Him; nevertheless, it is entirely gracious of God in relation to the sinner to justify him. God is declared just in His nature and government in justifying the ungodly by faith. But the whole plan of redemption is gracious as far as the sinner is concerned. It is pure, undeserved love that leads God to provide a Saviour for sinful men. It is grace that provides the Righteous One to work out in man's stead a righteousness for them. It is of His graciousness toward men that God the Son takes human nature and by years of humiliation and obedience and the depths of agony works out that robe of righteousness with which to clothe the sinner. It is gracious on the part of God the Father to willingly accept the righteousness of another in lieu of the righteousness which the sinner is unable to offer in himself. If justification as its basis be the man or his works, or his outlooks, it is of debt, not of grace. But with one accord, the Scriptures proclaim a salvation that is of the Lord and a justification by faith that is of grace, grace, grace to the utmost—grace to the unrighteous, whereby they are declared righteous in Christ—righteous as clothed in His spotless robes of righteousness.

Now as we cut away all centers, or subsidiary centers, of reliance on ourselves and our sinful hearts, and as we rest entirely and alone on the grace of God, and on the God of grace we place ourselves in faith's true attitude—we open our hearts for the streams of living water to flood our souls. As we see that we are saved entirely by the graciousness of God, that we rest entirely on Jesus Christ, and are accepted *in toto* for what He has done for us, the ocean of gratitude for this grace rises in a tidal wave that has real volume in lieu of the tiny, intermittent rivulets of thanks that have been trickling from our hearts. As we deny self and rest alone on Jesus Christ, we realize the appropriate relationship in which close fellowship may exist, we draw really close to Him, we cling indeed, we hide in the riven rock, we seek to be crushed to His bosom, and in the warmth and depth of living fellowship with the ever-present loving Redeemer we begin to live His life and manifest the reality of His power, the blessedness of His grace.

9. WITHERSPOON AND DOCTRINE[1]

John Witherspoon, the leader of the evangelical party in the Kirk of Scotland, was called to this land in 1768 as president of Princeton College. Here he helped re-organize the Presbyterian Church and was instrumental in forming the first General Assembly. He wrote the Parliamentary Principles which transformed a "branch" of an established Church into a free Church.

The only minister to sign the Declaration of Independence, Dr. Witherspoon labored so mightily for the American cause that the state of New Jersey proclaimed 1975 as John Witherspoon Year: "In tribute to this man of God, patriot, educator and signer of the Declaration of Independence, and to encourage a return to God, patriotism, fidelity in government, true education and the spirit of 1776."

Dr. Witherspoon wrote a pamphlet on the connection between the doctrine of justification by the imputed righteousness of Christ and holiness of life. In testimony to the Gospel he preached, the following summary is presented.

The Reformation doctrine of justification by the imputed righteousness of Christ was attacked on the grounds that it loosened the obligations to practice Christian living. Dr. Witherspoon replied, "On the contrary, the belief and acceptance of justification by the grace of God through the imputed righteousness of Christ makes men greater lovers of purity and holiness and fills them with a greater abhorrence of sin."

Experience shows that those who deny their own righteousness and hope for justification through Christ are the most tender, the

[1] WCR, *Presbyterian Journal,* September 22, 1976.

most fearful of sinning, and the most holy in their lives.

Using Scriptural language, Dr. Witherspoon described the doctrine thus: "All have sinned and come short of the glory of God, therefore, by the deeds of the law there shall no flesh be justified in His sight. But we are justified freely by His grace, through the redemption that is in Christ Jesus, whom God set forth as a propitiation, through faith in His blood, to declare His righteousness for the remission of sins that are past, through the forbearance of God."

"Where is boasting then? It is excluded. By what law? Of works? Nay, but by the law of faith. Therefore we conclude that a man is justified by faith without the deeds of the law. Moreover, the law entered that the offense might abound; but where sin abounded, grace did much more abound; that as sin hath reigned unto death, even so might grace reign through righteousness unto eternal life by Jesus Christ our Lord."

In support of this Biblical truth, Dr. Witherspoon argued this way: First, one who expects justification by the imputed righteousness of Christ has the strongest convictions of *the obligation of the holy law of God* upon every reasonable creature. What Christ did for the salvation of sinners magnifies the law of God; He obeyed its precepts and endured its penalty.

Second, he who believes in Christ and expects justification by His imputed righteousness must have the deepest and strongest sense of *the evil of sin* in itself. Even though God is the God of love, He does not forgive sin without an atonement. The greatness of the price, "the precious blood of Christ," shows God's abhorrence of sin. The dignity and glory of the Redeemer, along with the greatness and severity of His suffering, testify to the heinousness of sin.

In order to save sinners, sin had to be expiated, even though God's own Son was the sacrificial victim. Therefore, the condemnation of sin was as truly in view as the salvation of sinners.

Third, he who expects justification only through the imputation of the righteousness of Christ has the most awful views of *the danger of sin.* He sees not only the obligation and purity of the law, but also the severity of the sanctions of that law, that is, the fear of the wrath and vengeance of God on account of sin. Those who flee to the propitiation of Christ for deliverance and rescue still believe that every sin deserves the wrath and curse of God both in this life and the one to come.

Fourth, those who expect justification by the imputation of the righteousness of Christ have the highest sense of *the purity and holiness of the divine nature,* and therefore the necessity of purity to fit them for His presence and enjoyment. Worshipers of God seek to be like Him. Even when God is inclined to mercy, the experience of mercy is obstructed until justice is satisfied as His Son stands in our place. Thus His mediation shows the purity of the divine nature.

Fifth, the motives of *gratitude and thankfulness* to God for His salvation lead to pure and holy lives.

Sixth, those who expect to be justified by the imputed righteousness of Christ must be possessed of a supreme and superlative *love to God* which is not only the source and principle but the very sum and substance—nay the perfection of holiness. His love for us begets our love for Him. We love because He first loved us. The supreme love of God is what is meant by holiness.

10. THE SAVIOUR OF SINNERS[1]

On the road to Damascus the Saviour met a sinner. The sinner was breathing out threatenings and slaughter against the people of God. His heart was filled with enmity toward Christ. Yet the risen Lord spoke to him in judgment and in mercy. Blinded by the light of His judgment Paul fell down as one dead. And at the same time the Lord whose Church he was persecuting spoke to Paul in mercy. The One who had prayed, "Father forgive them," appeared to Paul to forgive this persecutor and to receive His chief opponent as His dear friend.

Paul's testimony runs about as follows: When I was dying under the unerring verdict of the law, then wonder of wonders, God revealed His Son in me. God revealed Him as crucified for my sins. He who knew no sin was made sin for me. Christ became a curse for me. The agony, the wrath, the death that my sin deserved were visited upon Him. But when sin and Satan and death had done their worst, when the one sacrifice for sins was finished once for all, when the whole debt was paid; then God Himself broke the shackles of death and raised His beloved Son in the blessedness of pure righteousness. As He was delivered for my offenses, so was He raised for my justification. He who was made my sin, is now my righteousness. As in Him I died for my sins, so in Him I am now alive unto God. As in His dying my debt was fully paid, so in His resurrection I am fully justified. As I the guilty sinner became a curse in Him, so I the penitent believer am now the righteousness of God in Him. What matters it if men condemn, GOD justifies.

In the Epistle to the Romans Paul expounds the plan of Scripture by inculcating the fact that Christ is their first principle. Never

[1] WCR, *Christ—The Bread of Life*, 43-66.

does the Apostle forget that he is the sinner for whom Christ died. In Romans God speaks in judgment until the Apostle cries: "O wretched man that I am! who shall deliver me from the body of this death?" "I know that in me, that is in my flesh dwelleth no good thing." But here also the God of judgment is the God of Grace: "If it is by grace, it is no more of works." "To him that worketh not but believeth on Him that justifieth the ungodly his faith is reckoned for righteousness." "Thanks be unto God who giveth us the victory through Jesus Christ our Lord." In the epistle which speaks of the feather line between departing to be with Christ and abiding in this life, the Apostle is still sure that he has not yet attained nor been made perfect. In his final letters to Timothy, Paul the aged, both confesses himself the chief of sinners and shouts in victory, "I have fought a good fight, I have finished my course, I have kept the faith."

The Lord who reigns at the right hand of Power revealed to and through His Apostle the same good news for sinners He had taught "in the days of his flesh." There is a gentle probe in Jesus' words: "I came not to call the righteous, but sinners to repentance." Our Lord did not mean that there is a sinful class of men who need, and another, a righteous class, who do not need repentance. If one insists on finding two classes he will be closer to the Gospels if he says that one class is composed of the self-righteous sinners who think they are saints and the other of the penitent saints who know they are sinners. "Side by side let us set the words of Jesus spoken to religious men who were bent on punishing a sinful woman: 'He that is without sin among you, let him first cast a stone at her', and the words of John, speaking of himself and others far on in the Christian life: 'If we say that we have no sin, we deceive ourselves, and the truth is not in us.'"[1]

In an examination of an American religious poll, *Time* (Nov. 1, 1948) concluded that "the average pollee sounded not unlike the Pharisee who went up into the Temple to pray." Such Pharisaism bodes no good for the individual or for the nation. For he that exalteth himself shall be humbled. And, as Augustine said, our fallen nature needs a true confession not a false defence.[2] "The Church is built not by the righteousness of the Pharisee, but by the contrition

[1] Smart, J. D., *What a Man Can Believe*, p. 210.
[2] Augustine, *On Nature and Grace*, LXII.

of the Publican."[1] The other of the two men who went up into the Temple would not so much as lift up his eyes unto heaven, but beat upon his breast crying: "God be merciful to me a sinner." And the Lord said: "That man went home justified." At the same time a *sinner* and *justified*.

> Lord like a penitent I stand
> And lift my heart to Thee;
> Thy pardoning grace, O God, command,
> Be merciful to me.

Beside the crucified Saviour a thief was dying. At first there was railing on his lips. But God revealed Himself in the Christ in whom He was reconciling the world unto Himself. A sense of the fear of the holy God came over the dying thief and with it a glimmer of hope in God's forgiveness. In penitence he cried to his fellow, "Dost thou not fear God, seeing thou art in the same condemnation? And we indeed justly, for we are receiving the just reward for our deeds. But this One hath done nothing amiss." Then in struggling faith, in naked faith without works or merit, he committed himself to the Saviour, thus: "Lord Jesus, remember me when Thou comest in Thy Kingdom"—Thy Kingdom of grace for poor sinners like me. I am so bad that I deserve to be crucified. Yet Jesus so completely bore that man's sin that He could justly say to him, "today shalt thou be with Me in Paradise." This is the Gospel of the Saviour of sinners.

Augustine

In Augustine's *Confessions,* "the biography of the saint never obliterates the autobiography of the sinner." This consummate teacher of the Gospel of the grace of God had several of the penitential psalms copied on broad sheets of parchment and hung on the walls of the room in which he was dying. Thus, the outstanding Doctor of Latin Christianity descended into the Jordan reading and weeping as he read:

> Have mercy upon me, O God, according to Thy lovingkindness: According to the multitude of Thy tender mercies blot out my

[1] Niebuhr, *Beyond Tragedy,* p. 60.

transgressions. Wash me thoroughly from mine iniquity and cleanse me from my sin.

Out of the depths have I cried unto thee, O Lord. If Thou, Lord, should mark iniquities, who could stand? But with Thee there is forgiveness, that Thou mayest be feared.

Blessed is the man whose transgression is forgiven, whose sin is covered. Blessed is the man to whom the Lord imputeth not iniquity.

I said, I will confess my transgression unto the Lord; and Thou forgavest the iniquity of my sin.

Pascal's Pensées

The revival of Augustinianism connected with the names of Jansen, Saint Cyran and Quesnel was crushed by the Roman Catholic Church, but not before it had produced "a bonnie fighter." Blaise Pascal was not a Protestant, but many of his weighty words plumb our hearts:

> The knowledge of God without the knowledge of our own misery produces pride. The knowledge of our own misery without the knowledge of Jesus Christ produces despair. The knowledge of Jesus Christ exempts us both from pride, and despair; because in Him we see God, our own misery, and the only way of recovery from it.
>
> We may know God without knowing our own miseries, our own miseries without knowing God; or we may know both without knowing the means of deliverance from the miseries which oppress us. But we cannot know Jesus Christ without at the same time knowing God, our own miseries and the remedy for them; because Jesus Christ is not only God, but He is God, the healer of our miseries.
>
> We ought therefore wholly to direct our inquiries to the knowledge of Jesus Christ, since it is in Him alone that we can hope to know God, in a manner that shall be really advantageous to us.
>
> He is the true God to us men, that is to miserable and sinful creatures: He is the centre of all and the object of all.

The Reformers

The Reformation was also a revival of Augustinianism. But here the teaching of salvation by grace alone was safe-guarded by justification reckoned or imputed to the sinner on the ground of the righteousness of Christ and received by faith alone, that is *propter Christum per fidem.* Here the believer is at the same time a sinner in himself and graciously forgiven or counted as righteous in Christ, and this marvelous mercy turns him to God for the dynamics of a new life. The grace of the Lord Jesus Christ reveals to the Christian that he is *semper peccator, semper justus, semper penitens* [for ever a sinner, for ever righteous, for ever repentant].

Luther

In *the Bondage of the Will,* Luther portrays the living, risen Lord Jesus Christ interceding for the sinner on the basis of what He did for man in His earthly ministry, and sending His Spirit to convict man of sin and bring him to faith in the promises of God. This work of *Christ in us* brings comfort to our hearts as it leads us to trust in the finished work of *Christ for us.* And conversely, it is this work of *Christ in us—* the Holy Ghost opening to Luther the meaning of Romans 1:16-17 in the Black Tower at Wittenberg—that enables us to understand that *God in Christ is for us* and is gracious to us.

As early as 1516, Luther writes to Spenlein, an Augustinian monk:

> I should be glad to know what is the state of your soul. When you were living with me we were both in the greatest of all errors, seeking to stand before God on the ground of our own works. I am still struggling against that fatal error. O, my dear brother, learn to know Christ and Him crucified. Beware of pretending to such purity as no longer to confess thyself the Chief of Sinners. If our labours, and obediences and afflictions could have given peace to the conscience, why should Christ have died on the Cross? You will never find true peace till you find it and keep it in this—that Christ takes all your sins upon Himself, and bestows all His righteousness upon you.

In his open letter *On Translating,* Luther insists that it is Christ's death alone that takes away our sins and not our works also. In *Table-Talk,* Luther says:

What we have, the same is also His; but the exchange is exceeding unequal; for He has everlasting innocence, righteousness, life and salvation which He gives to be our own, while what we have is sin, death, damnation and hell; these we give unto Him, for He has taken our sins upon Him ... All the prophets well foresaw in the Spirit, that Christ, by imputation would become the greatest sinner upon the face of the earth, and a sacrifice for the sins of the whole world; would be no more considered an innocent person and without sin, or the Son of God in glory, but a notorious sinner.[1]

Again Luther says

A Christian is at the same time a sinner and a saint; he is at once bad and good, for in our own person we are in sin and in our own name we are sinners. But Christ brings us another name in which there is forgiveness of sins, so that for His sake our sin is forgiven and done away. Both are true. There are sins ... and yet there are no sins. For Christ's sake, God will not see them. Thus our Lord Jesus Christ alone is the garment of grace that is put upon us, that God our Father may not look upon us as sinners but receive us as righteous, holy, godly children and give us eternal life.

Calvin

Calvin's rule of faith is "to divest ourselves of all ground of glorying that God alone may be eminently glorious and that we may glory in Him."[2] For there is no worthiness in us why God should either shew His power to help us, or use His merciful goodness to save us.[3] The question is not how we can be righteous, but how though unrighteous we can be considered as righteous. And the answer is that "Christ alone must be proposed for righteousness who exceeds all the perfection of the law." "When we are facing the tribunal of God, we must dismiss all thoughts of our own works in reference to justification, we must embrace the Divine mercy alone, and turning our eyes from ourselves fix them solely on Christ."[4]

[1] *Table-Talk,* translated by W. Hazlitt, London, 1948, pp. 82, 84.
[2] Dedication to the *Institutes.*
[3] Calvin's Catechism, II, in Dunlop, *Collection of Confessions,* II. 142; Cf. Calvin's Commentaries on I Peter 1:1-2; and on Ephesians 1:4-5.
[4] *Institutes,* III.xix.2.

"We obtain justification before God, solely by the intervention of the righteousness of Christ. Which is equivalent to saying, that a man is righteous not in himself, but because the righteousness of Christ is communicated to him by imputation; and this is a point that deserves an attentive consideration. For it supersedes that idle notion, that a man is justified by faith, because faith receives the Spirit of God by whom he is made righteous; which is too repugnant to the foregoing doctrine, ever to be reconciled to it." "Our righteousness is not in ourselves but in Christ." Calvin called on regenerate man to think on everlasting righteousness, not on the basis of the good works to which he devotes himself, but solely on the intervention of the right-eousness of Christ given one by the mercy of God *"Christi nomen omne meritum excludit"*[1] [the name of Christ excludes all merit].

For Calvin,

> The whole of our salvation and all the branches of it are comprehended in Christ ... if we seek salvation we are taught by the name of Jesus that it is found in Him; if we seek any other gifts of the Spirit they will be found in His unction; strength in His dominion; purity in His conception; indulgence discovers itself in His nativity, by which He was made like us in all things that He might learn to condole with us; if we seek redemption it will be found in His suffering; absolution, in His condemnation; remission of the curse, in His cross; satisfaction in His sacrifice; purification in His blood; reconciliation in His descent into hell; mortification of the flesh, in His resurrection; the inheritance of the celestial kingdom, in His entrance into heaven; protection, security, abundance, and the enjoyment of all blessings in His kingdom; a fearless expectation of the judgment, in the judicial authority committed to Him. ... Blessings of every kind are deposited in Him, let us draw from His treasury, and from no other source, till our desires are satisfied.[2]

Bugenhagen

When there was no room in England for William Tyndale to translate the Bible, he fled to Wittenberg. Luther's colleague Bugen-hagen interested himself in the English refugee and wrote for

[1] *Institutes,* III.xi.11-13,16,23.
[2] *Institutes,* II.xvi.19.

him the first Reformation tract addressed to the English-speaking people. Bugenhagen admits that there are many erroneous statements, charges and calumnies leveled at the Reformers. He does not stay to answer them, but boldly declares. "We have but one doctrine: Christ is Our Righteousness."

English Faith

Small wonder that the Gospel bore fruit on English soil. There are no finer testimonies to the righteousness of God our Saviour than these words of the judicious Hooker:

Christ hath merited righteousness for as many as are found in Him. And in Him God findeth us, if we be believers; for by believing we are incorporated into Christ. Then, although in ourselves we be altogether sinful and unrighteous, yet even the man who is in himself impious, full of iniquity, full of sin—him being found in Christ through faith, and having his sin in hatred through repentance—him God beholdeth with a gracious eye and accepteth him in Jesus Christ as perfectly righteous as if he had fulfilled all that is commanded him in the holy law of God—shall I say accepteth him as more perfectly righteous than if himself had fulfilled the whole law? I must take heed what I say; but the Apostle saith: "God hath made Him to be sin, for us, Who knew no sin, that we might be made the righteousness of God in Him." Let it be counted folly or frenzy or fury, or whatsoever; it is our wisdom and our comfort: we care for no knowledge in the world but this—that man hath sinned and God hath suffered: that God hath made Himself the sin of men, and that men are made the righteousness of God in Him.[1]

Bread from Bunyan

Pilgrim's Progress is not quite forgotten. Written in Bedford Jail it played to packed houses in the Royal Theatre at Covent Garden, London, in 1948. Perhaps, the most moving scene in the play is where Pilgrim comes up with the Cross and the burden falls from his back and tumbles into the emptied Sepulchre.

[1] Richard Hooker on *Justification*, 1585.

> Blest Cross! blest Sepulchre! blest rather be
> The Man that there was put to shame for me.

In *Grace Abounding to the Chief of Sinners*, Bunyan tells us of the seven abominations that seared his heart, and of God's grace that brought relief. Here are some crumbs from the table God spread for this servant:

I remember that one day, as I was traveling into the country, and musing on the wickedness and blasphemy of my heart, and considering of the enmity that was in me to God, that scripture came to my mind, "He hath made peace by the Blood of His Cross." By which I was made to see, both again and again that day, that God and my soul were friends by this Blood; yea, I saw that the justice of God and my sinful Soul could embrace and kiss each other through this blood. This was a good day to me; I hope I shall not forget it.

But as I was walking up and down in the house, as a man in a most woeful state, that Word of God took hold of my heart, "Ye are freely justified by His Grace, through the redemption that is in Christ Jesus." But oh, what a turn it made in me!

And as I was thus in a muse, that Scripture also came with great power upon my Spirit, "Not by works of righteousness that we have done but according to His mercy, He hath saved us." Now was I got on high; I saw myself within the arms of Grace and Mercy.

But one day, as I was passing in the field and that too with some dashes on my conscience, fearing lest yet all was not right, suddenly this sentence fell upon my soul. Thy righteousness is in heaven, and me thought I saw with the Eyes of my Soul, Jesus Christ at God's Right Hand. There, I say, was my righteousness; so that whatever I was, or whatever I was doing, God could not say of me, He wants my righteousness, for that was just before Him. I also saw, moreover that it was not my good frame of heart that made my Righteousness better, not yet my bad frame that made my Righteousness worse; for my Righteousness was Jesus Christ Himself, the same yesterday, today and forever.

Now did my chains fall off my legs indeed; I was loosed from my afflictions and irons; my temptations also fled away; now went I also home rejoicing, for the grace and love of God. So when I came home, I looked to see if I could find that sentence. Thy righteousness is in Heaven, but could not find such a saying; wherefore my heart began to sink; only that was brought to my remembrance. He is made unto us of God Wisdom and Righteousness and Sanctification and Redemption, by this Word I saw the other sentence true.

For by this Scripture, I saw that the Man Christ Jesus, as He is distinct from us, as touching His bodily presence, so He is our Righteousness and Sanctification before God. Here, therefore, I lived for some time, very sweetly with God through Christ. Oh me thought, Christ! Christ: there was nothing but Christ before my Eyes.

Now was I as one awakened out of some troublesome sleep and dream and listening to this heavenly sentence; I was as if I had heard it thus expounded to me: Sinner, thou thinkest that because of thy Sins and Infirmities I can not save thy Soul: but behold my Son is by me, and upon Him I look, and not on thee, and deal with thee according as I am pleased with Him.

John Wesley

Whatever differences there are in systematic theology between Calvinism and Evangelical Arminianism,[1] in the field of historical theology a Presbyterian remembers the miracle of grace by which the Wesleys led the evangelical movement that saved eighteenth century England from rationalism. In this movement they had the stimulus and inspiration from such American Calvinists as Frelinghuysen, the Tennents, and Jonathan Edwards, such Welsh Calvinists as Howell Harris and Daniel Rowland, and such Scottish worthies as Halyburton and Boston. They had the Calvinist Whitefield as their associate and Lady Huntington as a patron. But English Presbyterianism in the eighteenth century was on the downgrade toward Arianism and Socinianism and much of Scottish Presbyterianism was engaged in a therapeutic preaching that left little room for a free offer of the Gospel to sinners.[2] The Marrowmen who protested against the Scottish condition received scant consideration from the Moderate machine in Scotland, and the Erskines corresponded with the Wesleys. John Duncan has said that Hyper-Calvinism is a house without a door and that Arminianism is a door without a house. Perhaps, the Erskines and the Wesleys were seeking both a door wide open in invitation

---

[1] Girardeau, J. L., *Calvinism and Evangelical Arminianism;* Lecerf, A., *An Introduction to Reformed Dogmatics,* p. 382.

[2] Macleod, John, *Scottish Theology in Connection with Church History.*

and a house in which the sheep might be safely folded. Indeed, a number of recent studies[1] in Wesley hold that he moved from a High Church Arminianism under the influence of Luther toward Augustinianism, and thereafter was sometimes more and sometimes less Calvinistic.

In his sermon on "The Lord Our Righteousness" John Wesley describes the righteousness of Christ as including both the *active* and the *passive* righteousness which Christ wrought for us in His human life and which is *imputed* to us when we believe. Moreover, "There is no true faith, that is, justifying faith, which hath not the righteousness of Christ for its object." "All believers are forgiven and accepted, not for the sake of anything in them, or anything that ever was, that is, or ever can be done by them, but wholly and solely for the sake of what Christ hath done and suffered for them." The faith which is imputed for righteousness is faith in the righteousness of Christ.

Wesley affirms that "this is the doctrine I have constantly believed and taught for near eight and twenty years," and which I have published over and over in the hymns, such as the following:

> Jesu, thy blood and righteousness
> My beauty are, my glorious dress:
> Midst flaming worlds in these array'd,
> With joy shall I lift up my head.

Further Wesley expressly cites Calvin as teaching the same doctrine he holds on this matter, "namely, that the righteousness of Christ, both his active and passive righteousness, is the meritorious cause of our justification, and has procured for us at God's hand, that upon our believing, we should be accounted righteous by him."[2]

In opposing Dr. John Taylor's attack on original sin, Wesley said: "If the sin of Adam was not imputed to us, neither is the righteousness of Christ." "A denial of original sin contradicts the main design of the Gospel which is to humble man and to ascribe to God's free grace, not man's free will, the whole of salvation." Wesley uses large

---

[1] G. C. Cell, *The Rediscovery of John Wesley;* A. W. Harrison, *The Evangelical Revival and Christian Reunion;* Franz Hildebrandt, *This is the Message;* Wm. Cannon, *The Theology of John Wesley.*

[2] *The Works of Rev. John Wesley,* N. Y., 1832, 1:169-177; cf. Harrison, A. W., *The Evangelical Revival and Christian Reunion.*

portions of Thomas Boston's *Fourfold State* to state his position here. In another place, Wesley insists on grace alone and comes "to the very edge of Calvinism" in ascribing all good to free grace, in denying all natural free will and all power antecedent to grace, and in excluding all merit from man for what he has or does by the grace of God.[1] It has become popular to assume that all men are naturally children of God. Like our own Robert A. Webb,[2] Wesley taught that we sinners become God's children by adoption, that is by faith in Jesus Christ.

William Law pressed mysticism in these words: "There is but one salvation for all mankind, and the way to it is one; and that is the desire of the soul turned to God. This desire brings the soul to God and God unto the soul: it unites with God, it cooperates with God, and is one life with God." But nothing so stirred Charles Wesley to indignation as the idea that man can save himself apart from the mediatorial work of Christ. And John Wesley declared: "All the other enemies of Christianity are triflers; the mystics are the most dangerous of its enemies. They stab it in the vitals; and its most serious professors are likely to fall by them. May I praise Him who has snatched me out of this fire likewise by warning all others that are set on fire of hell." A Gospel without Christ? Why Wesley's description of his own preaching runs thus: "I have been offering Christ to men for three hours."[3]

The sun arose for England's tireless evangelist in that strange warming of his heart in Aldersgate Street Mission when: "I felt I did trust in Christ, Christ alone for salvation, and an assurance was given me that He had taken away *my* sins, even *mine,* and saved *me* from the law of sin and death." At his dying bed, this great campaigner for souls testifies, "There is no way into the holiest but by the blood of Jesus." A scholar, who has traced the story of Wesley's dying further than the account in the *Journal,* says that when the evangelist became too weak to speak his lips were forming these words of the Apostle: "The chief of sinners, I."

[1] *The Works of Rev. John Wesley,* 5:647-48 and 8:285.
[2] Webb, R. A., *The Reformed Doctrine of Adoption.*
[3] Cited, F. Hildebrandt, *This is the Message.*

Thomas Adam

Another English evangelical of Wesley's century is Thomas Adam. After suffering under the toils of the law, Adam found the Gospel in Romans and began to preach salvation through faith in Jesus Christ alone to man who is always a sinner. In his *Private Thoughts on Religion,* he confesses, "Sin is still here, deep in the centre of my heart and twisted about every fibre of it." "The moment we think we have no sin we shall desert Christ, for Christ came to save sinners." "If I were to live to the world's end and do all the good that man can do, I must still cry, Mercy."

No, this does not mean easy acquiescence in sinning, "I would rather be cast into the burning fiery furnace, or the lion's den, than suffer sin to lie quiet in my spirit." Christ never comes into the soul unattended. He brings the Holy Spirit with Him and the Spirit His train of gifts and graces. Christ comes with a blessing in each hand, forgiveness in one and holiness in the other. "Christ's forgiveness of sins is complete at once, because less would do me no good; His holiness is dispensed by degrees and to none wholly in this life lest we should slight His forgiveness."

"On earth it is one of the hardest things in the world to see sin and Christ at the same time, to be penetrated with a lively sense of our desert of punishment and absolute freedom from condemnation; but the more we know of both, the nearer approach we shall make to the state of heaven." "It is a great paradox but the glorious truth of Christianity that a good conscience may consist with a consciousness of evil." And Warfield who has culled these testimonies from Adam adds: "Sin and Christ; ill desert and no condemnation; we are sinners and saints all at once! That is the paradox of evangelicalism. The Antinomian and the Perfectionist would abolish the paradox—the one drowning the saint in the sinner, the other concealing the sinner in the saint." We must ever see both members of the paradox and see them whole. "Though we can have no satisfaction in ourselves, we may have perfect satisfaction in Christ."[1]

The God in whom we trust is the pardoning God, God in Christ. And every step of our salvation is His work. The work He has

[1] B. B. Warfield, *Perfectionism,* I. 126-132.

undertaken is now in process. Neither for the individual nor for the world is God's work complete.

We share in this process by working out our own salvation with fear and trembling, for it is God who worketh in us to will and to do for His good pleasure. We reign with Him in righteousness, His righteousness imputed to us. And in His Kingdom, the light of His Grace sanctifies every relation in life.

Words from Old Scotia

The Scottish divines are not wanting in such confessions. Samuel Rutherford has been called "the saint of the covenant," but Rutherford's own word is: "Woe, woe is me that men should think there is anything in me. The house devils that keep me company and this sink of corruption make me carry low sails … But howbeit I am a wretched captive of sin, yet my Lord can hew heaven out of worse timber than I am if worse there be."

When he heard that his colleague of the Westminster Assembly, George Gillespie, was dying, Samuel Rutherford wrote him: "My reverend and dear brother, look to the East. Die well. Your life of faith is just finishing. Finish it well. Let your last act of faith be your best act. Stand not upon sanctification, but upon justification. Recollect that your apprehensions are not canonical." And George Gillespie replied: "There is nothing that I have done that can stand the touchstone of God's justice. Christ is my all. I am nothing."

In Scotland, there are no names more celebrated by picture, statue, or story than Thomas Chalmers. How eloquent he was in preaching and in praying! And yet when Chalmers came to die, he declared: "What could I do if God did not justify the ungodly."

Scotland's tale would not be told without a word from John Duncan. The beloved teacher tells us:

God showed me a biography, an autobiography—and a heart, my heart. There are seven abominations in a man's heart. And mine eye was fixed on that heart for horror. For it was not simply my eye fixed on the heart but God showed me His own eye looking on it and saying, "See thy sin under My eye; see My eye sees that." God be merciful to me a sinner!

Methought then I stood at Calvary and heard these words! "It is finished." God said, "Look into the heart of Christ and behold Him in His vicarious death. Behold Him and know the grace of the Lord Jesus Christ, that, though He was rich, yet for your sakes, He became poor, that ye through poverty might be rich … Return unto Me, for I have redeemed thee. And the Lord showed me a heart into which He had put a new song."

It was the song of a soul known to God; and many such there are. It was the song of one to whom much had been forgiven, and who therefore loved much; and many such there are. But it was the song of the chief of sinners; of the one to whom most had been forgiven, and who loved most.[1]

---

[1]Macleod, John, *Scottish Theology*, pp. 284-286.

11. THE SHEPHERD OF THE FLOCK[1]

OUR Lord Jesus Christ is the Alpha and the Omega (*Rev.* 22:13). Before the foundation of the world, God chose His only-begotten Son as the beginning of all His ways and works with men. He ordained Him as the Shepherd of Israel, the Messiah of His people, the Head of His body, the Church. In Christ as our Shepherd and Saviour God chose a flock or congregation and calls individuals into this fellowship. The flock of God includes the patriarchs, the congregation of ancient Israel, Jesus and His disciples, the Christian Church in history, and the heavenly Jerusalem.

The close relationship between the shepherd and the sheep is an analogy richly drawn upon the scriptural revelation to make clear the fellowship between God and His people. When Sankey sang "The Ninety and Nine" to a Scottish audience, men understood. From that land of shepherds and sheep had come the story of old Wrottley who was found frozen beside his sheep that white winter, a man's loyalty to the dumb animals that trusted him. And beside the old shepherd was found the body of Wullie, his faithful dog, dead of a broken heart: an animal's loyalty to his master. Here in America where sheep herding is declining because men are becoming weary of living with nothing but sheep, it may be doubted whether the biblical picture can so easily be followed. But if we are to know the revelation God makes of Himself through His Word, we cannot neglect the Shepherd of Israel, the Good Shepherd, the Great Shepherd of the Sheep, and the Chief Shepherd of the Flock.

---

[1] WCR, *Christ—The Bread of Life,* 170-90.

The Shepherd of Israel

In His dealing with Jacob, with Moses and with David, the LORD showed Himself the true Shepherd of His people. "Thou leddest thy people like a flock by the hand of Moses and Aaron" (cf. *Gen.* 48:15 in Hebrew). Thereafter, through the prophet Ezekiel God rebukes the false shepherds, and promises to come as the faithful Shepherd who searches out His own sheep, ministers to their needs, gathers them into the fold (*Ezek.* 34). If in judgment He scatters Israel, He will gather him again and keep him as a shepherd does his flock (*Jer.* 31:10).

At the same time as Jehovah promises to be the Shepherd of Israel He also promises to set up one shepherd for them, even His servant David. He shall feed them and shall be their shepherd (*Ezek.* 34:23f). After condemning the shepherds that scatter the flock, Jehovah promises to gather them and raise up for them a righteous Branch who will be to His Israel, Jehovah our Righteousness (*Jer.* 23:1-6). Isaiah promises a herald to prepare the way of the LORD that all flesh may see the glory of God and this coming of the Lord Jehovah is both with a mighty arm and with a shepherd's care. "He will feed His flock like a shepherd, He will carry the lambs in His arm, and will gently lead those that have their young" (*Isa.* 40:3-11). This Isaianic promise is applied by John the Baptist and by Mark to the coming of our Lord Jesus Christ. Micah sees the coming of a ruler to feed His flock in the strength of Jehovah, in the majesty of the name of Jehovah, His God. And this One, whose goings forth are from of old, from everlasting, is to come to Israel from Bethlehem (*Mic.* 5:2-5; *Matt.* 2:6). Jehovah of hosts calls the sword to awake against "my shepherd," against the man who is "my fellow." "Smite the shepherd and the sheep will be scattered" (*Zech.* 13:7).

In the Old Testament times the ancient congregation gathered around the Holy One of Israel singing: "the LORD is my shepherd, I shall not want." "Give ear, O Shepherd of Israel, Thou that leadest Joseph like a flock." "We are His people and the sheep of His pasture." "We are the people of His pasture and the sheep of His hand" (*Psa.* 23; 80; 100; 95). As they praised Him for His loving care and cried unto the LORD for salvation, Israel received His promises that the LORD Himself would come to save and shepherd His flock. This

Shepherd of Israel is the mighty One, the fellow of Jehovah of hosts, whose goings forth are from eternity, He will come as the Branch of David and as such be the LORD our Righteousness. The Shepherd picture carries the truth that the government was upon His shoulders in the Old Testament theocracy and that He would come and reveal in our human life the shepherd's care.

The Good Shepherd

The presentation of Christ as the Shepherd is common to the Synoptic Gospels as well as to John. The scribes tell Herod that He who is to shepherd God's people Israel is to be born in Bethlehem (*Matt.* 2:6). Jesus recognizes Himself as sent to the lost sheep of the house of Israel (*Matt.* 10:6). In answer to the charge of His enemies that He receives sinners and eats with them, He gives the parable of the Shepherd who leaves the ninety and nine and goes to the desert to find his lost sheep (*Luke* 15). On another occasion, the Saviour told the same parable to vindicate the interest of the heavenly Father in the least of those who were coming to Him (*Matt.* 18:10-15). There is joy over the sheep which is found more than over the ninety and nine that went not astray, and this joy is nothing less than the joy of heaven. Heaven rejoices as the lost sheep of the house of Israel—publicans and sinners—hear the Voice of the Good Shepherd and gather about Him.

> Was there ever kinder shepherd,
> Half so gentle, half so sweet,
> As the Saviour who would have us,
> Come and gather round His feet.

The disciples are as sheep in the midst of wolves (*Matt.* 10:16) and are sent in the first instance to the lost sheep of the house of Israel (*Matt.* 15:24). As the shadows gather about the Shepherd, He comforts the little band of followers with this promise: "Fear not little flock, it is your Father's purpose to give you the kingdom" (*Luke* 12:32), and warns them of the impending catastrophe in the words of the prophet Zechariah, "It is written, I will smite the shepherd and the sheep shall be scattered" (*Matt.* 26:31; *Mark* 14:27).

In the Fourth Gospel our Lord presents Himself as the Door to the sheep by which if any man enter in he shall be saved and go in and out and find pasture. He is come that we might have life and have it more abundantly. He is the Good Shepherd who knows His sheep and is known of them. Though some heed not His call, His sheep hear the Voice of the Good Shepherd and follow Him. And the voice of a stranger will they not follow, for they know not the voice of a stranger. Other sheep He has which are not of this fold, them also He will bring and they shall hear His voice, and there shall be one flock, one Shepherd. The Good Shepherd is not a mere hireling, who sees the wolf coming and flees, because he is a hireling and not the shepherd. The Good Shepherd, whose own the sheep are, gives His life for the sheep. "I lay down My life for the sheep" (*John* 10:1-28).

As our Lord ministered to the needy sheep of Israel the picture of the Good Shepherd was filled and overflowed in loving kindness. He preached the Gospel to the destitute, He received and forgave sinners, He broke the shackles of Satan, He gathered the lost sheep, He gave them rest from the exactions of men, He brought them into the glorious liberty of the children of God, He healed the sick and raised the dead, He gave sight to the blind and hearing to the deaf, He bore our griefs and carried our sorrows, He brought the joy of heaven to earth. Out of discordant notes He wrought the harmony of a fellowship. Because He was the center the centripetal forces outweighed the centrifugal. He was the ladder down which the love of heaven came to earth: "God so loved the world that He gave His only begotten Son." "As the Father has loved Me so have I loved you." "Love one another as I have loved you."

When Peter made his great confession that Jesus was the Messiah, the Son of the living God, Jesus ascribed it to the Father's revelation and added, "And upon this rock I will build my Church" (*Matt.* 16:18). Later when a humbled Peter renewed his pledge of love, our Lord said: "Feed my lambs ... tend my sheep ... feed my sheep" (*John* 21:15-17). In his message to the Ephesian elders Paul wove these two representations into an explicit unity: "Take heed unto yourselves and to all the flock, in which the Holy Spirit has made you overseers, to feed the Church of God which He purchased with His own blood" (*Acts* 20:28). As the shepherd implies the flock, as the hen gathers her chickens under her wing, as the bridegroom is the center of the wedding party, as the cornerstone is the foundation for the building, as the Son of Man stands for the Kingdom of the saints of the Most High (*Dan.* 7), as the Messiah represents the Israel of God, as the Servant of the Lord justifies many, as the King implies the kingdom, so the Christ has His twelve disciples and the Lord His Church. Thus an increasing sense of the significance of Jesus as the Messiah has meant a recovery of the integral relation of the Church to Him. Jesus is central to the Church as He is to the Kingdom. His invitation is "come unto ME" and His warning is against those who cast a stumbling-block before one of the least of these "who believe in ME." As He is the door of the sheep, and His yoke is the yoke of the Kingdom, so as soon as Peter has confessed His Messiahship, Jesus says, "I built MY Church." That is, our Lord did found the Church, or more accurately He re-founded the old Church on faith in His own Messiahship.

The Great Shepherd

As the voice of the Good Shepherd gathers the sheep and as the love of the Good Shepherd binds them together in the fold, so the risen presence of the Great Shepherd renews and sustains the flock.

The God of peace brought again from the dead the Great Shepherd of the sheep through the blood of the everlasting covenant and sent our Lord Jesus to re-gather the flock which had been scattered by the shock of the arrest and the crucifixion. "It is in Him and especially in His resurrection that the basis of the Church appears. The word *Christ* itself implies the community over which the Messiah reigns."[1] The forgiving grace of the risen Lord Jesus appears in His first commission: "Go tell His disciples *and Peter*." As John also is to discover on lonely Patmos and Stephen at his stoning, the same loving heart beats in the bosom of the risen Lord as in that of the suffering Saviour

By the evening of Easter the firstlings of the flock are gathered, a week later even Thomas is present, ere the time of the Ascension over five hundred brethren meet the King on the mountain.

By His Ascension Christ was removed from a single earthly locality and exalted to the Throne at the right hand of God. Thus He

[1] Ramsay, *The Resurrection of Christ.*

was able to be present at every place in the power of the Spirit. At Pentecost the coming of the Holy Spirit from the exalted Christ constituted the assembled disciples the Church of God. As the vicar of Christ the Spirit came to be the life, the guide, the comforter of the flock until the return of Christ. He anointed, sealed, or christened every member of the gathering. As from the right hand of God Christ continued to pour forth the Spirit, the Church lived and grew. After Pentecost the Lord added together those who were being saved by the thousands. "It is not we who maintain a Church, nor was it our forefathers, nor will it be our posterity; but He it has been, is and will be, who says, I am with you always, even unto the end of the earth" (Luther).

As the Spirit is the inward power, so also the Lord provided for His people outward means to guide the flock—the apostles, the Word, the sacraments. At one and the same time the Church is the dwelling place of the living Christ and the guardian of the tradition set up by the humiliated Christ. As a Church having the Word without the Spirit would be dead, so a fellowship of the Spirit without the Word would run into subjectivism and fanaticism. Both the Apostles and the Spirit are sent by Christ. At Pentecost, the Word was present in the form of the Old Testament, the remembered words of Jesus and the preaching of the Apostles as His witnesses. In due time an apostolically guided Church added the New Testament as an accretion to the Old Testament. Baptism which was once for all and the Lord's Supper which was recurrent sealed one's participation in the death and resurrection of Christ and in the Christian fellowship. The whole Christian worship was directed towards the Lord's Supper and its culmination was the old Aramaic prayer, Maranatha, "Come, Lord Jesus!" This petition was breathed in the confidence that the Christ who had broken the bread at the Last Supper and had supped with them after His Resurrection would be in the midst of His flock as they communed with Him, and would finally come in His glory. And keeping His promise Christ ever comes to sup with His people as they open the door to sup with Him (*Rev.* 3:20).

Somewhat as the Lord described Himself as the Vine and the disciples as the branches, so the Apostle Paul speaks of Christ the Head and the Church as His body. The figure occurs in the major epistles and is amplified in the epistles of the imprisonment. As a branch does not live of itself and as a heap of branches do not constitute a living vine, so the disciples isolated from Christ are not the Church. As the branches must be in living union with the Vine so the body must be in vital union with the Head.

Accordingly, the unity of the Church is not in her earthly organization but in her heavenly Head; it is not horizontal, it is vertical. For Rome the Christ is only where the Church is, while for Protestantism the Church is where the Christ is. According to Thornwell, "the Church of Rome undertakes to exhibit Christ as well as His members, to exhibit the body in its unity with an earthly head; the Presbyterian Church exhibits in visible unity on earth the body only and connects it with a heavenly head."[1] Our first General Assembly said: "The unity of the Church does not require a formal bond of union among all the congregations of believers throughout the earth." Our Book of Church Order affirms that the division of the one Church into denominations, though it obscures, does not destroy the visible unity of the body of Christ. We express this unity when we share with one another in the ministration of the Word and of the sacraments—the God-given marks of the Church.

The Church is the organ of Christ's activity in the world, and the instrument of and witness to His reign. The very existence of the Church universal witnesses to the Reign of Christ at God's right hand. As the figure of the head and body is related to that of the vine and the branches on the vital side, so the same figure is related to that of the King and the kingdom on the potent side. As the Head Christ is the center of authority which every member is to serve and obey. The plentitude of power and authority is in His hand. He reigns at the right hand of God, every principality and power being made subject to Him and in the fullness of His august power He is given to be Head over His body the Church.

Over against all human claims the Apostle places the sole authority of Christ over His Body the Church. In the struggles in Scotland, the Episcopal and the Erastian party sought a mere recognition of a mystical Headship of Christ. But the Presbyterian and Evangelical party insisted that the Headship was also juridical and kingly. As the

[1] Thornwell's *Collected Writings*, IV: 136.

Head, Christ is the only King, the sole lawgiver in Zion. He sits on the throne of David to govern and rule His Church and the banner of Christ's crown and covenant is to be lifted against the effort of every king, secular lord, ecclesiastical leader, party majority that presumes to usurp that lordship which belongs to Christ alone. The booklets issued by the Confessing Church of Germany, the Reformed Churches of Holland, the Church of Norway, and the Church of Denmark show that Christ was the living Lord and power of His Church in enabling her to resist the efforts of the Nazi to dominate the Church.

In its organization and through its ninety years of organic life the Southern Presbyterian Church has been a living witness to Christ as the one and only King in Zion. This appears in the moderatorial sermon of Dr. B. M. Palmer in 1861, in the "Address to all the Churches of Jesus Christ" issued by the 1861 Assembly, and in our Book of Church Order.

This Book has restored the preface to the old Westminster Form of Presbyterian Government and made it the first paragraph of a magnificent chapter on Christ as "The King and Head of the Church." Here Jesus, the Mediator, is presented as the sole Priest, Prophet, King, Saviour and Head of the Church, as "the only lawgiver in Zion." "It belongs to His majesty from His throne of glory, to rule and teach the Church through His Word and Spirit, by the ministry of men: thus mediately exercising His own authority, and enforcing His own laws." As King, Christ has given His Church officers, oracles and ordinances, wherein He has ordained His system of doctrine, government, discipline and worship and to which He commands that nothing be added and from them naught taken away.

The function of the Church is to proclaim, administer and enforce "the law of Christ revealed in the Scriptures," while the Church courts themselves "can make no law binding the conscience." The power of the Church courts is to minister the law of Christ; not to make laws but to declare and enforce the laws the King has made. And Church power has the divine sanction only when it is "in conformity with the statutes enacted by Christ, the Lawgiver, and when put forth by courts or officers appointed thereunto in His Word."

We rejoice in the life and work of every branch of the Church universal; for every denomination, every congregation, every group meeting in Christ's Name is a witness to Him. We invite every other branch of the one Church of Christ to consider the particular witness God has given our branch to bear, namely, that Jesus Christ is the sole King as well as the only Head of the people of God, the only rightful ruler, the sole lawgiver in Zion. In this testimony we are standing in the line of John Wycliffe, John Hus, Martin Luther, John Calvin, John Knox, Josias Welch, Andrew Melville, Alexander Henderson, George Gillespie, John Witherspoon as well as of our Southern Presbyterian worthies.

The Chief Shepherd

In the fifth chapter of First Peter the presbyters are exhorted to shepherd the flock in view of the coming of the Chief Shepherd to give crowns of glory to His faithful witnesses. A similar thought is expressed by the Apostle Paul to the elders of Ephesus: "Take heed to yourselves and to all the flock, in which the Holy Spirit has made you bishops to shepherd the Church of God which He has purchased with His own blood." Thus the shepherd heart and the shepherd work of our Lord Jesus Christ are transmitted as a measure and example to His under-shepherds. In our several responsibilities as presbyters, as bishops, as witnesses to the sufferings of Christ and the glory that shall be revealed, as servants of the Church, in our homes, our congregations, our denominations we are to follow the Chief Shepherd. "Both in His ministry and in His death, Christ transcends us. But, none the less, He is our pattern, and we are to be changed into His image. Let us rejoice that He is power as well as pattern. He goes before us, but He dwells within us too. His life will create our lives anew, till we are signed with His autograph and transfigured into His glory."

Among other things, looking to the Chief Shepherd means that we are to labor in the Church "not as lords over God's heritage but as examples to the flock." Here is the mind of Christ: He who was in the form of God took the form of a servant that in the form of a servant we might see the heart of God (*Phil.* 2:5-9). "Those who seem to rule over the nations lord it over them, and their great ones exercise authority upon them. But it shall not be so among you. But whoever would be great among you, must be your servant, and whoever would be first among you must be slave of all. For even the (heavenly) Son of Man came (to earth) not to be served but to serve, and to give His life a ransom instead of many" (*Mark* 10:42-45). Following in the train of the Chief Shepherd the Apostle to the Gentiles reminds us that we preach not ourselves but Jesus Christ as Lord, and ourselves your servants for Jesus' sake. "In that Kingdom, service is not a stepping stone to nobility; it is nobility, the only kind of nobility that is recognized."[1] The Christian, then, is not to reach for leadership but for service. He is not to be dominated by ambition for position or prestige, but to be consumed by zeal for the flock. Whether God gives to the particular servant large success in the eyes of the world, or at the behest of an adulteress to be beheaded in a dungeon prison, is beside the point. The servant is to minister with an eye to his Lord, not with an eye to the plaudits of men.

Again in this service of Christ we are to help one another. Peter's exhortation is as a fellow presbyter and Paul lifts before the presbyterate of Ephesus the years of his own service as a ground of exhortation. The business of discipline is to help one another. When a man is overtaken in a fault it is the duty of his brethren to restore him, but to do so in a spirit of meekness remembering that he has but stumbled in the path we have all too weakly trod.

Again the thought of the Chief Shepherd leads our eyes onward to the consummation ordained by God. The Chief Shepherd is to be manifested, His glory is to be revealed, and the fruitful undershepherds are then to receive unfading crowns of glory. In between the years of our lives, here on earth and the coming of the Chief Shepherd there is given us a vision of saints gathered about the throne of God.

In that other land Christ is still the Shepherd of the sheep. "For the Lamb that is in the midst of the Throne shall shepherd them, and shall lead them unto living fountains of water; and God shall wipe away all tears from their eyes" (*Rev.* 7:17). Those who have heard His voice here and have been held through life in His nail-pierced hands—despite all the efforts of Satan's wolves to tear them away—

[1] Manson, T. W., *The Church's Ministry,* p. 19.

go to be folded by their Shepherd under the tabernacle of the Most High (*Rev.* 7:15).

> Blessed that flock safe penned in Paradise;
>> Blessed this flock that tramps in weary ways:
> All form one flock, God's flock; all yield Him praise
>> By joy or pain, still tending towards the prize.

The Good Shepherd laid down His life for the sheep, and the God of Peace raised again from the dead our Lord Jesus Christ that Great Shepherd of the sheep. For to this end Christ both died and rose again that He might be Lord both of the dead and the living. When He did lay down His life in our stead, He drew the sting out of our death. Yea, though I walk through the valley of the shadow of death I will fear no evil, for Thou art with me. The Shepherd, who has been through His death for us and thereby conquered death, who rose for our justification, goes through our death with us.

> Far, far away, like bells at ev'ning pealing,
>> The voice of Jesus sounds o'er land and sea,
> And laden souls by thousands meekly stealing,
>> Kind Shepherd, turn their weary steps to Thee.

To be sheep of God's flock means to have our souls restored by the Good Shepherd who gave His life for the sheep, cared for through this life and accompanied through the valley of the shadow by the Great Shepherd whom the God of peace raised again from the dead, to tabernacle before the Throne with the Lamb as the heavenly Shepherd, and to look forward in the blessed hope of the epiphany of the Chief Shepherd. The Word of His patience is: "Fear not little flock it is the Father's purpose to give you the Kingdom."

The Church looks forward to the marriage feast of the Lamb, when the Lord who gave Himself up for the Church shall present His bride unto Himself without spot or wrinkle or any such thing. Least of all in this day when Marxian communism has turned idealism into dialectic materialism and yet has retained in this dialectic a materialistic messianism—a promise of a good time coming—can Christianity forget the spires of the New Jerusalem. "Only Christian eschatology quiet and confident, can stand up to this messianism." "The return of

Christ to judge the living and the dead, must be trumpeted with all St. Paul's and St. John's glory in the splendour of Christ, the Christ by whom and for whom all things are made."[1]

To a race whose speech had been broken into a thousand jarring tongues, to an earth that had been covered with violence and blood, the Reconciler came.

Planting His cross as the great magnet of earth, He draws to Himself His purchased seed, incorporates them into a society of love, and sends them forth to throw its bands around a shattered world. Prophecy, through her roll, shows in the dim perspective this church embracing all lands and tongues and tribes within her arms, and "the kingdoms of this world becoming the kingdoms of our Lord and of His Christ." The reconciliation ends not here. When this militant Church shall be transfigured ... to her visible worship and fellowship will be added the "innumerable company of angels" whom sin has never soiled. The sad breach is forever healed; the cherubim and a flaming sword shall no longer guard the way of the tree of life against guilty man. He who has made reconciliation for iniquity and brought in everlasting righteousness, has also "made an end of sins."

Sin, death and hell are cast into the lake of fire: the redeemed Universe is brought into one under Him who is Head over all. Saints and angels shall blend in a harmony of praise around the throne, and the schism of sin be cancelled forever in the Church fellowship of the New Jerusalem.[2]

---

[1] Maury, P., *The Church's Witness to God's Design.*
[2] Palmer, B. M., Sermon to the 1861 General Assembly, *Minutes,* pp. 69-70.

12. THE JUDGMENT SEAT OF CHRIST[1]

The Manifestation of the Seriousness of Life

The judgment seat of Christ lends a seriousness to all life. The things we do are not trivial and unimportant, they will be judged by God. "Each man's work shall be made manifest: the day shall declare it" (*1 Cor.* 3:13). Our daily doings are not to be dismissed as mere deeds of the body; these are the very things that are to make us manifest before His judgment. In the risen body each one is to receive the things done in the body, whether it be good or bad (*2 Cor.* 5:10). The idle talk and gossip in which we too easily indulge is not inconsequential. James warns us that the tongue is a world of iniquity, set on fire of hell. The thoughtless, spontaneous, unguarded word reveals the abundance of the heart, so that for every idle word that men speak they shall give account in the day of judgment (*Matt.* 12:35-36). The judgment seat of Christ enhances the meaning and importance of every thought, word and act. It is an impetus to all holy desires, all good counsels and all just works, and a deterrent from the lusts of the flesh, the pride of the eye and the pride of life. The judgment casts its shadow over death as the final event in one's day of grace. "As the tree falleth, so shall it lie." Accordingly, "we must learn to speak more seriously and severely of death. It is the wages of sin and the portal to judgment."

Only as grace restores our vision of the Judgment shall we seriously seek to enter through the strait gate and to walk in the narrow way. Only the judgment can revive in our hearts a concern for either

[1] WCR, *Christ—The Hope of Glory: Christological Eschatology,* 261-81; abridged by *The Banner of Truth,* 178 (July 1978): 1-6 and 181 (October 1978): 29-32.

the weightier matters of justice, mercy and the love of God, or for the jots and tittles of His law. Only the realization that we must give account to God will deliver us from being time-servers and men-pleasers. Only the faith—that the Lord is our Judge, the Lord is our Lawgiver, the Lord is our King (*Isa.* 33:22)—will bring us back to serious exegesis of God's Word, that our social and individual conduct may be determined, not by the opinions of the hour, but by the law of the Lord; that our confession of faith may be reformed not by the wish of the Church, but by the Word of our God; that our order of service may not be a will-worship, fashioned by human aesthetics or expediency, but that we may tread His courts in the ways warranted by His Word. We shall be more zealous, in our personal lives, to sanctify Christ as Lord in our hearts, and, in our official positions, to minister the gifts of His bounty as good stewards of the manifold grace of God, when we realize that each shall give account to Him that is ready to judge the living and the dead (*1 Pet.* 4:5). When the Apostle Paul came to the end of his course and sought to lay on his successor the most solemn obligation to carry on, he wrote, "I charge thee in the sight of God, and of Christ Jesus, who shall judge the living and the dead, and by His appearing and His kingdom: preach the word."

A sense of responsibility to God, a realization that one must give account to God at His throne for every moment of his life, moved John Wesley to unceasing service and moulded him in methodical piety. A conscience sensitized to the judgment seat of Christ will quicken in each of us something of the zeal and urgency in our ministerial vocation which characterized Wesley, Asbury or "Brother Bryan" of Birmingham who died lamenting that there were so many people out of Christ.[1]

At the passing of our great Christian warrior, B. M. Palmer tenderly said, "Whilst Dabney sleeps with the honoured dead in the rural graveyard in Prince Edward, those who stood by his side, fighting for the truth of God in his generation, are standing at the edge of their own graves opening at their feet. Together with their departed brother they will awake in the triumphant resurrection morn. Will those who take their places be faithful to the trust, and hold the

---

[1] J. A. Bryan of Birmingham, Alabama.

truth of God in this age of empiricism, in which human devices are substituted for the power of Divine truth, and artificial combinations usurp the functions of the Church of God?"[1] At Dabney's funeral, Moses D. Hoge affirmed, "No church on this continent has been more favoured of heaven in having at its very organization three such men as Thornwell, Palmer and Dabney." The judgment seat of Christ calls us to build worthily on the heritage God has given us through them.

The Judgment Faces Christians

Some well-meaning people have robbed the judgment seat of Christ of its Christian application by forcing Scripture to conform to their theological schemes. It is all too easy to set up our systems, over-simplify them and then force the fuller and richer truths of the Word into the petty grooves of our making. Thus, all too often the shadow of little man limits the fullness of God's revelation. The true process must ever be to reform our thinking, our systems, our preconceptions and assumptions by the fullness of God's Word.

In 2 Corinthians 5:10, the text which has furnished the theme for this lecture, some have said that the Greek word, translated judgment seat, is used in classic Greek only for the bench used by the judges of a contest, such as the Isthmian games, who award prizes to the victors. From this alleged usage it has been affirmed that the Christians appear here only to receive their rewards. However, a study of the New Testament shows that the word *bema* is frequently used of the judgment seat of an official who heard criminal cases, such as Pilate, Gallio, Festus and Caesar (*Matt.* 27:19; *John* 19:13; *Acts* 18:12, 16, 17; 25:6, 17).

In His Gospel teaching, our Lord declared, "The Son of man shall come in the glory of His Father with His angels; and then shall He render unto every man according to his deeds" (*Matt.* 16:27). And speaking from heaven to the Church in Thyatira, "These things saith the Son of God, who hath His eyes like a flame of fire ... I am He that searcheth the reins and the hearts: and I will give unto each one

[1] B. M. Palmer, "The Christian Warrior" in *Southern Presbyterian,* January 20, 1898.

of you according to your works" (*Rev.* 2:18, 23).

No one stated the doctrine of salvation by free grace and justification by faith alone more vigorously than Paul or Luther. Yet Paul says, "He that judgeth me is the Lord. Wherefore judge nothing before the time, until the Lord come" (*1 Cor.* 4:4-5); and "Every man shall receive his own reward according to his own labour" (*1 Cor.* 3:8). He further states that we are stewards of the mysteries of God and "it is required in stewards that a man be found faithful." In commenting on Psalm 6, Luther writes, "So in a just man there must always be the fear of the judgment of God, because of the old man within."

Among the evangelical theologians of today, Professor W. D. Wendland of Kiel recognizes that "the Christian church cannot anticipate this judgment, especially as it must itself appear before the judgment seat of Christ."

On a re-study of the whole matter, Professor Koberle, a Lutheran theologian of Tubingen, states the case thus:

> It is impossible to restrict the statements of the New Testament concerning the final judgment to the ungodly or to self-righteous zealots for the Law, to say nothing of trying to explain theirs as remnants of Jewish ideas in the theology of St Paul. The Son of Man will require a special reckoning from those who have been engaged in His service and have been endowed with His gifts. That the returning Judge would reward every man according to his work was told to the disciples. Every idle word spoken by man must be accounted for at the last day. St Paul regards every earthly tribunal and every earthly self-judgment as unimportant, whether it be approval or disapproval, for that day shall declare it; the day in which the Lord will judge. Then will man's work first be revealed, of what sort it is. Each one will reap what he has sowed. All must appear before the judgment seat of Christ to receive the final judgment on this earthly life. Whoever in the earthly congregation continues to serve evil shall not inherit the Kingdom. Accordingly, at the end of days the judgment will actually be passed on the works of the sinner and of the righteous, and so the fear of displeasing God must accompany even the life of the believer as a holy fear and as an aid in overcoming temptation. Insincere life, an unbridled tongue or body, impure passions, implacable enmity which faith that possessed the Spirit might have restrained or turned aside will go with us and accuse us before God. But when the idea of judgment on the entire attitude of one who is justified has been maintained, there will

be no room for the ancient antinomian misunderstanding which has always accompanied Paulinism and Lutheranism like a dark shadow; the question of whether the Christian cannot continue in sin because of the working of grace would thus become so much more mightily evident (*Rom.* 6:1 *seq.*). If even the justified sinner must face the judgment it is no longer a matter of indifference as to the degree in which he has allowed himself to be purified by the Spirit from the "defilement and evil of the flesh."[1]

The Judgment in respect to Justification

If our theology is to be conformed to the Word, we cannot allow even the great doctrine of grace to obliterate or remove the Judgment. And properly understood there is no reason why it should. Justification is an anticipation of the judgment, a piece of realized eschatology, a taste of the powers of the world to come. It presupposes the judgment and does not dispense with it. The Jew looked for the judgment at the last day; the New Testament sees Christ taking our curse, removing the handwriting in ordinances that was against us by nailing it to His Cross, and proclaims the justification, here and now, of everyone that believeth on Him. But this anticipation of the final judgment does not make that unnecessary or a mere duplication. There are several differences.

The soteric principle is foremost in justification; and its great truth is that *God is for us.* The ultimate principle in the judgment is theological, a vindication of God by showing that the justified have been *for God* in their faith, testimonies and lives. There is no disharmony between justification by faith alone and the manifestation of the believer's faith by his obedience and love and service in the final assize. There the whole process of redemption is seen in its outcome in such a way as to vindicate God's wisdom, power and grace in the method He has adopted, in His patience and long-suffering toward His fallen creatures. The Judgment manifests the glory of God, showing that His plan of salvation has been a success, not a failure.

[1] Koberle, A., *The Quest for Holiness*, pp. 165-66. Citing *Luke* 19:11-26; *Matt.* 16:24-27; 25:32; 12.36; *1 Cor.* 4:3; 3:13 seq.; 6:9 seq.; *Gal* 6:7 seq.; 5:19-21; *2 Cor.* 5:10; *2 Thess.* 1:8-10; *Rom.* 2; *1 Pet.* 4:17-19.

Again justification is a secret thing occurring in the forum of human conscience. It is a dealing between God and the soul, unseen by the world. The sinner *believes on Him that justifies the ungodly,* and is justified by faith, not by sight. On the other hand the Last Judgment is a public acknowledgement of those who have put on Christ. Then each man and his work shall be manifest, for the Day will declare it. When God judges the secrets of men, there will be nothing hidden that is not made manifest. Further, God the Father is the author of justification; while Christ presides at the great judgment (*John* 5:22; *Acts* 17:31; *Rom.* 2:16; *Matt.* 25:31f.).

In the present justification, the sinner's works are entirely out of consideration. We reckon that a man is justified by faith, apart from the works of the law (*Rom.* 3:28). We know that a man is not justified by the works of the law but through faith in Jesus Christ (*Gal.* 2:16). But in the future judgment his work done under the impulse of God's grace will enter into the judgment as a factor upon which the decision is made (*1 Cor.* 3:15). However, there is a basic difference between the Judaistic principle that God gives a man a stipulated equivalent for his own works, and the Pauline principle that a man being justified by grace through faith alone is moved to express his gratitude to God who saved him by doing the good works God before ordained. God works in us to will as well as to do these good works (*Phil.* 2:13); in Christ Jesus faith works by love (*Gal.* 5:6). Now that we have been made new creatures, His Spirit works these good deeds as the expression and outcome of a living faith. Thus Paul sees an organic connection between faith and works. It is not as though good works, atomistically considered, make a good man; but a man justified and sanctified by a saving fellowship with God does good works. And these works shine before men to the glory of God, and the vindication of His salvation. These good works are not the exact equivalent of the reward. The Apostle's figures—a race and a prize, sowing and reaping, sons and an inheritance—suggest a real connection between the antecedent and the consequent, but not an exact equivalent. The prize is more than exact wages, the harvest than the sowing, the inheritance of a son than the wages of a labourer. And even the Saviour's parable of the labourers employed at different hours in the vineyard represents full reward for those who have laboured only briefly. Grace is resplendent in the glory of the judgment, as it is in the act of justification.

Using the figure of two sets of books employed in Revelation (20:11-15), Professor Albertus Pieters pictures the clerk of the heavenly court calling off a name: "One angel looks in his book to see what the works were of the one named. He finds, in the midst of a sad and shameful record of failures and offences, as a precious jewel in the rubbish, this entry: 'He believed on Jesus Christ as his Saviour.' He looks further, and finds works on record in accordance with this faith. Then he turns to the angel with the Book of Life, and asks: 'Is his name written there?'—'It is.'"

Thus, as Alford says, "we should say that those books and the Book of Life bore independent witness to the fact of men being or not being among the saved: the one, by inference from the works recorded: the other by inscription or non-inscription of the name in the list. So the 'books' would be, as it were, the vouchers for the Book of Life."

Works are an indication of the reality of our faith, a measure of the servant's fidelity; and hence, in the parable of the talents, an indication or scale of the honours he receives; but the ground of righteousness is here also all that which the Lord Jesus did for us. Our faith, our testimony, our service, our ministries to His brethren, the fruits of His Spirit in our lives, testify that in our weak and imperfect ways we confessed Him here below; and in that awful day He will confess us before the Father and the holy angels.

The Generations in the Judgment

Believers and unbelievers, Jews and Gentiles, men who were entrusted with the oracles of God and men who only had the law written on their consciences, men who knew their Lord's will and men who knew it not, all shall stand before Him who is no respecter of persons, when God shall judge the secrets of men by Jesus Christ (*Rom.* 2:11-16; *Luke* 12:48). Angels and men, sinners and saints, the quick and the dead, shall all be there. "Not one of all God's rational creatures shall be missing." Moreover one generation shall appear with another; and the children shall report in the presence of the fathers the use they have made of their patrimony, physical and spiritual. When one is giving account of his own stewardship to God, perhaps we shall be less caustic of those who witnessed valiantly for the faith in past generations—Thornwell, Dabney and Warfield. These men who laboured and we who enter into their heritage and draw support from the foundations and convictions they established shall stand together before the judgment seat of Christ. For,

> In one vast conflux rolled,
> Wave following wave, are men of every age,
> Nation and tongue: all hear the warning blast,
> And led by wondrous impulse hither come.

The Puritans shall rise in the judgment to meet their detractors, the Reformers to confront their critics, pious Methodists to face grand-children who fancy they have out-grown their Methodism, the dour Covenanters to accuse those who have forgotten that the unborn children were pledged to the faith of the covenant. If King Saul bowed his face to the ground at the mention of the shade of Samuel, what will Adolph Hitler do when he meets Martin Luther, or Rosenberg when he sees the Preceptor of Germany [Melanchthon], Bertrand Russell when Jonathan Edwards rises, John Broadus Watson when John A. Broadus comes? How shall our generation which barely reproduces itself face the pioneer parents who supplied the children to build this nation? How shall this generation of champagne and cocktails look to the fathers who had the courage to prohibit the manufacture and sale of intoxicating liquor?

If we glance at only some of the specific references in Scripture we find that Sodom and Gomorrah, the generation of Abraham, the Queen of Sheba, a generation a thousand years later, Nineveh of the generation of Jonah are to stand in the judgment with the generation to which Jesus preached. Those who heard Noah will rise in the judgment to confront the men of Capernaum who heard Christ (*1 Pet.* 3:20; 4:6). Paul and his converts will be there to meet their persecutors (*2 Thess.* 1:4-10). The martyrs under the altar wait for their brethren to fulfil their course, perhaps in the Great Tribula-tion; then all who were persecuted for righteousness' sake shall be avenged together (*Rev.* 6:9-11). Abraham and Jacob shall enter into the Kingdom of God with men from the north and the east and the south and the west, while many of the children of the Kingdom are being cast out. Those who are persecuted for Christ's sake are to be greatly rewarded in heaven with the Old Testament prophets who suffered *causa Dei* (*Matt.* 5:11-12). It is generally agreed that the Bible was not more than fifteen hundred years in writing. And yet it mentions generations from the days of Abraham, and the days of Noah, millenniums before Christ, to the Christian centuries that shall stand together in the judgment.

The earth and the sea shall give up their dead. And hell shall disgorge her minions. The devils shall not be absent, but shall stand condemned by the Lord who Himself took the nature and status of a creature and therein met and conquered the Accuser of His brethren. The Devil shall be cast into the lake of fire and brimstone where are also the beast and the false prophet; and they shall be tormented day and night for ever and ever (*Rev.* 20:10). Indeed, the eternal fire has been prepared for the Devil and his angels (*Matt.* 25:41) and needs not men to rush past the Gospel of grace and the Cross of atonement to feed its flames.

Thus, even in the fearful judgment scene there are intimations of grace and the preaching of judgment is a call to repentance. Heaven is a kingdom prepared from the foundation of the world for those blessed of the Father, God would have all men to be saved, there is to be a great host that no man can number who have washed their robes and made them white in the blood of the Lamb, who are arrayed in white linen which is the righteous acts of the saints.

The judgment throne of Divine glory is specifically described as "the judgment seat of Christ." This great event will be the vindication of the Person, the work and the claims of the humiliated Saviour before an assembled universe. It is the teaching of the Gospels as well as the Epistles, of the Synoptics as well as John, that the function of judgment is committed to Jesus Christ. This is so generally the rule in Scripture that the exception in Romans 14:10-12 is to be understood as explaining the rule. "God is here mentioned as Judge (see 2.16). He judges the world through Christ."

The Sermon on the Mount closes with men pleading with Christ as *the Lord* who has the final word concerning their destiny, and departure from whom is Hell. The eschatological discourse in Matthew repeatedly emphasizes the same thought. When the Son of man comes in His glory, His angels shall gather His elect. We, His servants, shall give account to our Lord at His coming of our diligence in the task He has assigned and for the talents He has intrusted to us. Except we be watching, our Lord will not take us in with Him to the marriage feast. The Son of man shall sit upon the throne of His glory and as King and Lord divide all the nations. From His word there is no appeal, only Heaven or Hell. According to John's Gospel, the Father has given all judgment to the Son (5.22).

For Paul, the Resurrection of Jesus is God's assurance to all men that He will judge the world by the Man whom He has raised up (*Acts* 17:31). Thus, the Apostle says, "He that judgeth me is the Lord"; and "God shall judge the secrets of men, according to my gospel, by Jesus Christ"; and "we shall all appear before the judgment seat of Christ." In Revelation, the Word of God, who is King of kings and Lord of lords doth judge and make war (19:11-16), even as in the earlier chapters He walks among the candlesticks judging the churches.

God shall yet make bare His mighty arm and vindicate His holy Child Jesus in the eyes of every creature. When He stood before the High Priest, Jesus said, "Hereafter shall ye see the Son of Man sitting on the right hand of power and coming in the clouds of heaven." Because He humbled Himself and became obedient unto death, even the death of the Cross, God has highly exalted Him and given Him a Name that is above every name. And as He sits upon the throne of His glory every knee shall bow at the name of Jesus, of things in heaven, and things on earth and things under the earth; and every tongue shall confess that Jesus, the Messiah, is Lord to the glory of God the Father (*Phil.* 2:9-11). Then men, demons and angels, assembled before the Great White Throne, shall bow in adoration and worship the Lord Jesus Christ. Having come in the form of a servant into this old world of sin and death, He shall come again in His native glory, a glory before which the fashion of this world shall be changed. At His shout the dead shall arise and death be vanquished; from His face the present earth and heaven shall flee away and there shall be a new heavens and a new earth in which dwelleth righteousness as the theatre for the manifestation of His Eternal Glory.

Today we offer Christ to men. In His Name we beg them to be reconciled to God. Those who reject His mercy, disdain His dying love, scoff at His Resurrection, spurn the record of His saving revelation shall prostrate themselves before the throne of His glory and wait in breathless agony His Word. The judgment-seat of Christ lends new meaning to the Gospel declaration, "This is the work of God that ye believe on Him whom He hath sent." It gives poignancy to the Saviour's warning, "Except ye believe that I am He, ye shall die in your sins." The redemption Christ won will not be fully applied until He comes to reign in glory. Until then there will be men living on this earth struggling against the world, the flesh and the Devil, while those who have departed to be with Him will not be publicly vindicated and received in their completed personalities into the everlasting kingdom of our Lord and Saviour Jesus Christ. The Church will still be a struggling, spotted, imperfect body made up of such imperfect believers, such foolish leaders as we are.

Only then will she be the Church glorious, without spot or wrinkle or any such thing. Only as she shares in the radiancy of His Appearing will she be the Church Triumphant, the Bride arrayed in fine linen pure and white for her marriage to the Lamb. Then will the holy temple in the Lord which is built upon the foundation of the apostles and prophets, Jesus Christ Himself being the chief cornerstone, be completed, her top-stone brought forth with shouts of grace. Then will the scaffolding of earthly worship be removed, for the tabernacle of God shall be with men, and the Lord God Almighty and the Lamb shall be the sanctuary of the Holy City, the New Jerusalem. God, who has begun a good work in us will complete it in that day of Jesus Christ. Of Him are we in Christ Jesus who is made unto us wisdom from God, and righteousness, and sanctification and final, complete redemption (*1 Cor.* 1:30).

When we shall see Him we shall be like Him, for we shall see Him as He is. And, according to the working of His mighty power, whereby He is able to subdue all things unto Himself, even these bodies of our humiliation shall be made like unto His glorious Body.

The judgment of God is the vindication of Christ. As we contemplate that glorious scene may we solemnly ask ourselves, Have I bound myself to Him with the cords of love, of faith and of hope?

Does the Lord who knows all things know that even this treacherous heart of mine has a real affection for Him who loves me? And have I expressed that affiance of my heart in ways that recognize His Lordship—in ways of His ordering? With the heart man believeth unto salvation and with the lips confession is made unto salvation (*Rom.* 10:10). God grant that we may each be engrafted into Christ and meet the Judgment in Him!

13. REGNUM GLORIAE[1]

The Lord of Glory

Glory is the most distinctively characterizing attribute of the God of the Old Testament. Jehovah is the God of glory, the King of glory, whom the heaven of heavens cannot contain, and who yet manifests His glory in His Shekinah Presence in the Holy of Holies. He is the glory in the midst of His people (*Zech.* 2:5). Israel is exhorted, "Arise, shine for the glory of Jehovah is risen upon thee and the LORD will be unto thee an everlasting light and thy God, thy glory" (*Isa.* 60:1, 19).

In the New Testament Jesus Christ is "the outshining of the glory of God" (*Heb.* 1:3), "the Glory" (*James* 2:1), "the Lord of Glory" (*1 Cor.* 2:8). He came trailing such unquenched clouds of Divine glory that the disciples recognized His glory, glory as of the only begotten of the Father (*John* 1:14). His triumphal Parousia shall be the epiphany of the glory of our great God and Saviour (*Titus* 2:13). Jesus Himself speaks of the Son of Man's coming on the clouds with power and great glory (*Matt.* 24:30) to sit upon the throne of His glory (*Matt.* 25:31), and of the regeneration in which His disciples shall also sit on thrones judging Israel (*Matt.* 19:28). Our Lord prayed that His disciples might see His glory (*John* 17:5, 22, 24). Those who partake of Christ's sufferings rejoice in the blessed hope of the revelation of His glory (*1 Pet.* 4:13). The light of the knowledge of the glory of God shined into Paul's heart from the face of Jesus Christ, so that he knew his Saviour to be the Lord of glory even when He was crucified (*2 Cor.* 4:6; *1 Cor.* 2:8). In his Patmos vision John sees the Lamb in the midst of the Throne receiving the worship of the four living ones and

[1] WCR, *Christ—The Hope of Glory,* 292-300.

the four and twenty elders, while myriads of angels sing, "Worthy is the Lamb that hath been slain to receive the power, and riches, and wisdom, and honor, and glory, and blessing" (*Rev.* 5:12). According to the New Testament the Word became flesh, Jesus Christ is the Shekinah Glory, God tabernacling among us, God manifest in the flesh. Thereafter, He ascended to the state of heavenly glory which was His before the foundation of the world and in this glory is receiving the worship of those who have washed their robes and made them white in the blood of the Lamb (*Rev.* 7:9-14).

"In the days of His flesh" this Divine glory was veiled by the form of a servant and the likeness of men, and it has not yet been publicly manifested to the world which crucified Him. Therefore, there shall be a manifestation of His glory, such a manifestation as, perhaps, this present form of the world with its law of sin and death is incapable of receiving. There shall be new heavens and a new earth as a fit theatre for the revelation of His eternal glory. All the might and magnificence of the God who created the innumerable starry hosts, the galaxies of heaven, the spiral nebulae, all the wisdom of the Spirit of God who ordered the light waves, the atomic structure, the electrical forces and the course of history, all the splendour of the Triune Jehovah before whom the heaven of heavens are unclean and the seraphim veil their faces, crying, HOLY, HOLY, HOLY, shall be brought into play to create a new world for the display of the glory of our King. And the glory of the King carries with it the glory of His Kingdom. According to His gracious word, we also shall see His glory; we shall share His glory; we shall reign with Him in the throne of His glory.

The Glory of His Grace

The glory of God's righteous justice is manifest in rewarding the faithful and punishing the wicked angels. But even the angels desire to look into the sufferings of Christ and the glories that shall follow them (*1 Pet.* 1:11-12), for the grace of God hath appeared in Him and that grace shall be fully brought to the redeemed at the revelation of Jesus Christ (*Titus* 2:11; *1 Pet.* 1:13). We have been redeemed unto the praise of His glory, that is, especially unto the praise of the glory of His grace which He freely bestowed on us in the Beloved (*Eph.*

1:12, 14). We are each one monuments of God's mercy, testimonies of His love to the unlovely, brands plucked from the burning by the redemption that is in Christ Jesus, children of wrath made alive together with Christ.

In the ages to come God will continue to shower His mercies upon us showing the exceeding kindness of the heart of Him who has made Himself our Father in Christ Jesus (*Eph.* 2:7). And every new act of mercy will testify the greatness of His love, the wonder of His grace. In these limitless aeons we shall learn the breadth and length and height and depth of the love of Christ which passeth knowledge (*Eph.* 3:18). God shall cloth His people with the garments of salvation and the robe of righteousness as the bridegroom adorneth himself with a garland and as the bride adorneth herself with her jewels. And with each new understanding of the plan of salvation, each new appropriation of the greatness of His heart, there shall go forth a paean of praise to Him who loveth us. There is a story of an old Scottish Divine to whom God spoke in a dream saying that he wanted this minister to know just how much God loved him. And ever after that experience there was a fragrance and a sweetness about that life such as one seldom sees. When we see Him as He is, when day by day He unfolds to us the wonders of His love, our lives shall also take on the fragrance and the beauty of His grace. By looking to Him we shall reflect His likeness.

The closing book of the Bible clearly indicates that He shall appear then, as He does now in Heaven in the character that marks Him as the Redeemer. In the first twenty-six books of the New Testament the Saviour is occasionally designated the Lamb; in the closing book which pictures Him in heaven and in the New Jerusalem He is given that designation some thirty times. And the Lamb is a term descriptive, not of His gentleness, but of His death. Thus the Apocalypse reveals the death of Christ as the center and heart of the throne of the universe today, the event that shares with creation itself the worship and praise of heaven (*Rev.* 5, 7). And the Kingdom of Glory is ushered in by the marriage of the Lamb (*Rev.* 21:22, 9; 19:7). The holy city, New Jerusalem, which cometh down out of heaven having the glory of God, is none other than the Lamb's wife, the glorious Church without spot, or wrinkle or any such thing (*Rev.* 21; *Eph.* 5:27). There is no temple in this holy city: for the Lord God the Almighty, and the Lamb, are the temple thereof (*Rev.* 21:22). The river of the water of life that brings healing for the nations flows clear as crystal from the throne of God and of the Lamb (*Rev.* 22:1-2). Redemption is the theme of heaven. Redemption will be the theme of the New Jerusalem. The blessings of that city flow to us from the green hill without the city wall of Jerusalem where the dear Lord was crucified who died to save us all. Accordingly grace is the never failing keynote of our praise. As we look to the pit whence we were hewn, and then to His image which His grace shall have pressed upon us, and to the Lamb standing as it had been slain, we shall praise the glory of His grace. All eternity will not be too long to thank the God of all grace who called us unto eternal glory in Christ and to praise the Lamb who loves us and who loosed us from our sins in His own blood.

> The bride eyes not her garment,
>   But her dear bridegroom's face;
> I will not gaze at glory,
>   But on my King of grace;
> Not at the crown He lifteth,
>   But on His pierced hand:
> The Lamb is all the glory
>   Of Emmanuel's Land.

The Glory of Holiness

For sinners all other glories flow out of the glory of God's grace. We can never cease to praise Him that He looked upon us in our sins and raised us up with Christ and made us sit with Him in the heavenlies until the revelation of His grace conforms us to His image. Yet the glories of the Kingdom that begin in grace issue in every spiritual virtue and every physical beauty. The glory of the only begotten of the Father was grace and truth (*John* 1:14). His life manifested the glory of perfect obedience to the Father, of love unspeakable, of humility, of righteousness, of compassion, of zeal for the Father's glory; and we shall be like Him. Yea, we shall be raised spiritual bodies; and the fruits of the Spirit are the virtues of Christ. The New Jerusalem shall be marked by such spiritual glories as truth, righteousness, peace, harmony, love, joy, gentleness, longsuffering, patience, faithfulness, kindness, goodness, meekness, temperance. It shall be resplendent in the peaceable fruits of righteousness. "According to His promise we look for a new heaven and a new earth wherein dwelleth righteousness" (*2 Pet.* 3:13). Kant used to say, "The starry heavens above me, and the moral law in me ... are the two things which fill the soul with ever new and increasing admiration and reverence." But what Kant's practical reason operating with the categorical imperative and the autonomous will of man have been unable to do, the grace of God in Christ will consummate. In the new world the glory of moral righteousness will shine from the redeemed children of men as the stars adorn heavens on a cloudless night. Truth shall spring out of the earth as righteousness looks down from heaven (*Psa.* 85:11). The Father's house will be glorious in the beauty of its order, and the blessedness of His bounty to His family. The Church shall be glorious and without blemish in purity, truth, peace, unity, concord, holiness. The City of God, resplendent in the glory of God, shall gather into her bosom the nations of earth and heal their wounds with the leaves from the tree of life.

The Glory of Happiness

His throne shall bathe this holy city Jerusalem with the glory of joy and blessedness. Happiness is ultimately dependent upon holiness. The pleasures of sin are fleeting, at His right hand there are joys forevermore. God chastiseth us today that we may be partakers of His holiness, and the chastisement that seemeth to be not joyous, but grievous yieldeth the peaceful fruits of righteousness (*Heb.* 12:10-11). For the joy that was set before Him Christ endured the cross, despising the shame; and our chastisements are signs that we also are sons beloved of the Lord, who is thereby preparing us for these eternal joys (*Heb.* 12:1-6). "Our light affliction, which is for the moment, worketh for us more and more exceedingly an eternal weight of glory" (*2 Cor.* 4:17). Yea, even in the trials of our faith Peter urges our great rejoicing in view of the exceeding joys of this celestial inheritance, incorruptible, undefined and unfading (*1 Pet.* 1:4-6). God Himself shall dwell with His people and be their God and wipe all tears from their eyes and death shall be no more; neither shall there be mourning, nor crying, nor pain any more; the first things are passed away and all things are made new. "For Jehovah will be thine everlasting light and the days of thy mourning shall be ended" (*Isa.* 60:20). Before the throne of the Lamb there shall be no more curse. And all the beatitudes of God shall be filled and overfilled in the city of God, as God maketh those who take refuge under the shadow of His wings to drink of the river of His pleasures (*Psa.* 36:7-8). God shall bless us with His presence, and the Saviour's joy shall be in us that our joy may be full.

"For behold, I create new heavens and a new earth: and the former things shall not be remembered, nor come into mind. But be ye glad and rejoice forever in that which I create; for, behold, I create Jerusalem a rejoicing, and her people a joy. And I will rejoice in Jerusalem, and joy in my people; and there shall be heard in her no more the voice of weeping and the voice of crying" (*Isa.* 65:17-19).

> For the darkness shall turn to dawning,
>   And the dawning to noonday bright,
>   And Christ's great Kingdom shall come on earth,
>   The Kingdom of Love and Light.

The Glory of Beauty

These glories of the Kingdom are not confined to spiritual relationships and moral integrity such as grace, holiness and blessedness. Glory means manifested beauty, light, splendor. "Rapt Isaiah" in the Old and the Seer of Patmos in the New Testament have not exhausted human language in their closing chapters without showing that there shall be a physical glory as the place for this spiritual loveliness. Men chose beautiful Lake Leman and the background of Switzerland's snow-capped peaks for the Palace of Peace. Shall God's Kingdom of Glory have a less resplendent setting? A visitor to Patmos says that, as one looks at this island nestling in the blue waters of the Mediterranean and rising against the brighter blue of an evening sky, he sees high in the mountains a beautiful white city. And when light clouds pass between, it seems that this city is just settling down out of heaven. So John saw the New Jerusalem coming down out of heaven, adorned as a bride for her husband, reflecting the splendor of the glory of God, her light like unto a stone most precious. How can one describe the City of God? The city was pure gold, like unto pure glass. The foundations of her walls were adorned with all manner of precious stones. Her twelve gates were twelve pearls; her street was pure gold like unto transparent glass. There is no night there; neither is there need for sun or moon; the glory of God lightens it and the Lamb is the lamp thereof. The LORD will be an everlasting light and thy God thy Glory. Her gates are open continually to bring in the glory and the honor of the nations. Her wall shall be called Salvation and her gates Praise. Her glory shall surpass that of Lebanon and Herman. She shall be a crown of beauty in the hand of Jehovah and a royal diadem in the hand of her God and His glory shall be seen upon her.

Thus the imagery drawn from our lives and observations is exhausted to set forth the glorious beauty of the New Jerusalem. Among all people the wedding is the occasion for the display of plenty and beauty. The City of God is garlanded as a bridegroom and adorned with jewels as a bride made ready for her husband, for "as the bridegroom rejoiceth over the bride so shall thy God rejoice over thee." Among nations we think of the Arch of Triumph and the Victor marching home with kings and princes swelling his triumphal procession. Even so "they shall bring the glory and the honor of the nations" into the Holy City. Nations "shall come to thy light and kings to the brightness of thy rising." Men will bring unto thee "the wealth of the nations and their kings led captive." When Jehovah makes Jerusalem a praise in the earth, the glory of God which lightens her shall eclipse the splendor of the skies, so that the city will have "no need of the sun neither of the moon to shine upon it." And "at evening time it shall be light" (*Zech.* 14:7).

We have no way of distinguishing which parts of this rich terminology are figurative and which parts literal. But the figures God employs are true figures; the reality is not less glorious than the figure indicates. Perhaps the glories are beyond the power of tongue to tell or pen to write, and the prophets have used the highest lights of our temporal language, the top flights of finite imagery to indicate eternal glories. The glories so indicated are set forth in a physical environment that is worthy of the Father's bountiful hand, and of the beauty of His holiness. "The world of nature is full of beauty." As we see and enjoy this beauty we learn that God, the Creator, is not only truth and love, but also beauty. "God creates not only living hearts, but also form and figure," color and contrast. "He establishes not only inwardness, but also corporeality, visible beauty. He will be glorified not only in His spiritual cosmos, in the living building of the Church which worships Him, but also in the visible cosmos of nature." Beauty is to be understood not only as a means to the true and the good, with which it is properly related, but beauty is a thought of God in its own right and consequently a special attribute of the reality of God. This truth is perhaps clearer if we remember that nature is more a scientific than a Biblical term, and that the Scriptural concept *creation* is related immediately to God. While the category of physical nature excludes the spiritual, the category of creature includes both the physical and the spiritual, and makes it easier to think of the one as well as the other reflecting the glories of the Creator. The foretastes of God's appreciation of the beautiful which we see in the tints of autumn, the fresh green of the spring, the dazzling diamonds of the skies, the rosy tints of the dawn, the glowing colors of the evening, and the radiant smiles of children's faces point to the beauty of the Infinite Artist. "The renovation glory of the Resurrection is not to be confined to the Lord Jesus Christ and the saints. It is to extend even to the material universe."[1] The holy city shall show forth the glory of God in her beauty as well as in her order, in her physical as well as in her moral and spiritual adornment. "Reborn Paradise shall in its visible form shine forth eternally and resplendently to the glory of God."[2] The King has a new heaven and a new earth of unutterable beauty and glory prepared for the blessed of His Father, in which every created form shall shine in a beauty that reflects God's glory and every redeemed child shall show forth the praise of Him who called us out of darkness into His marvelous light.

[1] Cameron, J. K., p. 167.
[2] Kuyper, A., *The Revelation of St. John,* p. 343.

14. PREDESTINATION[1]

For Christian faith, predestination is a vision of the King in the glory of His grace, and a warning against transposing the revelation of the majesty of His mercy into any concatenated scheme of human logic. It proclaims the freeness of God's saving grace in Christ, without making of His will an arbitrary fatalism. The ways of Him who predestines are past our tracing out, and the mystery thereof bids us worship where we cannot fathom.

Historically, Augustine of Hippo formulated triple predestination, that is: general predestination or providence, which magnifies God's wisdom in governing all things; special predestination or election in which His free grace is seen in the choice of His people; and preterition or reprobation by which He passes by and leaves other sinners to the due desert of their guilt for the manifestation of His power and justice.

In the English Bible, the verb "predestinate" occurs in the eighth chapter of Romans and in the first chapter of Ephesians. The Apostle introduces us to this high theme from the viewpoint of a pastor and in the context of a congregation, rather than as a logician of a philosophical school. In this setting, we confront not abstract decrees set and established in the distant past, but the living God and Father of our Lord Jesus Christ predestining and gathering to Himself His family, adopting them in the Son of His love, and leading them to the praise of the glory of His unspeakable grace. Thus considered, predestination is *personal, Christocentric,* and *gracious.* This revelation of the living God, Who personally predestines, delivers us from an impersonal petrification of predestination. Its center in Christ gives

[1] WCR, "Predestination," in *Basic Christian Doctrines,* ed. Carl F. H. Henry (New York: Holt, Rinehart and Winston, 1962), 49-55.

us the assurance of faith and saves the believer from that deadly labyrinth which swallows up the speculative thinker. And its sheer grace protects from Pelagianism and Pharisaism and fills the heart with gratitude. The rhythm of grace and gratitude, of *God for us* and consequently of *us for God* is the Christian life.

Predestination is the personal decision of the God who elects

The most important thing in the Apostle's statements on predestination in Romans and in Ephesians is that it is God who chooses. The doctrine is not primarily predestination, but God who predestines; the decrees are only after God's decreeing. In Ephesians 1:3, it is God who is showering His blessings upon us. In verse 4, the Greek verb is a middle which indicates God selecting for Himself, as an old patriarch might look over his heirs—including his in-laws, adopted children, and grandchildren—and say to them all: You are just the ones Mother and I chose for ourselves to make up this, our whole family. Since God's choosing was before the foundation of the world, when He alone existed, this can be nothing but God's own act. The fifth verse continues the stress on the decision and action of the divine personality, by declaring it to be according to the good pleasure of His own will.

In Romans 8, God is working all things for good to those who are called according to His own purposes. The golden chain which ties together the acts of God, from their foundation in His eternal purpose to their consummation in His making us who are sinners like unto the image of His Son, is nothing else than just *God Himself.* He loved us; He foreknew us; He predestined us; He called us; He justified us; He glorified us. It is God Who is for us. It is God Who justifies. In the hands of Paul, as of Augustine, Luther, Calvin, and Edwards, this teaching brings God into the center of the picture— God, the Person who wills, who decides, who acts for us, even for our salvation.

A speculative consideration of the eternal decrees may well issue in a mode of thinking that treats them as abstractions apart from God and thereby depersonalizes them. And when either decree or grace is construed without God Himself, then the quest for a personal element lights upon man, and what started as God's free grace ends as man's decisive will. Eternal predestination according to decrees established before the foundation of the world may be turned into a form of "orthodox" deism. On the other hand, the sovereignty of God meant for Luther and Calvin God in action here and now, His hand at the helm even in the most violent storm. God has not gone fishing or golfing or to an Ethiopian banquet. He is not asleep. He is not otiose. He is *activissimus.* We are not following the Reformers when we treat God as an absentee deity. Their God was the God of Elijah.

Indeed, the thought of God who personally wills, decides, and acts is close to the heart of the Gospel. It rings in the finite verbs in the Creed. It shines in the great passives by which John Wesley describes the strange warming of his own heart. It is a genuine part of the restudy of the *kerygma,* which is blessing the Church today.

Again, this God, who personally predestines, acts in His love. In mercy, He chose for adoption into His family of children even us rebellious sinners. The man who wrote Romans and Ephesians describes himself as the chief of sinners. In Ephesians 1:5, the choice to be God's children is according to the purpose of His own will, with which the phrase *in love* may well be linked. Or, if that phrase belongs to verse 4, nevertheless in Ephesians 2:4, the riches of God's saving mercy rest upon "His great love wherewith He loved us." In Romans, the verb "predestinate" occurs in the context of God working all things for good, of both the ascended Christ and the Holy Spirit interceding for the saints, and of the purpose of God bringing them into the fellowship and likeness of Jesus Christ. In Ephesians, the God who blesses His people with every spiritual blessing, according to His choosing of them before He made the worlds, is none other than *the Father of our Lord Jesus Christ.* The God Who predestines is the God before Whom Jesus lived, in Whom He trusted, to Whom He prayed "Abba," and to Whose right hand as Lord and Christ He has been exalted that He may actively accomplish the loving program of eternal election in the history of world affairs and carry the host of His redeemed into the gates of the New Jerusalem.

Predestination is in Jesus Christ

According to Romans 8, we are predestined to be conformed to the image of His Son that He may be the firstborn among many brethren, and we know that God is for us by His not withholding His own Son. According to Ephesians 1:3, Christ is the ground and reason of the divine blessing; in verse 4, He is the meritorious cause of our election; in verse 5, through His mediation, our adoption is realized; and in verse 6, the grace of God is revealed and bestowed. Salvation is the act of the Holy God doing justice to His own righteousness at any cost to Himself. In Christ we have redemption through His blood—the forgiveness of sins through His giving of Himself for us.

Augustine turned away from that neo-Platonic scheme, in which the "lower parts" of God and the "higher parts" of man somehow make contact, to Jesus Christ, Who as man is the way and as God is the goal of man's pilgrimage. Staupitz told Luther to find himself in the wounds of Christ, and then predestination would be to him inexpressibly sweet. To the request of a troubled woman, Luther replied, "Hear the Incarnate Son. He offers thee Himself as Predestination."

Likewise, Calvin exhorts men "to flee straight to Christ in whom the salvation is set forth for us which otherwise would have lain hidden in God." That we may call boldly on God as our Father, "our beginning is not at all to be made from God's determination concerning us before the creation of the world, but from the revelation to his fatherly love to us in Christ and Christ's daily preaching to us by the Gospel" (*Consensus Genevensis*). Calvin prays that we may be "led to Christ only as the fountain of election," even as truly God, He is "the author of election" and as truly man, He is "the brightest example of election." And, "it is beyond all controversy, that no man is loved by God but in Christ; He is the Beloved Son in Whom the love of the Father perpetually rests, and then diffuses itself to us so that we are accepted in the Beloved."[1]

One may compare this with the declarations of neo-orthodoxy in the *Scottish Journal of Theology*,[2] to the effect that election is *in Christo*

---

[1] Calvin, *Institutes,* III.xxii.7; III.i; III.ii.32.
[2] *Scottish Journal of Theology,* I, pp. 179-181.

in the sense that Christ is the Chooser; that it is *per Christum* in that He is the Chosen One who imparts salvation to those committed to Him, the Head who communicates to His members; and that it is *propter Christum* because He takes upon His shoulders our condemnation and bears for us the damnation we deserve.

The neo-orthodox, however, extend this last point further than do the classical Augustinians. Indeed, their view of Christ, as taking reprobation for the whole human race, would seem to leave no place for any discriminatory choice by God. When all is said and done, there remains the biblical picture of God Who chooses, God Who elects, God Who predestines in Christ and for His sake saves a great host that no man can number, including the last, the least, and the lowest of those who take refuge under His wings; but He does not save those who continue to love darkness rather than light, because their deeds are evil; nor those for whom the preaching of the Gospel is a savor of death unto death; nor those who despise the riches of His goodness, longsuffering, and forbearance, and fail to consider that the goodness of God leads to repentance. When the cities of His day rejected Jesus, He rejoiced in the Father's sovereign discrimination, and continued to sound forth His gracious invitation: "Come unto *me,* and find rest for your souls."

Predestination is the election of free grace

The Lord of the hosts whom He predestines to be His children in Jesus Christ is the God of grace. In Ephesians, predestination is rooted in and magnifies the sheer grace of God.

Ephesians begins, as it ends, with grace. God has blessed us with all spiritual blessings in Christ. All these flow from His gracious choosing. He predestines according to His loving purpose, to the praise of *the glory of His grace* which He has *graciously* bestowed upon us in the Beloved, in Whom we have redemption through His blood, even the forgiveness of our sins according to *the riches of His grace* which He has lavished upon us.

There is no place here for human conceits. God did not bestow His electing love upon us before the foundation of the world because of any fancied "infinite value of the human soul." We had no value;

indeed, we had no existence. God, Who alone was before creation, is the God of love, of pure grace. The riches of His mercy were bestowed upon us *on account of His great love wherewith He loved us.* There was no goodness nor worthiness in us to cause Him to choose us. Rather were we hateful and hating one another, when the kindness and love of God toward men appeared in Christ. God so loved the world, which slew the babies of Bethlehem and crucified Jesus, that He gave for it His only begotten Son. In Ephesians, it is quite definite that God foresaw us and must needs have seen us only in Christ in order to choose such rebellious sinners to be holy and without blame before Him in love.

Grace means that God is for us, yes, for us even when we were against Him. In sheer grace He chose to create men who were capable of denying the love which He bears them. The unfathomable depths of that grace are revealed in God's giving for this rebellious race the Son of His bosom. It is Christ coming into the world to save sinners, to identify Himself with us, to pick up the ticket for our responsibilities, to give Himself on the cross as the ransom price for our deliverance—the propitiation which diverted from us the divine wrath.

Those who come to Christ were already God's sons in His heart while they were yet in themselves enemies. Again and again that grace is made conspicuous. The risen Christ intervenes to confront His chief opponent and turn him into His trusted friend. Grace is Christ's love for Saul of Tarsus, even when Saul was persecuting Him in the treatment he was meting out to Jesus' brethren. Thus, grace is prevenient; it comes first, before any response by the sinner. We were dead in trespasses and sins, but God made us alive and raised us up together with Christ. Thus were we born "not of the will of man but of God," born of the Spirit who works faith in us and thereby unites us to Christ in our effectual calling.

Grace is the heart and center of the Gospel. It is the expression of the electing love of God and the parent of faith. It issues in the inward work of the Holy Spirit, illuminating our hearts to appropriate the love of God revealed in Christ dying for the ungodly. It is this love reaching out to forgive the guilty. It is not that we loved Him, but that He loved us and sent His Son to be the propitiation for our sins. It is the forgiveness which justifies the ungodly, through the redemption that is in Christ Jesus. It is the Father's welcome to the prodigal, which gives him a place in the family of God by adoption and by regeneration.

Because it is *sola gratia,* therefore, it can only be *sola fide.* Grace leads to faith, to unwavering trust of the heart in Him Who has given Himself to us as our Father and our Saviour in Jesus Christ. Faith wrought by the grace of the Spirit lays aside trust in self; denies all self-confidence, renounces any thought of merit even in our faith; and entrusts the believer as a helpless, undeserving, ill-deserving, hell-deserving sinner wholly to the goodness, mercy, love, kindness, and grace of God revealed in Jesus Christ.

15. THE CHRISTIAN FAITH ACCORDING TO THE SHORTER CATECHISM[1]

In *The Christian Faith According To The Shorter Catechism* Dr. Robinson includes questions 1-38 and 84-87. His material from questions 29-38 and 84-87 appears below.

Q. 29. How are we made partakers of the redemption purchased by Christ?

A. We are made partakers of the redemption purchased by Christ by the effectual application of it to us by His Holy Spirit.

Christ died for us over nineteen hundred years ago and over five thousand miles away. How do we receive the blessing He won for us by His death? Christ is a matter of past history and an object of cold thought until the Holy Spirit brings the living Christ and His redemption to us. The Holy Spirit as the hand of God unites us to Christ, the heart of God. By the inward work of the Spirit we become members of Christ's Body and share in the blessings that belong to the Head of the Body. The Holy Spirit is the key who unlocks the treasures of Christ's merit to us. The preacher and the teacher are the outward teachers, the Holy Spirit is the Inward Teacher showing the things of Christ to us. Thinking of the work of the Holy Spirit, Spurgeon used to close his sermons with these lines:

> We have heard the preacher,
> Truth by him has been made known;
> But we need a greater Teacher
> From the everlasting Throne.
> Application is the work of God alone.

[1] WCR, *The Christian Faith according to the Shorter Catechism*, 31-36, 40-43.

Partakers are sharers, those who are given a part in Christ and His redemption. Redemption is a purchasing, a buying back, a deliverance. "The Son of man came to give His life a ransom for many. Now a ransom is a price paid to release those who are held in bondage or captivity ... The fallen state of man is a state of guilt and bondage, from which Christ redeemed His people by laying down His life as a ransom for them. We are bought with a price. We are not redeemed with corruptible things as silver and gold, but with the precious blood of Christ" (A. Whyte). He bought us back from the dominion of Satan for the Kingdom of God. He delivered us from the penalty of sin and brought us into the privilege of forgiven children.

If you have a bad infection you apply a poultice to the sore spot. The Holy Spirit applies Christ and His benefits to the soul. The work of Christ for us is redemption. The work of the Holy Spirit in us is application. We sinners need all that Christ did for us and all the Holy Spirit does for us—that we may be saved.

Q. 30. How doth the Spirit apply to us the redemption purchased by Christ?

A. The Spirit applieth to us the redemption purchased by Christ by working faith in us and thereby uniting us to Christ in our effectual calling.

Apply means to join, or fold together, or lay on as a salve is put on an injured part. The Holy Spirit lays upon the soul the fruits of Christ's redemption by uniting us to Him. And the Holy Spirit does this by shedding abroad the love of God in our heart. He shows God's own love in that Christ died for us. Thus we come to trust and confide in the loving heavenly Father, to believe in Him. Believing means receiving Jesus Christ as our Saviour (*John* 1:12). Believing means coming to God in Christ (*John* 6:35). Believing means looking to Christ for our salvation (*John* 3:14-15). When the Holy Spirit comes into a sinful heart it turns in faith to the Lord Jesus Christ as certainly as the sunflower turns to the sun and as freely as the hurt child runs to his mother. Faith is running to Christ with the feet of the heart, embracing Him with the arms of the spirit, feeding upon Him with the mouth of the soul, resting upon Him alone for salvation. Faith is the empty hand of the beggar that receives Christ for forgiveness.

"Christ has merited [earned] righteousness for as many as are found in Him. In Him God finds us, if we are believers; for by faith we are incorporated [included] in Him. Then, although in ourselves we be altogether sinful and unrighteous, yet even the man which in himself is impure, full of iniquity, full of sin; him being found in Christ through faith, and having his sin in hatred through repentance, him God beholdeth with a gracious eye, puts away his sin by not imputing it [to him], takes quite away the punishment due by pardoning it; and accepts him in Jesus Christ as perfectly righteous as if he had fulfilled all that is commanded him in the law ... God made HIM to be sin for us WHO knew no sin, that we might be made the righteousness of God in HIM" (Hooker).

Faith unites us to Christ or makes us one with Him. He is the head and we are His members so that we are one body with Him. As the Holy Spirit makes us one with Christ in this living union with Him, so God gives us all the blessings Christ purchased for us by dying in our stead. What He gained by acting for us He makes over to us. He gave Himself for us that He might forgive us. He gives Himself to us by His Spirit that His forgiveness may be ours here and now. To Him all the prophets bear witness that whosoever believeth on Him has the forgiveness of sins. The next question will explain our effectual calling.

Q. 31. What is effectual calling?

A. Effectual calling is the work of God's Spirit, whereby convincing us of our sin and misery, enlightening our minds in the knowledge of Christ, and renewing our wills, He doth persuade and enable us to embrace Jesus Christ freely offered to us in the Gospel.

This is a very personal way of describing our conversion. God is a person, I am a person. He calls me and I come to Him. "He saved us and called us with a holy calling." An effectual call is one that gets results. When Mr. Curtis Green was a boy and played with our boys, his mother would call "Curtis." And often there was no response. When the call "Curtis Green" became more insistent he would lift an eye. But whenever it became "Curtis Vance Green," he would say: "Now she means business, I must go." The last was an effectual call.

Effectual calling is a work, not merely an act. Indeed several steps or stages may be distinguished in it. In one step the Holy Spirit convicts or convinces us of our sin. It is all too easy to think about somebody else's sins and to excuse ourselves. When the Holy Spirit works upon our hearts we see our own sin in its wickedness and baseness and misery. We stop excusing ourselves and hate our disobedience to and rebellion against God. We see our sin as that wicked thing God hates. Misery and shame take the place of self-satisfaction and conceit.

More important still, the Holy Spirit shows us Christ. We must all be taught of God. The Inward Teacher enlightens the eyes of our understanding so that we see the Lord Jesus as our loving Saviour. The natural man receives not the things of the Spirit of God for they are foolishness to him. The Spirit removes the ignorance and the prejudice from our minds so that we see Christ as the One who loved us and gave Himself up to save us.

Yet another thing the gracious Spirit does. Jesus said: "No man can come unto me, except the Father which sent me draw him." "Ye will not come unto me that ye might have life." Our fallen nature is dead in trespasses and sins. Our wills are held in bondage to our evil desires, pleasures, lusts, and sins. Here is a steel needle on a pivot. It turns this way and that as the various currents of air strike it. But magnetize that needle and it will settle down in a steady point to the magnetic North. It has now become a useful compass. What magnetizing does to the needle, the Holy Spirit does to the will. He gives it a new purpose and a new direction. Instead of letting it wander hither and yonder over the things of this world, He directs it to Christ and the things of God.

Thus the Spirit persuades and enables me to embrace Jesus Christ. The Patriarchs embraced the promises and the promises are all yea and amen in Christ. As faith is elsewhere described as coming to Christ, so here it is embracing Christ, clasping, taking, receiving Him. "As many as received Him to them gave He power to become the sons of God even to them that believe on His Name."

The Gospel is the Good News of salvation. It is God's own story of Christ, His beloved Son. And God freely offers Christ to everyone. Christ is the bread of life. The banquet is spread. Come and eat! You are guilty of no presumption in coming or in eating. The Spirit and bride say, "Come." And he that heareth, let him say, "Come." And he that is athirst let him come. And he that will, let him take of the water of life freely.

Q. 32. What benefits do they that are effectually called partake of in this life?

A. They that are effectually called do in this life partake of justification, adoption, and sanctification, and the several benefits which in this life do either accompany or flow from them.

Out of God's great heart of love came His only begotten Son to be our Saviour. The living Christ at the right hand of the Father sends the Holy Spirit to unite us to Himself. From this union with Christ the Holy Spirit brings us exceeding great and precious blessings. Some of these benefits or good things come in this life, some at death, and some at the resurrection. This question is the beginning of a group or section of seven questions, 32-38. This question and those through 36 deal with the blessings for this life, 37 with the blessings at death, and 38 with those at the resurrection. Each item in this answer is to be expounded in the following questions: justification or forgiveness in 33, adoption or being accepted as children of God in 34, sanctification or holy living in 35. According to the thirty-sixth answer, the benefits which go with or come from these three blessings are: being made sure of the Father's love, peace in our consciences, joy in the Holy Spirit, increase or growth in grace, and being continued or kept by the power of God unto final salvation.

Q. 33. What is justification?

A. Justification is an act of God's free grace, wherein He pardoneth all our sins, and accepteth us as righteous in His sight, only for the righteousness of Christ imputed to us and received by faith alone.

In the fifth century, Paulinus, Bishop of Nola, expended all his large estates in redeeming from captivity his brethren enslaved by the Goths. When his resources were exhausted, a poor widow came pleading her destitute condition due to the fact that the barbarians had carried her only son away to Africa as a slave. Paulinus immediately went over to Africa. There he found the young man and entered into an agreement with his master to take the young man's place as a slave. Accordingly, the youth returned to care for his mother and Paulinus continued for months under the yoke. Later when the master heard of his high standing Paulinus was released.

Finding us in bondage to sin and the law, Christ volunteered to take our place that we might be freed. He was made under the law, and God laid on Him the iniquity of us all. He was made sin for us that we might be made the righteousness of God in Him. Because of all Christ did and suffered for us, God forgives us, pronounces us just, accepts us as righteous in Christ.

Justification is an act, not a slow process, not a long work. It is the act of a judge. When a man stands accused before a court, the judge either declares him condemned or pronounces him acquitted, freed from condemnation, forgiven. It is an immediate, a full act. A man is completely justified. "There is therefore now no condemnation to them that are in Christ Jesus." This is God's act. When God justifieth who is he that condemneth? And God's act to us is of His free grace. We do not deserve this great mercy. We are undeserving sinners, rebels who deserve punishment. But God has been pleased to bind us up in the covenant of grace and the bundle of life with His only begotten Son, Jesus Christ. God looks upon Christ and His righteousness and accepts all those who trust in Christ as righteous for His sake. He was punished that we might be forgiven. He obeyed the law 100 percent perfectly. And God counts His perfect obedience to us. God reckons Christ's righteousness to us, He puts it to our account. He imputes it to us. In this way we are regarded as righteous and treated as just by God. Since Christ did give perfect obedience and did endure the full penalty for His people, since He paid our full debt, therefore, God is just even when He justifies the sinner who trusts in Christ. But to us it is an act of overflowing love and mercy.

In this act of grace God pardons all our sins and accepts us as righteous in His sight. Our sins were laid on Jesus and He satisfied all our obligations. Now His righteousness is laid on us and for His sake God forgives our sins and accepts us as righteous in His sight. The publican in the Temple bowed his head and cried: "God, be merciful to me a sinner." And that man went home justified. The dying thief said: "We two thieves are receiving the just reward of our deeds. We are so bad we deserve to be crucified." Then he entrusted himself to Jesus, saying: "Lord, remember me when Thou comest into Thy kingdom." And the Lord Jesus said to him: "Today shalt thou be with Me in Paradise." So bad he deserved to be crucified and yet so fully justified that he was immediately received into Paradise!

Now this great change comes to us, not from any work we have done or can do to earn it. It comes to us when we admit we cannot earn righteousness, and trust Christ to do for us what we cannot do for ourselves and what we cannot do without. We entrust ourselves to our Saviour, we confess Him as our Lord.

Q. 34. What is adoption?

A. Adoption is an act of God's free grace, whereby we are received into the number, and have a right to all the privileges of the sons of God.

Justification is a deed of God acting as a judge and pronouncing me, a sinner, righteous for the sake of the righteousness of Christ imputed to me. Adoption is an act in which God as a Father receives me, the sinner, as His child and gives me the liberties and privileges which Christ, the elder brother, has won for me. No human story can fully illustrate the Gospel. This one goes part of the way:

King Zaleucis of the Locrians made a law that if anyone was convicted of a certain crime he should have both his eyes put out. One of the first persons convicted was his own son. What was Zaleucis to do? If he were only a King he could execute the penalty and forget the matter. If he were only a father he could forgive the offense and receive his son into his arms. But he was both a king whose honor was pledged to the fair enforcement of his laws and a father whose heart yearned for his son. King Zaleucis solved the problem by having one of his own eyes put out and one of the eyes of his son. Thereafter when men looked into the empty socket in the king's face they remembered the sanctity of the King's law and the love of the father's heart.

God our heavenly Father, the Lord of heaven and of earth, did more than take the half of our punishment. In the person of His own Son He took our place and bore all our punishment in His own body on the Tree. He did this that we might be forgiven children rather than guilty subjects.

In adoption a man takes into his family one who was not originally a part of it and gives him his name, the enjoyment of his home, the right of inheriting his property. The adopted child has the full standing of a son or a daughter in the home.

God made Adam in His own image and put him on probation in order that if he stood he might have an established place in the family of God. But Adam fell and was driven from the presence of God. What Adam lost, Christ won for us. The eternal Son of God became also the Son of Man that in our human nature He might live the life of a loving, obedient child of God. He kept His state of loving sonship unbroken through the difficulties of our life. Now He gives us this high and blessed standing He maintained for us. And He regenerates us, or gives us a new heart—a heart that loves and serves God. "As many as received Him to them gave He the power, the right, the authority, to become the sons of God, even to them that believe on His Name. Who were born not of blood, nor of the will of the flesh, nor the will of man—but of God." "We are all children of God by faith in Jesus Christ." God for Christ's sake receives us into His family and assures us of a share not only in His bounty but in His heart. God our Father loves us more than our earthly father does. He knows better what is good for us and He is more able to care for and protect us than are the parents in our homes.

When the papers carried the story of an American advance led by a division in which a son served, the earthly father definitely committed the lad to his heavenly Father. For the heavenly Father knows better, loves more and can do more than the earthly parent.

Moreover, the heavenly Father was present and did save the son from anything worse than a minor wound—while the earthly father was thousands of miles away and would have been powerless to save even had he been present.

Q. 35. What is sanctification?

A. Sanctification is the work of God's free grace, whereby we are renewed in the whole man after the image of God, and are enabled more and more to die unto sin, and to live unto righteousness.

Justification, Adoption, Sanctification, are all of God's free grace—of His undeserved love to sinners. "If it is of (God's) grace it is no more of our works: otherwise grace is no more grace." "To make a man a saint, grace is absolutely necessary; and whoever doubts this does not know what a saint is, nor what a man is" (Pascal).

But while justification and adoption are acts, sanctification is a work that continues throughout life. Justification and adoption are complete at once, sanctification is a gradual process. They change our relation to God, sanctification changes our lives to accord with the new relation. "In adoption we are taken into the family of God, and in sanctification we take on the family features" (Whyte). God took Israel out of Egypt rather quickly, but it took forty years to get Egypt out of Israel.

The ground of justification and of adoption is the work of Christ for us. The life of sanctification is the work of the Holy Spirit in us. The power of the Spirit in the life of a Christian may be compared with the wind that moves a sail boat. Let the wind stop. The boat will stagger on a few lengths but very soon it ceases to move forward and then drifts backward with the current.

As the Holy Spirit comes into our hearts He brings a new life. By His power the soul that was dead in sin is born again, regenerated. Thereafter He nourishes the new life and so renews the whole man after the image of God. He makes the tree good and then causes good fruit to grow on the good tree. His gifts are faith, hope and love. The fruits He brings into our lives are love, joy, peace, longsuffering, gentleness, goodness, meekness, faithfulness, temperance.

Even when we fall into sin and grieve Him He does not wholly forsake us. Wherever there is a penitent heart to be comforted and restored there is the blessed Comforter. And all holiness or separation from sin is His work. In most cases sanctification is not a steady progress upward, but in spite of our many falls He patiently leads us onward towards God's idea of a man. And Christ is God's idea of a man.

Justification and sanctification have been compared thus: "Christ never comes into the soul unattended, He brings the Holy Spirit with Him, and the Spirit His train of gifts and graces." "Christ comes with a blessing in each hand, forgiveness in one and holiness in the other, and never gives either to any who will not take both. But Christ's forgiveness of all sins is complete at once, because less would do us no good; His holiness is dispensed by degrees, and to none wholly in this life, lest we should slight His forgiveness." "It is the joy of my heart that I am free from guilt, and the desire of my heart to be freed from sin." "Whenever I die, I die a sinner; but by the grace of God, penitent, and, I trust, accepted in the Beloved" (Thomas Adam).

Q. 36. *What are the benefits which in this life do accompany or flow from justification, adoption, and sanctification?*

A. The benefits which in this life do accompany or flow from justification, adoption, and sanctification, are: assurance of God's love, peace of conscience, joy in the Holy Ghost, increase in grace, and perseverance therein to the end.

A good Bible commentary on this answer is found in Romans 5:1-11; and 8:26-39. When we come to God in Christ we find Him the gracious Father whose hands are always overflowing with kindnesses to us.

The Holy Spirit sheds abroad the love of God in our hearts when He fixes our eyes on Christ, the gift of God's love. All about us there are the sick, the needy, the hurt. Pain, sorrow, accidents are everywhere. In the changing experiences of life we need to keep ourselves in the love of God. Luther asked but one thing to live by: the certainty that God was gracious and merciful toward him. This assurance may not come to everyone at once. One can be a Christian believer without being entirely sure that he is. But as we keep looking unto Jesus the author and finisher of our faith God gives us a sure faith in Him.

"Then I began to give place to the Word, which, with power, did over and over make this joyful sound within my soul, Thou art my love, thou art my Love; and nothing shall separate thee from my love: and with that Romans 8:39 came into my mind. Now was my heart filled with comfort and hope, now I could believe that my sins would be forgiven me. Yea I was so taken up with the love and mercy of God, I could not tell how to contain till I got home. I think I could have spoken of His love and of His mercy to me, even to the very crows that sat upon the ploughed land before me, had they been capable to have understood me" (Bunyan).

And from the same look comes peace of conscience. Every one of us knows that he is responsible for his sins. And the only way to gain a sense of forgiveness is to trust in the Lamb of God who took our responsibilities and answered for our sins on Calvary. For His sake the Father forgives us and gives us peace in our consciences.

> Look, Father, look on His anointed face,
>   And only look on us as found in Him;
> Look not on our misusings of Thy grace,
>   Our prayers so languid, and our faith so dim;
> For lo! between our sins and their reward
>   We set the Passion of Thy Son our Lord.

The Christian loses his love for the pleasures of this world, but he is the man who has true joy. God has made us for Himself and our hearts are restless until they rest in Him. The kingdom of God is not meat and drink, but love and peace and joy in the Holy Ghost. When we sin we grieve the Holy Spirit, but our prayer of confession is: "Take not Thy Holy Spirit from me; restore unto me the joy of thy salvation." As He stood in the shadow of the Cross, Christ prayed that His joy might be in His disciples and that their joy might be full. Paul wrote from a Roman prison: "Rejoice in the Lord always and again I say rejoice."

The story is told of an aged minister who received a letter containing a check for $50.00 and a statement, "more to follow." Some days later another letter, exactly similar and others of the same nature. When God gives us one gift of His grace He always adds this note, "more to follow." We have so far received only the down payment, the earnest of the Holy Spirit. When people buy an expensive property they generally pay only a part, a small first part, and then gradually the balance. God has given us only a portion of the grace and blessing of the Holy Spirit. He will continue to give us more and more of His blessings. In *Pilgrim's Progress* there is a picture of a fire on which Satan is continually pouring water and yet ever and again the fire leaps up more brightly. On the other side of the wall Pilgrim sees the Holy Spirit ever and again pouring oil on the fire. By grace of the Spirit, by the keeping power of God we are preserved in the Christian faith. Our Lord says that He knows His sheep and gives them eternal life and that no one is able to take them out of His hand. We are kept through faith unto salvation.

Q. 37. *What benefits do believers receive from Christ at death?*

A. *The souls of believers are at their death made perfect in holiness, and do immediately pass into glory; and their bodies being still united to Christ do rest in their graves till the resurrection.*

Death does come into our homes and into our classes sometimes from age, sometimes from accidents, sometimes from sickness, sometimes from war. What happens to a Christian believer at death? Our catechism is so clear here that some ministers use the thirty-seventh and thirty-eighth answers in their burial services. We want a definite word and these words have comforted many hearts. Briefly, they mean that Christ has changed the face of death.

Perhaps you boys and girls would like an illustration drawn from the days of knighthood and chivalry. Each knight carried a shining sword. Sometimes he wore it in the scabbard hanging at his side, sometimes he grasped its flashing blade in his hand. When the sword was in the knight's hand it was separated from its scabbard, but in either case both sword and scabbard were united to the person of the knight. Let us compare the soul of a Christian to the sword and his body to the scabbard, and let us think of the Person of Christ as like the person of the knight. When the Christian lives he is like the sword in the scabbard, body and soul joined together and attached to the Person of Christ. When the Christian dies it is like the knight taking the sword out of the scabbard and holding it up in his hand, for, then soul and body are separate one from the other. But here is the glorious thing: both soul and body are still united to the Person of Christ as both the sword and the scabbard are still united to the person of the knight.

As God changed Paul on the Road to Damascus from an enemy of Christ to a devoted apostle, as the Holy Spirit changed Peter at Pentecost from a coward to a hero, so at death God breaks this evil self-will of ours and frees us from the sinful desires of the flesh. As Jesus assured the thief on the cross that he would be with HIM in paradise that day, and as Paul departed to be with Christ, so those who die trusting in Jesus go to be with HIM in glory. We do not know too much about their place or condition. We know that heaven is one of the mansions of the Father's House and that it is with Christ.

> My knowledge of that life is small,
> The eye of faith is dim,
> But 'tis enough that Christ knows all
> And I shall be with Him.

When one of our loved ones dies we carefully lay his body in a coffin as if we were tucking a child in to sleep. We are not saying goodbye forever. Because Jesus died and rose again those who sleep in HIM, He will bring with Him when He returns in glory. Until then we trust them body as well as soul to their loving Saviour's keeping. He watches over them whether their bodies sleep in the graveyard at home or in beautiful cemeteries the Government has made for the soldiers in Holland or in Australia. Elizabeth Barrett Browning wrote:

> And, friends, dear friends, when it shall be
> That this low breath is gone from me,
> And round my bier ye come to weep,
> Let one, most loving of you all,
> Say, "Not a tear must o'er her fall—
> He giveth His beloved sleep."

Q. 38. What benefits do believers receive from Christ at the resurrection?

A. At the resurrection believers being raised up in glory, shall be openly acknowledged and acquitted in the day of judgment, and made perfectly blessed in the full enjoyment of God to all eternity.

Railroad men call the end of the line the terminal. In railroad terms, death for a believer is not a terminal but only a tunnel with the throne of God and of the Lamb at the other end. Or to return to the illustration we used in our last study: as the knight returns the sword to its scabbard; so when He comes again, Christ will raise up our bodies and return our souls to them. God made the whole man, body and soul, and in Christ God saves the whole man body as well as soul. Of course, it is only God who can raise the dead. So when we believe in the Resurrection we are necessarily believing in God, in His Almighty Power that did raise Christ up from the dead.

When we entrust ourselves to Christ, our Saviour, He says to us as He did to the paralytic: "Son [Daughter], be of good cheer, thy sins be forgiven thee." Now this occurs in the hidden places of the heart. When Christ comes in His glory He is to sit upon the throne of His glory and before Him are to be gathered all nations. "We shall all appear before the judgment seat of Christ to render account of the deeds done in the flesh." The word of forgiveness spoken in the secret of our hearts is now to be publicly declared.

Jesus says that those who confess Him before men, He will confess before His Father in heaven. As a name is read out, the recording angel reads from the books that he believed in Christ, that he confessed the Saviour with his lips and with his life. And then the Saviour Himself reads out that name as one of His own written in the Lamb's book of life.

> Jesus, Thy blood and righteousness
> My beauty are, my glorious dress:
> 'Midst flaming worlds in these arrayed
> With joy shall I lift up my head.

> Bold shall I stand in that great day:
>> For who aught to my charge shall lay?
> Fully absolved [freed] through these I am
>> From sin and fear, from guilt and shame.

The enthroned Christ will say: "Come ye blessed of My Father inherit the Kingdom prepared for you from the foundation of the world." "And these shall go into everlasting life."

Everlasting life is a perfect blessedness in God and with God. It is not only that we are to find God in heaven, but that in God we are to find heaven. "To sit down with Abraham, Isaac, and Jacob was the phraseology of the Old Testament, but to sit with US—with Father, Son and Holy Ghost—this is Christ's language, this is New Testament language" (Goodwin). God is the portion of His people. He has made us for Himself and we are restless until we rest in Him. The psalmist speaks of God as "my exceeding joy." In Thy presence there are joys forever more.

The return of Christ and the resurrection of His people is the great event of the future. All the eyes of prophecy are fixed upon it. The Christian life is like a bird supported by two wings. One of these is the precious faith resting on what Christ has done for us, the other is the blessed hope directed to His return in glory and all He will do then. This answer gives four specific things which He will do then: raise us up, acknowledge us, acquit us in the judgment, and make us perfectly blessed in enjoying God forever.

Q. 84. What doth every sin deserve?

A. Every sin deserveth God's wrath and curse, both in this life, and that which is to come.

Between the last question we discussed and this question our Shorter Catechism gives a full treatment of the Ten Commandments. By studying the Commandments and applying them to our thoughts, words and deeds, we see how many sins we have. This question brings before us the seriousness of every sin. Some sins are worse than others, but there are no little sins, for there is no little God to sin against. Every sin is against the great God of heaven and earth, and so every sin is a great sin. If you steal from the corner grocer you have robbed him, but you have also broken God's law and you have sinned against God.

God's wrath is different from our getting mad. His wrath is free from those imperfections of passion, resentment, fury, unreasonableness and inconstancy which make anger so evil in us. Indeed, the wrath of God denotes the effects of righteous indignation rather than the feeling of anger. Our wicked opposition to God calls forth His holy opposition to us, that is, to our wickedness. "In God, who is the living good, wrath appears as the holy disapprobation [disapproval] of evil, and the firm resolve to destroy it."

As His wrath is not rage, so God's curse is not violent language or cruel treatment. It is the punishment due to sin. "The wages of sin is death." "The wrath of God is revealed from heaven against all unrighteousness and ungodliness of men." Notice that the Books of Isaiah, Ecclesiastes and Malachi close on the solemn warning of God's judgment. The Sermon on the Mount and the Sermon on the end of the world close the same way (*Matt.* 7:27; 25:46). There are solemn words in the last chapter in the Bible.

Owen says that the curse of God consists, first, in the sentence of death, temporal and eternal; second, in the loss of the grace and the favor of God; third, in guilt and horror of conscience, despair and anguish here; with, fourth, eternal damnation hereafter.

The Bible uses such solemn terms as "everlasting fire," "everlasting punishment," "everlasting destruction," "shame and everlasting contempt," "the outer darkness," "the blackness of darkness," "the lakes of fire and brimstone" to warn us of the wrath to come. It does this to deter us, to turn us away from Hell and turn us to the arms of the Saviour. God tells us to meet our sins and find forgiveness here and not to have them meet us in the world to come. Now is the accepted time, today is the day of salvation. Christ can save the last, the least and the lowest who will come to God by Him. "Justice reigns in hell, and grace in heaven. Men's merit makes hell, and Christ's merit makes heaven" (Traill).

Q. 85. What doth God require of us, that we may escape His wrath and curse due to us for sin?

A. To escape the wrath and curse of God due to us for sin, God requireth of us faith in Jesus Christ, repentance unto life, with the diligent use of all the outward means whereby Christ communicateth to us the benefits of redemption.

If you have followed our study so far you know that we are all guilty before God, that none of us can free himself of his guilt, and that God has set before us a Saviour who can put us right with God. Now we are considering how we can lay hold on the Redemption Christ secured for sinners. The wages of sin—the thing that sin deserves—is death. The wrath and curse of God is due to us for every sin. And each of us has many sins. But there is a Saviour who has met and satisfied all the conditions of the Covenant of Grace. Christ Jesus has done enough to save everyone who trusts in Him. We have also seen that the Holy Spirit takes the things of Christ and brings them to us. How do we on our part lay hold of Christ and His salvation?

Even when the gift is freely offered the giver requires that the gift be accepted. God offers us salvation in Christ. He asks that we accept Christ and His salvation. The inward means by which we accept are faith in Jesus Christ and repentance unto life. The outward means which our wise and loving heavenly Father has given to keep us in touch with Christ are: the Word (the Bible), the sacraments of baptism and the Lord's Supper, and prayer. As we use these inward and outward means God gives or imparts to us the blessings of salvation or the benefits of redemption. In the next two questions we will learn the meaning of faith and of repentance.

Q. 86. What is faith in Jesus Christ?

A. Faith in Jesus Christ is a saving grace, whereby we receive and rest upon Him alone for salvation, as He is offered to us in the Gospel.

Let us put this answer together with those to the thirtieth and thirty-first questions. Then we will see that faith is the work of the Holy

Spirit Who persuades and enables us to embrace Jesus Christ, and also that in it we receive and rest upon Christ alone for salvation. The Gospel is God's offer of Christ. The Holy Spirit effectually calls us to accept Him. By the grace He gives we do accept Christ and this acceptance is our faith.

The Bible sometimes calls faith a looking to the Divine Redeemer. "Look unto Me and be ye saved." "Behold the Lamb of God." Sometimes it is described as a coming to Christ. "Come unto Me all ye that labor." "He that cometh to Me shall not hunger, and he that believeth on Me shall never thirst." Again it is a receiving of Him. "As many as received Him to them gave He power to become the sons of God, even to them that believe on His name."

Finally it is a fleeing for refuge and a resting or relying upon God our Saviour. Faith is assenting to and approving of God's way of saving us sinners. But this assent passes into personal trust. Faith is trust in a person. We accept the word of a man, we trust our friend to help us when we are in need. We bring our sick brother or sister and entrust him to our doctor. If we trust a friend, how much more ought we to trust the best friend a sinner ever had—the Saviour who died for sinners. We receive Christ and live in reliance upon Him alone for salvation. That is, we trust ourselves to Him believing that He and He alone can and will save us.

It is not Christ and our efforts that saves. It is Christ alone. It is not Christ and the prayers of the Virgin Mary or of the saints. It is Christ alone. It is not Christ and the worship of the Church. It is Christ alone. It is not even Christ and faith, it is Christ alone who saves and faith is only trusting in Him alone to save us. "It is not thy joy in Christ that saves thee—it is Christ. It is not thy hold on Christ that saves thee—it is Christ. It is not thy assurance of salvation that saves thee—it is Christ. It is not even thy faith in Christ, though faith is the means—it is Christ."

Faith is the empty hand of the beggar that putteth on Christ for justification. "The principal acts of saving faith are accepting, receiving and resting upon Christ alone for justification, sanctification and eternal life, by virtue of the covenant of grace."

Q. 87. What is repentance unto life?

A. Repentance unto life is a saving grace, whereby a sinner, out of a true sense of his sin, and apprehension of the mercy of God in Christ, doth, with grief and hatred of his sin, turn from it unto God with full purpose of, and endeavor after, new obedience.

Repentance is a change from the mind of self to the mind of Christ. As one turns to God in Christ he turns from sin. Faith and repentance are thus two sides of one act. "Repentance is the act of a believer; and faith is the act of a penitent. So that whoever believes repents, and whoever repents believes" (C. Hodge).

Jesus came preaching: "Repent ye, and believe the Gospel." "This is the work of God, that ye believe on Him Whom He hath sent." "Except ye repent, ye shall all likewise perish." He told the disciples that "repentance and remission of sins should be preached in His name among all nations." Peter declared that God had exalted Christ a Prince and a Saviour to give repentance and the remission of sins. Paul testified "repentance toward God and faith in our Lord Jesus Christ."

Repentance unto life is distinguished from a mere outward change or a momentary regret or remorse. True repentance is a change of heart, wrought by the Holy Spirit. He renews our wills so that we freely come to God asking His forgiveness. When the Holy Spirit brings a sinner face to face with the Holy God, he cries with Job: "I have heard of Thee by the hearing of the ear; but now mine eye seeth Thee: wherefore I abhor myself and repent in dust and ashes."

The Spirit sheds abroad the love of God in our hearts. He shows us God's own love in that Christ died for the ungodly. In this way He enables us to apprehend, or to lay hold on, or to understand the mercy of God in Christ. In the light of the lovingkindness of God sin looks worse than anywhere else. I have sinned against God who so loved me as to die for me in Christ. "When this amazing love is fully comprehended and distinctly realized, the stoutest heart of the proudest sinner will yield to its mighty influence. Love is the talisman by which God subdues the sinner's heart and gains his supreme affection. Let him firmly believe and strongly realize that Jesus was indeed the Lamb of God slain for the sins of the world, and that it was Love, almighty Love, which occasioned the awful sacrifice, and he will bow his soul in the depths of humility and give his heart to God" (Thornwell).

16. GOD INCARNATE FOR SUFFERING MEN[1]

As a nation we are standing on the threshold of a great victory. But the hour of victory is the moment to see ourselves in the light of God's presence and to humble ourselves under His almighty hand. Otherwise we shall give ourselves to such boastings as the Gentiles know. And lest we forget, the war has given us solemn reminders of the fearful cost at which victory comes. The Battle of the Bulge at the 1944 Christmas season piled up the longest casualty list in American history. The problem of pain which has long been with you at Warm Springs has become a nation-wide problem. Has the Church an answer to this chorus of suffering and heartache that is rising from every home? Blessed be God she has. To suffering man we offer the suffering Saviour. For the torn in body, for the shocked in mind, for the broken in heart the Gospel presents God who became incarnate that He might suffer with us and for us in our human flesh.

The solace for the sorrow and the suffering of the war is in the first Christmas and in the first Christian Easter. It is precisely this—that "the Lord of glory of His own will entered into our life of grief and suffering, and for love of men bore all and more than all that men may be called to bear." "God, the Almighty and Eternal God, has shared our experience in its depths of weakness and pain."

The *Lord* who in the beginning laid the foundation of the earth and who upholds all things by the Word of His power laid aside the glories of heaven and took our flesh and blood that in our nature He might suffer. In Himself God is the Being of pure activity living in a blessedness and glory which no creaturely force can attack. But God willed to put Himself into our frail and suffering humanity that

[1] The sermon was printed in the *Southern Presbyterian Journal* and added to *Christ—The Bread of Life,* 99-109.

therein He might be susceptible to the slings and arrows of man's rage and hate, to all the suffering brought on by the creature's rebellion against his Maker, and by man's subsequent inhumanity to man. Jesus was made a little lower than the angels for the suffering of death that by the grace of God He might taste of death for every man. He entered into our life with all its miseries. The joy of heaven and the Lord of angels became the man of sorrows and acquainted with grief. While He was here He was so busy healing the sick and ministering to the suffering that Matthew remembered what was written by the prophet: He took our infirmities and bore our sicknesses.

It pleased God in bringing many sons unto glory to make the Captain of our salvation perfect through suffering. Have your nerves twitched and pained where some limb was twisted or lacking? His nerve centers, His very hands and feet, were pierced with cruel spikes. Have your temples throbbed with a fever that would not abate? His throbbed with thorns crushed into them. Have the implements of war torn and lacerated your body? The war-spear of the soldier was thrust into His side.

In the long days of agony are you asking why does He not work a miracle and restore you at once as He healed the multitudes in old Galilee? In *The Robe,* Lloyd Douglas has fancied the story of Miriam, a bed-ridden Jewess lass, whose body He did not heal, but in whose heart He placed a song. The Gospels have a surer story than Douglas' fancy. There is one Person for whom Jesus did not work a miracle to avert suffering. That Person fasted forty days until He was tempted to turn the very rocks into bread. That Person was mocked and scourged and spat upon, but He never whimpered and He never beckoned for the twelve legions of angels that were at His call. When He suffered He threatened not. My brother, if He does not heal you with a word, He is inviting you to follow in the steps He Himself has trod without a single miracle to ease one bit of His agony. Refusing the deadening effect of the ancient drug He drained the bitter cup the Father gave Him to drink.

With the suffering, sorrowing people of Holland Pastor Koopman pleaded: "Why so much suffering comes no one can say. But one thing I know and whoever knows it has the true faith in life and in death—it does not happen outside the merciful will of Jesus Christ.

He understands your suffering because He has borne it all before you did."

Yes, Christ bore our suffering, all that we bear and more. For He suffered not only the cruel scourging and the agonizing crucifixion by which His form was marred more than any man and His visage more than the sons of men. He who knew no sin was made sin for us. Thus He endured the wrath of God revealed from heaven against all unrighteousness and ungodliness of men. He suffered as the Lamb of God for the sins of the world. It pleased the Father to bruise Him for our transgressions. And all this suffering with us and for us He freely took of His own loving and sovereign will. He who was God freely became man that His flesh might be torn and His body mangled for us men and for our salvation. And today:

> He, who for men in mercy stood,
> And poured on earth His precious blood ...
> Our fellow-sufferer yet retains
> A fellow feeling of our pains ...
> In every pang that rends the heart,
> The Man of sorrows had a part;
> He sympathizes in our grief,
> And to the sufferer sends relief.

God incarnate in Jesus of Nazareth not only suffered our bodily pains, His breast also throbbed with our heart-aches. He who numbers the stars heals the broken in heart. He who marshals the spiral nebulae binds up our sorrows. The vast diamond-studded Milky Way is but as "dust from the Almighty's moving Chariot Wheels." And yet in all our afflictions He is afflicted and the Angel of His Presence saves us.

The Epistle to the Hebrews shows the Saviour walking by faith as we walk, beset by our anxieties and fears. So really did He share our flesh and blood that these words express the faith He placed in God: "I will put my trust in Him." "Who in the days of His flesh, having offered up prayers and supplications with strong crying and tears unto Him that was able to save Him from death and having been heard for His godly fear, though He was a Son, yet learned He obedience by the things which He suffered." In becoming our complete and compassionate High Priest Christ passed through the whole curriculum of temptation, trial, patience, fear, anxiety and heart agony we face. Therefore He is a faithful and merciful High Priest who can bear gently with the ignorant and erring in that He Himself was also compassed with infirmity.

In the days of His flesh our Lord showed the deepest concern for the heart anxieties, the worries and the fears of those about Him. When He stood with Mary and Martha at the tomb of Lazarus their sorrow so moved His heart that Jesus wept with them. The last week shows Him time and again weeping over Jerusalem. "O Jerusalem, thou that killest the prophets and stonest those that are sent unto thee, how often would I have gathered thy children as a hen gathereth her chickens under her wings, and ye would not." At the last when the women bewailed and lamented Him, Jesus turned and said unto them: "Daughters of Jerusalem weep not for Me, but weep for yourselves." The dreadful punishment in store for Jerusalem brought tears that His own cross was not then extorting from His eyes.

The acme of tender consideration is in Jesus' treatment of Jairus. As He goes to heal the daughter the report arrives that the child is dead and there is no need to trouble the Master further. But before the father has time to answer, Jesus' word of encouragement is steadying Jairus' wavering faith: "Fear not, only believe, and she shall be made whole." Though the weight of a world's redemption is upon Him, the anxieties of Mary are all met as her crucified Son says: "Mother, behold thy son." And (to John): "Son, behold thy mother."

Nor has this concern for our anxieties been dimmed by the glories and blessedness of heaven. When Stephen is stoned the Son of Man rises from His seat at the Father's Throne and so manifests Himself to His dying martyr that Stephen's face shines like the face of an angel. When He manifested His glory to John on Patmos, He was quick to manifest with it His understanding grace. "And He laid His right hand upon me, saying, Fear not: I am the first and the last, and the Living One; and I was dead, and behold I am alive forevermore, and I have the keys of death and of Hades."

As little children in their games stand in a circle about a common center so we all face one great fear, the fear of death. And that is the particular fear our Lord came to face with us and for us. He was made a little lower than the angels for the suffering of death, that by the grace of God He might taste of death for every man. He died that through death He might destroy him that had the power of death, that is the devil, and deliver them who through fear of death were all their lifetime subject to bondage.

On land, on sea, under the sea, and in the air the Lord Christ is entering into the hearts of His men when they find terror on every side. A letter was recently received from a lieutenant in the Seventy-ninth Division telling how depressed he was as he contemplated the near approach of D-Day. Then God spoke to him through the chanting of the ninety-first, the soldier's Psalm. When the Ninth Army was advancing on the Roer, we had a letter: "Mother, Dad: The terror by night and the arrow that flieth by day, the pestilence that walketh in darkness and the destruction that wasteth at noonday are no mere figures of speech over here. But deeper than the dangers of war there is the calm of the presence of the Lord, the steadying touch of His hand, the understanding assurance of His voice: 'I will never leave thee, nor forsake thee: so that we may boldly say, The Lord is my helper and I will not fear what man may do unto me.'"

Let us then draw near the Table with Gospel viands for our sorrows spread. And as He gives us beauty for ashes, the oil of joy for mourning, the garment of praise for the spirit of heaviness, let our overwhelming wonder be:

> That the Great Angel-blinding light should shrink
> His blaze, to shine in a poor Shepherd's eye;
> That the unmeasur'd God so low should sink,
> As Pris'ner in a few poor rags to ly;
> That from his Mother's Breast he milke should drink,
> Who feeds with Nectar Heav'n's faire family,
> That a vile Manger his low Bed should prove,
> Who in a Throne of stars Thunders above;
> That he whom the Sun serves, should faintly peepe
> Through clouds of Infant Flesh! that he, the old
> Eternall Word should be a Child, and weepe;
> That he who made the fire, should feare the cold,
> That Heav'n's high Majesty his Court should keepe
> In a clay cottage, by each blast control'd;

> That Glories self should serve our Griefs and feares,
> And free Eternity submit to years.

The ever-blessed God became incarnate that He might suffer the pangs of our torn flesh, the ever-active Creator became a man that He might be susceptible of the creature's fears and tears. But the Great Gospel paradox is yet to be put: He who has life in Himself and who giveth life to whom He will became mortal man that for our sins He might die. He whose years shall not fail became obedient unto death and that the death of the Cross. To the dregs He drank our cup of woe that we might quaff His cup of salvation. That He might bring many sons unto glory He tasted death for every man. Christ both died and rose again that He might be Lord, both of the dead and of the living. Thus, He calls us to go through no darker room than He has gone through before us. Yea though I walk through the valley of the shadow of death, I will fear no evil, for Thou art with me and even death is no new way to Thee.

With rare literary skill John Hay, sometime Secretary of State, portrayed death as *The Stirrup Cup* which the cavalryman used to drink as he mounted his steed:

> My short and happy day is done,
> The long and lonely night comes on:
> And at my door the pale horse stands
> To bear me forth to unknown lands.

General E. P. Alexander took up the figure and wrote something of his own dauntless daring into it:

> But storm and gloom and mystery
> Shall only nerve my courage high.
> Who thro' life's scenes hath borne his part
> May face its close with tranquil heart.

The lines came into the hands of James Powers Smith who, as an aide-de-camp to Stonewall Jackson, had passed through many a valley of the shadow. Dr. Smith put into the figure the tranquil heart that Christ gives:

> The pale horse stands and will not bide,
> The night has come and I must ride;

> But not alone to unknown lands,
>   My Friend goes with me holding hands.

This friend has gone through the strait gate of death, His own death, before He goes through the gate of death with us. And in that going through of His own death He drew the sharpest sting out of our death. For the sting of death is sin and the power of sin is the law. But Christ died for our sins, the Just for the unjust. There is, therefore, now no condemnation to those who are in Christ Jesus. Thanks be unto God who giveth us the victory through our Lord Jesus Christ!

Compare the death of Jesus with the death of Stephen and you are immeasurably struck with the contrast. Why should the face of Stephen shine like the face of an angel while the visage of Jesus was so marred more than any man? Why? Because Jesus who had no sin of His own was made sin for Stephen in order that Stephen who had no righteousness of his own might be made the righteousness of God in Christ. Because He is the answer for sin, therefore Christ has the answer to death. He was delivered for our offenses and raised for our justification. Therefore:

> In peace let me resign my breath
>   And Thy salvation see:
> My sins deserved eternal death,
>   But Jesus died for me.

It is a proper thought that one draw the veil of charity over the shortcomings of those who die, especially of those who die in faith. For the spirits of those who die in the Lord are beautified, made perfect in holiness. By the grace of the Lord their spirits are glorified like Him who takes them to Himself. That noble, fine, generous, loving spirit is changed into His likeness and all that was base and wicked is done away. Thus we properly think of them as pure and kind all through like the angelic spirits which surround the throne.

> All rapture, thro' and thro'
>   In God's most holy sight.

The Christ who pierced the mystery of the tomb rose again from the dead and ascended to the right hand of the Father where He ever liveth to intercede for us. There His understanding heart, His unceasing prayers, His constant grace, keep our faith from failing and carry onward the Church of God until that day when He shall appear a second time apart from sin unto salvation. By tasting death for us He drew its sting. By rising from the dead and ascending to the right hand of the Majesty on High He has given us an anchor sure and steadfast. Even so them also that sleep in Jesus Christ will God bring with Him.

At Easter 1942, the Old First Church in Birmingham held a memorial service for a lad who went down in the S-26 near Panama. On that occasion his mother wrote:

> God has given me a guiding Light,
>   A star called Faith
> "That substance of things hoped for,
>   That evidence of things not seen."
> And now within me peace and joy are born,
>   For some day there shall come a Resurrection morn
> And I shall see again and know my son.

17. THE JOY OF THE LORD[1]

Nehemiah 8:10—"The joy of the Lord is your strength."

When the walls of Jerusalem were rebuilt, the people gathered to worship the LORD, and the Levites expounded to them the law of God. As the Word of the LORD lay bare their sin they began to mourn and weep under the just judgment of God. But Nehemiah and Ezra stopped them, saying, "The Day is holy unto the LORD your God; weep not, neither mourn, for the joy of the LORD is your strength." The Word of God ever judges us, but blessed be the LORD our God, His Word of judgment is at the same time His Word of grace. He wounds, but He also heals. He convicts of sin, but He graciously pardons through the redemption which is in Christ Jesus.

The Bible is a book of life, presenting people in every conceivable difficulty, suffering, sin, disappointment, need—but through it all and over it all is the sound of rejoicing. God brought forth His people with joy, His chosen with singing. David appointed singers to lift up their voices with joy and brought the Ark into Zion with such joy that his wife thought he danced too gaily. The people offered for the Temple with joy. Hezekiah's passover feast was celebrated with such great joy that Jerusalem had not seen the like since the days of Solomon. The foundations of the new Temple were laid with the shout of joy and the house of the LORD was dedicated with joy. When the walls of the city were dedicated God made His people to rejoice with such great joy that the joy of Jerusalem was heard afar off. Blessed is

---

1 "The Joy of the Lord," appeared in the *Presbyterian Journal,* August 1943, 11-13. In it Dr. Robinson outlines a biblical theology of joy that is breath-taking in its beauty and scope.

the people that know the joyful sound, for the city of God is the joy of the whole earth.

> Saviour, if of Zion's city
>   I, thru' grace, a member am,
> Let the world deride or pity,
>   I will glory in Thy Name.
> Fading is the worldling's pleasure,
>   All his boasted pomp and show;
> Solid joys and lasting treasure
>   None but Zion's children know.

The living God is the only source of true joy. "In Thy Presence is fullness of joy; at Thy right hand there are pleasures for evermore." Those that walk in the light of His countenance know the joyful sound. Those that gather in His solemn assembly hear Him say, "The LORD thy God in the midst of thee is mighty; He will save, He will rejoice over thee with joy; He will rest in His love, He will joy over thee with singing." Therefore, O God, send out Thy light and Thy truth and let them lead me to Thy Tabernacles, unto God my exceeding joy.

> Praise to God immortal praise,
>   For the love that crowns our days,
> Bounteous source of ev'ry joy,
>   Let Thy praise our tongues employ.

The Joy of Our Lord's Ministry

The joy of heaven was brought to earth when God became man for us men and for our salvation. Luke has caught the gladness of that hour in the fragrance of song with which He welcomes the Saviour. He ushers us as it were into a beautiful cathedral, on one side of which are the women, Elizabeth with her *Benedicta*, and Mary with the *Magnificat*; and on the other the men, Zacharias with the *Benedictus*, and Simeon with the *Nunc Dimittis*, while above is the angel chorus singing, "Glory to God in the highest, and on earth peace, good-will to men." When Mary comes to visit Elizabeth, John leaps for joy, while Mary's spirit rejoices in God her Saviour. The angel brings the shepherds good tidings of great joy which shall be to all people. When the Wise Men saw the star they rejoiced with exceedingly great joy. When all men began to come to Jesus, John's joy was made full. The friend of the bridegroom rejoiced greatly because of the bridegroom's voice.

The Father gave not the Spirit by measure to the Son, and one of the primary gifts of the Spirit is joy. When Jesus admonishes the disciples to rejoice because He goeth to the Father, for the Father is even greater, He is tacitly saying that up to that time He has been their joy. Our Lord began His miracles by making wine that there might be more joy at the wedding feast. When He healed the woman whom Satan had bound eighteen years, the ruler of the synagogue became indignant, but the multitude rejoiced for the glorious things that were done by Him. When the seventy returned from their mission of preaching, teaching and healing, they rejoiced that even the demons were subject unto them in Christ's Name. Jesus told them rather to rejoice that their names were written in heaven. In the midst of His own rejection by the critics of Galilee our Lord rejoiced in the Holy Spirit and said: "I thank Thee, O Father, Lord of heaven and earth, that Thou didst hide these things from the wise and understanding and reveal them unto babes; yea, Father; for so it seemed well-pleasing in Thy sight."

When what was foreshadowed in the rejection in Galilee occurred in Jerusalem also, Jesus gathered His disciples close about Him, and in the shadow of Gethsemane and Calvary He spoke unto them that His joy might be in them and that their joy might be full. Passing rapidly by the agonies of His own going He promised to see them again and cause their hearts to rejoice with a joy that none could take from them. From His emptied tomb the women departed quickly with fear and great joy to bring the disciples word. The Epistle to the Hebrews tells us that for the joy that was set before Him, Christ endured the Cross despising the shame. At Pentecost Peter sees Him seated at God's right hand made full of gladness with the Father's countenance.

Even before the Resurrection Jesus lived in such communion with the Father, such delight in doing His will, that as He tasted death for every man, His spirit overflowed with a joy that was sufficient to make the joy of disciples full. Now that He is enthroned in the joy of the Father's presence, surely earth hath no sorrow that can quench the joy He giveth.

> Jesus, Thou joy of loving hearts!
> > Thou Fount of Life! Thou Light of men!
> From the best bliss that earth imparts
> > We turn unfilled to Thee again.

The Joy of our Lord's Salvation

The Psalmist continually speaks of rejoicing in God's salvation, and out of the depths of sin David pleads, "Take not Thy Holy Spirit from me and restore unto me the joy of Thy salvation." There is joy in the presence of the angels of God over one sinner that repenteth more than over the ninety and nine that need no repentance. There was much joy in Samaria when Philip proclaimed unto them the Christ. The same evangelist began at the fifty-third of Isaiah and preached unto the Ethiopian Eunuch that Jesus was the lamb led unto the slaughter, who was wounded for our transgressions and bruised for our iniquities, and with whose stripes we are healed. The Ethiopian accepted the Gospel, confessed Christ, was baptized and went on his way rejoicing. Paul stopped the Philippian jailor from killing himself and told him, "Believe on the Lord Jesus Christ and thou shalt be saved." This man heard the Word of the Lord, believed in God, was baptized and rejoiced greatly with all his house. Friend, would you know the joy of salvation? Believe on the Lord Jesus Christ, receive His atonement, hide in the Rock of Ages that was cleft for thee, lay aside all confidence in yourself, entrust yourself to Him. Christian, would you taste again the joy of the Holy Ghost? They that go forth and weeping bearing precious seed, shall doubtless come again with rejoicing bringing their sheaves with them. Be helpers of others' joy and they will be your crown of rejoicing in the day of Jesus Christ. In that day He shall come in glory, but now

> Jesus comes to hearts rejoicing,
> > Bringing news of sins forgiven;
> Leading souls redeemed to heav'n;

'PLEADING FOR A REFORMATION VISION'

Alleluia! Alleluia!
Now the gate of death is riven.

The joy of His salvation carries with it the assurance of the Father's love and wisdom and care in every circumstance of life. The Bible is not a book of airy castles in the nebulous blue, it is not a vain clutching after Platonic ideas, it is the story of the joy of God in the serious problems of real life. Over the heart-burns, the sorrows and sufferings of life we see the Father's heart and know that His hand is upon us in chastening only to work out in us the peaceable fruits of righteousness. From the midst of physical sufferings the Apostle writes: "I am filled with comfort, I overflow with joy in all our affliction." James bids us count it all joy when we fall into manifold trials, knowing that the proving of our faith worketh patience. Peter calls us to rejoice greatly even in grief, for these trials prove our faith. As gold is refined in a furnace so our faith, being more precious than gold, though it is proved by fire, shall be found unto praise and glory and honor at the revelation of Jesus Christ, on whom believing we now rejoice greatly with joy unspeakable and full of glory. Facing the reality of famine, the Old Testament prophet cried:

> Although the fig tree shall not blossom,
> Neither shall the fruit be in the vines;
> The labour of the olives shall fail,
> And the fields shall yield no meat;
> The flock shall be cut off from the fold,
> And there shall be no herd in the stalls:
> Yet will I rejoice in the LORD,
> I will joy in the God of my salvation.

Weeping may endure for a night, but joy cometh to the people of God in the morning.

> O Joy that seekest me thru' pain,
>   I cannot close my heart to Thee!
> I trace the rainbow thru' the rain,
>   And feel the promise is not vain
> That morn' shall tearless be.

Yes, God's salvation has promises not only for this life, but also for that which is to come. As we look at the invisible things which God has for His children we find that our present afflictions work for us a far more exceeding and eternal weight of glory. Jesus tells us that when we are reproached for the sake of the Son of Man we are to rejoice and leap for joy, for great is our reward in heaven. We are not to think a fiery trial a strange thing, but as we are partakers of Christ's sufferings we are to rejoice, for at the revelation of His glory we shall rejoice with exceeding joy. We have a Saviour who died and rose again that He might be the Lord both of the dead and of the living. He is the Lamb who shepherds the souls in the heavenly pastures, the Son who prepares for us the many mansions of the Father's house. Therefore to depart and be with Him is far better for the believing soul, however hard it may be for those who remain. And in the final consummation we have the blessed hope of His appearing bringing with Him the tens of thousands of His saints, the New Jerusalem which occupies the City that has the glory of God for a light and the Lamb for a temple, new heavens in the new earth, where God dwells with His people, and wipes every tear from their eyes.

> Jerusalem the golden,
>   With milk and honey blest,
> Beneath thy contemplation,
>   Sink heart and voice oppressed;
> I know not, O I know not
>   What joys await us there,
> What radiancy of glory,
>   What bliss beyond compare.

Rejoice in the Lord!

One of the finest examples of rejoicing in the Lord is Paul's experiences with the Philippian Church. At Philippi he was arrested and scourged without a trial, his feet were thrust into stocks, he was hungry; but at midnight he and Silas were praying and singing hymns to God. Is it any wonder that God used his testimony to bring the joy of salvation to the jailor? Some years later Paul writes to this Church from the bonds of a Roman prison a letter that is simply running over with joy. He always prays for these Philippian Christians with joy, he looks forward to seeing them that their rejoicing may be more abundant, he asks them to make his joy full by being of one accord, he rejoices greatly in their thought for him and repeatedly bids them rejoice in the Lord. With the Epistle to the Philippians we may place a number of other Christian writings that have come from prisons redolent with the joy of the Lord: Revelation, *Pilgrim's Progress*, Rutherford's letters. The Confessional Minister in a Concentration Camp has a joy to which the master of Berchtesgaden is a stranger. Our own Dr. J. V. N. Talmadge stayed behind to care for our foreign mission property in Korea and was incarcerated several months. On his return he told us that the joy of the Lord had been his strength through those trying days.

We are bidden by the Saviour to ask in His Name and we shall receive that our joy may be full. Through His great mission access to the Father has been opened. He is the way by whom we come to the Father. As we come by this new and living way the Father receives us, the joy of fellowship with God is ours.

> There is a place where Jesus sheds
>   The oil of gladness on our heads,
> A place than all beside more sweet:
>   It is the blood-bought mercy-seat.
>
> O eyes that are weary and hearts that are sore
>   Look off unto Jesus, and sorrow no more.

Again our Lord says, "These things have I spoken unto you, that my joy may be in you and that your joy may be made full." The Book of God is the book of joy. And the way to joy is the study of the Word. In this hour of the world's travail even the secular press is pointing to the Book that gives a light to every age. From the *Saturday Evening Post* we read:

> A fighting man speaks from the floor of a storm-tossed raft. "Is there a Bible among us?" On a burning African desert a voice reads quietly, and a thousand heads bow reverently ... In the silence of night on a Kansas farm a mother finds solace in its thin, worn pages ... Quietly its words of comfort are spoken in solemn requiem as rough hands grown tender lower a hero's body overside.
>
> In the search for peace through generations man has turned to

the Bible. For the things men live by are found in this book that is the Word of God. In its pages men have found help for their deepest needs. Comfort for their shattered spirits. Light for their darkest hour. Always the Bible has inspired the noblest courage and the most sublime actions of man. Heroes have dedicated their lives to its principles. Martyrs have died with its words on their lips.

Now, an anguished world turns to this book that has molded the life of man. For its lessons of mercy, humanity, tolerance, charity. For a restoration of the spirit torn with grief. For return of the hope and faith grown weak under the whip of despotism. And here in its pages to seek the flame that lifts men's souls. The courage to face tomorrow. The faith, that in good time the sound of war will end and men shall live again in brotherhood and peace.

For the words of this Book are written that ye may believe that Jesus is the Christ, the Son of God, and that believing ye may have life through His Name. In the dim and distant centuries Abraham rejoiced to see His day, and he saw it and was glad. The faithful children of Abraham believed the promise that in his seed all the nations of the earth should be blessed and this faith in the Christ to come was accepted for righteousness. Now it was not written for his sake alone, that it was imputed to him; but for us also to whom it shall be imputed, if we believe on Him that raised up Jesus our Lord from the dead; who was delivered for our offenses, and was raised for our justification. In Jesus Christ there is a righteousness that can avail for the foulest sinner, a salvation for the most guilty. "Therefore, I will greatly rejoice in the LORD, my soul shall be joyful in my God; for He hath clothed me with the garments of salvation, He hath covered me with the robes of righteousness, as a bridegroom decketh himself with ornaments, and as a bride adorneth herself with her jewels."

18. UNDER HIS WINGS[1]

"Because he hath set his love upon Me, therefore will I deliver him: I will set him on high, because he hath known My name."—Psa. 91:14

Gypsy Smith visited Ira Sankey in his final illness. "Is there anything I can do for you?" asked the visitor. "Yes," replied the sick man, "sing for me, 'Under His Wings.'" And so the man who had sung so many into the fold passed into the valley of the shadow with a refrain he had himself written and with these words of comfort warming his heart:

> Under His wings I am safely abiding;
> Though the night deepens and tempests are wild,
> Still I can trust Him, I know He will keep me;
> He has redeemed me, and I am His child.

The Bible's first reference to the wings of the Almighty is in the blessing a wealthy Hebrew farmer passed upon a poor, foreign-born maiden who gleaned in his field. Boaz said to Ruth, the Moabitess: "The Lord recompense thy work, and a full reward be given thee of the Lord, the God of Israel, under whose wings thou hast come to take refuge." And for those who love a love story—as we all do— this cordial greeting had a much happier ending than the somewhat similar romance which an American poet saw nipped in the bud as the wealthy judge watched Maude Mueller rake the hay. Out of the pastoral romance of Boaz and Ruth came Obed and then Jesse and then David, the king.

No doubt David heard as a child the thrilling story of the love-making of his great-grandparents and with it the wings of the Lord

---

[1] This sermon appeared in the *Christian Observer,* December 13, 1944, 4-5.

which Boaz had spread over Ruth that day. At any rate, this sheltering figure of God's love and care became very precious to the poet king of Israel. It occurs in five Psalms attributed to David, as well as in the ninety-first, which is ascribed to no author.

Standing on Mount Olivet overlooking Zion, great David's Greater Son took up the same figure that His distant ancestor had used: "O Jerusalem, Jerusalem, which killest the prophets, and stonest them that are sent unto thee; how often would I have gathered thy children together as a hen doth gather her brood under her wings, and ye would not." What Jerusalem refused is our only refuge. All the grounds of our acceptance, our forgiveness, our righteousness, our peace, our adoption of a merciful hearing of our prayers are in Christ. We take refuge under the covert of His sacrifice and beneath the shield of His intercession. He did for us what we could not do for ourselves and what we cannot do without. He was delivered for our offenses and raised for our justification. As we take refuge under His wings, we have redemption through His blood, even the forgiveness of our sins. By His obedience we sinners are declared righteous.

Moreover, as we Gentile believers take refuge under the robes of His righteousness we may well pray for the time when He shall gather more of His ancient people, the Jews, as a hen gathereth her chickens under her wings. After the American army liberated Cherbourg the Jews gathered again and worshiped in their synagogue for the first time since the fall of France. A Christian caretaker had hidden the sacred scroll and the pieces of synagogue furniture; the Jews had been taken into Christian families and had temporarily adopted Christian names. In the hour of danger Cherbourg Jewry—that is, those who survived—took refuge under the wings of Christ and so escaped the wrath of the Nazi. May this be a parable and a prophecy that these and many others of the flesh of Abraham may take refuge for time and for eternity under the wings of their own Messiah, Jesus the Son of David, and be hidden from the wrath of God by His blood and righteousness sealed to them by baptism in His Name!

A Habitation for Trust.

Our text presents to us the overshadowing wings of the Almighty as a habitation in which to trust:

> He that dwelleth in the secret place of the Most High
> Shall abide under the shadow of the Almighty …
> He shall cover thee with His pinions,
> And under His wings shalt thou trust.

Many of our American fliers on Guadalcanal began every mission by repeating this ninety-first Psalm. Generally they came back, sometimes "on a wing and a prayer." And those that came not back went out, like Ira Sankey, under His wings. Some months ago, when the minister called, a mother had a glad cablegram that her son had completed the awful shuttle trip from England across Germany to North Africa and back in safety. Later that lad was one of the handful who returned safely to this country after the air battle of Munster and the terrific toll of duty accomplished in his plane, the "Rose Marie." When he left his mother had given him the eleventh verse of this Psalm: "For He shall give His angels charge over thee, to keep thee in all thy ways." Several papers have carried the letter of a Pennsylvania officer to his sister telling how he was shot down, but saved because the bullet was stopped by his Bible at this other verse from the same Psalm: "A thousand shall fall at thy side, and ten thousand at thy right hand; but it shall not come nigh thee."

Two years ago we read the ninety-first Psalm at my mother's table before two brothers went overseas. They have written back no stories of narrow escapes but one was several times on Anzio and was protected. So now with my own son in the combat area we would keep our trust under the shadow of His wing.

> There is a safe and secret place
> Beneath the wings divine,
> Reserved for all the heirs of grace—
> O be that refuge mine!

The Christian's consolation is "to apprehend that His Heavenly Father restrains all things by His power, governs all things by His will, and regulates all things by His wisdom, in such a manner that nothing can happen but by His appointment. Moreover God has taken him under His protection, and committed him to the care of angels so that he can sustain no injury from water, or fire, or sword, any farther than the Divine Governor may be pleased to permit." "Surely He shall deliver thee from the snare of the fowler, and from the noisome pestilence ... Thou shalt not be afraid for the terror by night; nor for the arrow that flieth by day; nor for the pestilence that walketh in darkness; nor for the destruction that wasteth at noonday." "The Lord is the strength of my life; of whom shall I be afraid? Though an host should encamp against me ... though I walk through the valley of the shadow of death, I will fear no evil. For Thou art with me."

> Be not dismayed whate'er betide,
> God will take care of you.
> Beneath His wings of love abide.
> Thro' ev'ry day, o'er all the way
> He will take care of you.

An Encouragement for Prayer.

The wings of the Lord were not only the psalmist's shield of protection, they were as well his encouragement in prayer. "He shall call upon Me, and I will answer him." In the hour when our loved ones are being committed to battle we pray for ourselves:

> Jesus, lover of my soul,
> Let me to Thy bosom fly.

And for them:

> Cover my defenseless head
> With the shadow of Thy wing.

In heat of mortal combat David lifted his heart in this prayer: "Shew Thy marvelous lovingkindness, O Thou that savest by Thy right hand them which put their trust in Thee from those that rise up against them. Keep me as the apple of the eye; hide me under the shadow of Thy wings from the wicked that oppress me, from my deadly enemies who compass me about" (*Psa.* 17:7-9).

As he hid from Saul in the Cave of Adullam and there seemed only a step between him and death, David cried: "Be merciful unto me, O God, be merciful unto me; for my soul trusteth in Thee; yea, in the shadow of Thy wings will I take refuge until these calamities be overpast. I will cry unto God, Most High … He will send from Heaven and save me from the reproach of him that would swallow me up."

Again when his heart was overwhelmed the fainting Psalmist prayed: "Hear my cry, O God; attend unto my prayer … lead me to the Rock that is higher than I. For Thou hast been a shelter for me, and a strong tower from the enemy. I will abide in Thy tabernacle; I will trust in the covert of Thy wings."

Finding our shelter in the covert of His wings, let us also pray:

> More things are wrought by prayer
> Than this world dreams of …
> For so the whole round world is every way
> Bound by gold chains about the feet of God.

When the American fleet joined battle in the Philippines the Presbytery and congregation lifted their hearts in the Navy Hymn:

> O Trinity of love and power!
> Our brethren shield in danger's hour
> From rock and tempest, fire and foe,
> Protect them wheresoe'er they go,
> And ever let there rise to Thee
> Glad hymns of praise from land and sea.

In praying, we know that God's gracious arms are over and about those we love, for we have an High Priest who ever liveth to intercede for us.

> High Priest of the Church dispensation,
> Lift up, we pray, Thy pierced hand,
> And bless Thy ransomed congregation
> In every place, by sea and land.
> Before Thy Father's face remember
> By name each individual member:
> Thy face now on us shine,
> Grant us Thy peace divine;
> For we are Thine.

A Refuge in Sorrow.

Under the wings of the Almighty the Psalmist hears the promises: "I will be with him in trouble, I will deliver him … I will shew him My salvation." As the reports come in of a dear one killed here, of another wounded there, of a third missing, let us all nestle nearer to the heart of the Eternal and find through Christ the God of comfort and the Father of consolations!

In the sixty-third Psalm David is out in the wilderness of Judah thirsting for God and longing to see His glory and power as he had seen it of old in the sanctuary. Before his plane was reported missing Captain Brooks Sheldon had written his father that the men in his squadron loved to sing: "Glorious things of thee are spoken, Zion, City of our God." Like David, these men long to see the glory and the grace of God as they saw it when His lovingkindness and His majesty were presented in the home church. But also like the Psalmist, they and we find solace under His wings. When the Lord took the youngest life we had on the campus, his mother found her anchor in these words of the Psalm: "Because Thy lovingkindness is better than life, my lips shall praise Thee."

David continues: "My soul shall be satisfied with marrow and fatness; and my mouth shall praise Thee with joyful lips; because Thou hast been my help, therefore in the shadow of Thy wings will I rejoice. My soul followeth hard after Thee: Thy right hand upholdeth me."

On another occasion David turned from the wickedness and the wrath of man to the lovingkindness of the Lord and His faithfulness which reacheth unto the skies (*Psa.* 36). And here he found solace in suffering: "How precious is Thy lovingkindness, O God, therefore the children of men put their trust in the shadow of Thy wings … Thou shalt make them drink of the river of Thy pleasure, for with Thee is the fountain of life; in Thy light we shall see light."

As the valley of the shadow of the bitter death which He was to endure for our sins closed around our Redeemer, He found a blessedness in communion with the Father and prayed that His overflowing joy might be in His disciples and that our joy might be made full. His work of removing our condemnation and opening the way of access to the Father so re-established communion with God that His servants were able to sing praises unto the Lord when their scourged bodies were fast in the stocks of the inner prison at Philippi. Later one of these same servants wrote from a Roman prison to the Philippian church: "Rejoice in the Lord, always; and again I say, Rejoice."

Under His wings, what a refuge in sorrow!
How the heart yearningly turns to His rest!
Often when earth has no balm for my healing,
There I find comfort and there I am blest.

O what precious enjoyment!
There will I hide, till life's trials are o'er;
Sheltered, protected, no evil can harm me.
Resting in Jesus I am safe evermore.

Under His wings, under His wings,
Who from His love can sever?
Under His wings my soul shall abide,
Safely abide forever.

19. THE LAMB IN THE MIDST OF THE THRONE[1]

The Church must needs have a focal center for her worship, and her Lord is not ignorant of this need and has never left this need to be supplied by the will-worship of man's devising. In the Old Testament the center of worship was the mercy-seat between the cherubim which covered the ark of the covenant. There the Shekinah Glory of the Lord dwelt; there the blood of propitiation was applied; there God reigned as King over Israel. This focal center was not visible to the eyes of all, but was carefully hidden behind the curtains in the most holy place. The worshiping Israelite saw only the veil. There was no image or likeness there of anything in heaven or on earth or under the earth which could become an idol for him. Even the Old Testament types were thus teaching some of the elements of a spiritual worship. And the time was hastening on when neither Mount Gerizim nor the Temple in Jerusalem nor any other place on earth should be the focus of worship. For God is a spirit and they who would worship Him must worship Him in spirit and in truth.

When the antitype came, the types, symbols and ceremonies of the Old Testament dispensation passed away. As old Israel had seen the angels of God descending and ascending upon the ladder let down from heaven, so the new Israelite was to enjoy this blessed communion with God through the Son of Man. In His saying about destroying the Temple and rebuilding it in three days, our Lord was pointing from the Temple on Mount Zion to the Temple of His own body. As the Temple had been the place of revelation, of worship, of audience, of government, where God dwelt between the cherubim at the blood-sprinkled mercy-seat, so Christ is the true Temple

[1] WCR, *Presbyterian Journal*, January 1944, 5-6.

or dwelling-place of God. "His body crucified and risen is the one medium of communion between God and man, as well as between man and God; and the acceptance of all Gospel worship depends simply on its relation to Him as the sole atonement for sin and Temple of God."

As the focal center of Old Testament worship was within the earthly veil—the Holy of Holies—so the focal center of New Testament worship is now within the heavenly veil, in the true tabernacle that God pitched and not man. When the Apocalypse unveils the worship of heaven it focuses upon the Lamb standing in the midst of the throne as it had been slain. When the Epistle to the Hebrews lifts our hearts in worship it centers them upon the High Priest of our profession who has passed through the heavens and ever liveth to make intercession for us at the Throne of Grace. And when the Word speaks of Christ as the sacrificial Lamb and the enthroned Priest, the faith to which the Gospel summons us hastens to take shelter under the covert of His sacrifice and the shield of His intercession.

Since the true Sanctuary is on high, on high is both the altar of sacrifice on which the blood of the Lamb slain from the foundation of the world has made propitiation for the world; and on high is the altar of incense where the heavenly High Priest mingles the fragrance of His intercession with the feeble and unworthy tribute of our thanksgiving and intercession so that they become an acceptable worship. And more than any sending up of our worship to heaven, God sheds down the light of His grace, mercy and peace from this heavenly sanctuary into the needy, the torn, the bleeding hearts of earth. The Church on earth is only properly the Church of God in Christ as she catches this healing light that filters down from Mount Zion which is above. And she does this by directing the hearts of her worshippers not to some "sacred" spot in an earthly sanctuary, but to the Lamb in the midst of the Throne—to the High Priest ministering in the heavenly Sanctuary.

It may well be that more of the beautiful Scriptural forms should be introduced into our liturgy, such as the Lord's Prayer, the Creed, a call to worship and a thankful dedication from the Psalter, a salutation from the Epistles, a prayer and an ascription after the sermon based on Ephesians 3:14-21, the recitation of Psalms of comfort and strength, a confession and assurance of absolution. But any acts of worship which only succeed in directing attention to themselves have miserably failed in their true end. Nothing aids worship that does not lift the soul to the Throne of God and of the Lamb. If we fancy that the aesthetic cleverness of our worship can supplant or supplement the righteousness of Christ—the sole ground of a sinner's acceptance with God— we are exchanging the lightning of Heaven for a slow combustion stove.

A religious masterpiece is one thing, the obedience of Christian faith is another thing. The first purpose for which the Westminster Assembly was called was to secure a Scriptural worship; and our Confession, Catechisms and Book of Church Order all declare that God has revealed in His Word all things necessary for His worship, and has commanded that nothing be added thereto. The desire for a religious masterpiece may invite men to erect an altar on earth with a picture and candles upon it as the focal center for worship. The obedience of Christian faith remembers that the Sanctuary which God pitched is in heaven where the High Priest of our profession ministers at the heavenly altar and that God has said, "Thou shalt not make unto thee any likeness of anything in heaven or on earth, thou shalt not bow down thyself to them nor worship them."

When the Reformation was lifting high the banners of the Word, the Reformers of Switzerland and of Scotland removed an earthly altar, a mediating priesthood and a sacrifice of the mass to make way for the table of the Lord, a Gospel ministry and a holy supper. The Scottish covenants condemned as a Romish error the consecration of altars. Zwingli, Calvin and Knox were concerned that no earthly trappings should deflect attention from the heavenly sanctuary where the sacrificial Lamb stands in the midst of the Throne of Grace, where the High Priest ever liveth to make intercession for us, where the Prophet like unto Moses reveals to us the will of God for our salvation, where the King of kings and Lord of lords rules over and defends us from all His and our enemies. As the Holy Spirit lifts our hearts to the worship center which God has erected, the Faithful Witness reveals to us the saving grace of God, and the heavenly High Priest ministers the mercy of His forgiving merit and offers His perfect intercession with the incense of our prayers, and the Prince over the Kings of earth takes us and our loved ones beneath the shelter of His loving wings.

Moreover, the worship of the New Testament is moving toward the Kingdom of Glory which is to be established in the New Heavens and the New Earth. The Holy City which comes down from God out of heaven has no temple, for the Lord God Almighty and the Lamb are the Temple of it. The New Jerusalem has no need of the sun neither of the moon to shine in it, for the glory of God doth lighten it and the Lamb is the light thereof. And there shall be no more curse, but the Throne of God and of the Lamb shall be in it. And His servants shall worship Him and they shall see His face and His Name shall be upon their foreheads—His own best name of gracious love.

20. OUR SOUTHERN PRESBYTERIAN BANNERS[1]

"In the Name of our God we will set up our banners."— Psa. 20:5

"Thou hast given a banner to them that fear Thee, that it may be displayed because of the truth."—Psa. 60:4

When Scottish Presbyterianism was threatened by Stuart totalitarianism the leaders of the Church renewed the Covenant, signing that hallowed document with blood drawn from their own veins. Recalling General Leslie from his service under Gustavus Adolphus, they marshaled an army to maintain their covenanted faith. As the blue stocking host gathered, flying before each captain's tent was a blue banner with this inscription, "For Christ's Crown and Covenant."

When Hampden C. Dubose returned from the Confederate War he found that the fathers had fallen asleep, that the generation of young men who had escaped the sword had missed a college education, that the theological seminaries were closed, that the colleges had lost their endowments, that few were left to lead in public prayer and that the songs of Zion were being sung by mourning women. But through the sorrows of war and the humiliation of Reconstruction, our Church was rich in God. The fathers had lifted their banners in God and the living God in whom they trusted did not forsake them.

In another hour of need, we are seeking to wave the banners which our heroic fathers lifted in the name of God. Under these banners there have come to our people blessing and increase, power and strength. The God of our fathers is equally potent today. He is the

[1] WCR, *Presbyterian Journal*, May 1942, 5-6.

all-sufficient God, all-sufficient for Himself and all-sufficient for His people. May His Spirit give us strength to keep these banners waving from every Southern Presbyterian Bethel, every place in which He hath caused His Name to dwell: the blue banner of covenanted loyalty to Christ as the only King in Zion, the only Head of His body the Church; the banner of His holy Word; the banner of the Westminster Standards which testify to His saving grace and sovereign glory; the banner of missions as the mission of the Church.

The Redeemer is the only King of Zion, the only Head over His Body the Church.

Alexander Henderson used Psalm 110:1 to set forth the truth that God had placed Christ at His own right hand to govern His Church. The Church is subject to Christ alone not to Caesar. As Benjamin Morgan Palmer declared at Augusta in 1861, God hath given Christ to be Head over all things to His body the Church. I owe allegiance as a citizen to the country and as a believer to the Church. God has established two governments—Church and State—but neither of these is subject to the other, while I am subject to both and God is over both.

The Church recognizes the Headship of Christ when she accepts the system of doctrine, government, discipline and worship which He has given her in His Word and obeys His command to add nothing thereto. Likewise when she confines her activities to the functions He has commissioned her to perform. God has not given to the Church the police functions of the magistrate, but the preaching of His Word, the enforcement of His law, the gathering and perfecting of His saints. The Headship of Christ is recognized in the acceptance of the sufficiency of the written Word, the architectonic principle of the Scottish Covenants. The Church is God's servant proclaiming His revealed will, not His confidential adviser presuming to supplement that Word in either worship, discipline or doctrine. The Headship of Christ is recognized in trying to govern the Church according to the pattern shown in the Mount of Scripture.

Presbyterianism is a system of church government by courts composed of elders (the presbyters of Scripture) called of God through the suffrage of His people. These courts are organized to represent the unity of the Church and to maintain the authority of Christ speaking in His Word. The Presbyterian officers receive their call, their authority, their gifts from Christ (*Eph.* 4).

The Bible is the Word of God written, the scepter of the King, the mouth of the Lord, the rule of faith, life and worship.

The fathers of the Southern Presbyterian Church maintained the infallible truth and Divine authority of the Holy Scripture in distinction from those critical views which deny that the Bible is what it professes to be and what our Lord Jesus Christ declares it to be. Our Church has had its part in making the South the Bible belt. In His infinite wisdom God has given this Book to be a lamp unto our feet, and where its light illumines the way, the freedoms of mankind flourish.

The very architecture of our Presbyterian Churches has testified that we have sought to be the Church of the Word. According to the Reformed Faith, the New Testament altar is in heaven where the great High Priest ministers, and that from this heavenly fount the blessings of the covenant of grace are dispensed by means of the pulpit where the Word is preached and the Table where the Lord's Supper is spread.

The Holy Spirit is the author of saving faith in Christ and in working faith He uses the instrument of His own forging, namely, the Word He hath inspired. It pleases God by the foolishness of preaching to save, so that faith cometh by hearing and hearing by the Word of Christ. Thus, "faith has a perpetual relation to the Word, and can no more be separated from it than the rays from the sun whence they proceed."

As the Apostle repeatedly called his readers to observe the pattern of doctrine delivered to them, so our fathers at their First General Assembly adopted the Westminster Confession and Catechisms as their confession of the living God.

Our standards recognize a God who is infinite in majesty and eternal in love, a sovereign Father and a fatherly Sovereign. They echo the Saviour's "Father, Lord of heaven and earth." The consistent

Calvinism of these standards is a vision of God in His majesty, of the King in His beauty and a consequent sense of our utter dependence upon Him. We depend upon God for truth and in the obedience of faith receive what He has revealed in His Word. We depend upon God for life and history as we state in the doctrines of foreordination, creation and providence. We depend upon God for religion, not seeking to construct human religious masterpieces, but worshiping the God who has graciously revealed Himself to Christian faith. Justification by faith alone means that we depend wholly upon the work of Christ for acceptance with God, that He is our Righteousness and that the Holy Spirit hath enabled us to receive and rest upon Him alone for salvation.

Our Confession sees God, the Father, first in creation; God, the Son, first in redemption; and God, the Spirit, first in regeneration; and seeks to give God all the glory of the whole saving process. In words that future events have proven prophetic Professor A. Lecerf of the theological faculty of the University of Paris brought this testimony from a Lutheran colleague to the Edinburgh Calvinistic Congress: "Our people need doctrine, a strong doctrine. I think God has something in store for His Church, something very dreadful. And because God knows that His Church needs a backbone, He is bringing her back to Calvinism which is the backbone of Christianity."

In immediate connection with the headship of Christ, our first General Assembly wrote upon our banner the Great Commission.

"Go ye into all the world and preach the Gospel to every creature" is the great end of our Church's organization and obedience to it is the indispensable condition of our Lord's promised blessing. Missions is the one grand comprehensive object a proper conception of whose vast magnitude and grandeur is the only thing which in connection with the love of Christ can ever sufficiently arouse the Church's energies and develop her resources, so as to cause her to carry on with the vigor and efficiency which true loyalty to her Lord demands those other agencies necessary to her internal growth and efficiency. The Southern Presbyterian Church is a missionary society and every member is a member for life of that society.

God has so blessed this banner lifted first by a Church hemmed in by hostile armies that today we have more members on the foreign field than we had when we started in the home field. And though many of our missionaries have had to leave under the pressure of Japanese conquest, the seed has been sown and the harvest is certain. It is interesting to notice that our three ministers who have done the most noteworthy social service have been men who most emphatically maintained that missions was the mission of the Church. While they were loyally preaching the Gospel in season and out of season, God gave to Hampden C. Dubose the added privilege of sharing largely in the suppression of the opium traffic, to J. Leighton Wilson to contribute the decisive article which stopped the African slave trade, and to Benjamin Morgan Palmer to deliver the eloquent civic address which crushed the Louisiana lottery. As these fathers of the Southern Presbyterian Church administered in the Church the task which the Founder laid upon the Church, God gave them the added privilege of accomplishing noteworthy things as citizens. They did not confuse the two distinct spheres in which men ought to serve the one God.

As my distinguished predecessor, Dr. R. C. Reed, well said, "the Church is an institution that did not originate in the will of man and that does not exist to further ends determined by the will and wisdom of men." "Its mission is to promote the glory of God and the salvation of men from the curse of the law." "The Church is an organization of which Christ is the Head and King, it can speak only what He has commissioned it to speak."

May the God of all grace give our feeble hands strength to hold aloft the mighty banners which the Fathers of the Southern Presbyterian Church lifted in the Name of our God!

21. GOD OF THE MARCHING CENTURIES[1]

God in History

In this centennial year (1961) of the Presbyterian Church, US, we unite our witness with the good confession our fathers have made to our great and gracious God. Our word today is EBENEZER! Hitherto the LORD in His mercy has led us. Thanks be unto God who has revealed Himself unto us in Jesus Christ, who has deposited this treasure in the clay vessels of our founding fathers, and kept this heritage alive in the yet more earthen vessels of us, their spiritual heirs. We come to join our celebration with that of the ancient Hebrews, when being delivered from Pharaoh at the Red Sea they cried,

> This is my God, and I will praise Him;
> My father's God, and I will exalt Him (*Exod.* 15:2).

Or, as one of our former pastors, Dr. D. P. McGeachy of Decatur, put it:

> God of the marching centuries,
>   Lord of the passing years,
> Leading a people's victories,
>   Sharing a people's tears,
> Seal us, as now we worship Thee
>   Here on this moment's height;
> Star of the way our fathers found,
>   Be still our guiding light.

The Biblical faith anchors in the living God, the God who has done mighty acts, who is active today, and who governs the future for

[1] WCR, *Presbyterian Journal,* October 18, 1961, 5-6, 8, 18.

His people in Christ Jesus. Ancient Israel laid hold of the God who made heaven and earth and who redeemed His people from Egypt with a mighty hand and an outstretched arm. Their confidence was in the God of the covenant, the shield of Abraham, the fear of Isaac, the Mighty One of Jacob.

In Luke 11:51, as in Hebrews 11, we seem to have sections of an old Hebrew Creed memorializing God's deliverances of His patriarchs and prophets. The writer to the Hebrews surrounds his tempted friends with this cloud of Old Testament witnesses and then adds those who had spoken unto them the Word of God and suffered as martyrs for Jesus under Nero—James, Peter, and Paul. In the crypt of Domitilla, a part of the Catacombs of Rome, there are pictures from the Old and New Testaments bespeaking the victorious power of God as He saved David from Goliath, gave perishing Israel the water from the rock, delivered Daniel from the lions and raised Lazarus from the grave. That is, the primitive Christians lived surrounded by the witness of the Old and the New Testament martyrs to the triumphs of the living God.

Out of that atmosphere comes the ancient Christian symbol which we now call the Apostles' Creed. God is the Father Almighty who created heaven and earth, and His gracious acts are all concentrated in the coming, the ministry, the death, the resurrection, the reign, and the return of our Lord Jesus Christ, whose saving work is carried forward by the Holy Ghost in the Church.

God in Redemption

True to their spiritual heritage, our fathers kept Jesus Christ at the center of their interest. They proclaimed the living God who did act in Jesus Christ, acted in His cross and resurrection to change the whole relationship between the Holy God and guilty sinners. In Christ He reconciled the world unto Himself. To this great new victory which God won in Christ, the Presbyterian Church, US, has, for a century, borne her testimony.

In 1897 Robert Lewis Dabney delivered his final addresses at Davidson College and Columbia Seminary on the theme: "Christ our substitute and sacrifice for imputed guilt." That is, the fundamental design of Christ's obedience and sacrifice is to make satisfaction to the justice of God, so that God may be just and the justifier of the ungodly who believe in Jesus. He suffered that sin might be righteously punished and the sinner forgiven. Earlier Thornwell proclaimed:

> Jesus made our curse, Jesus made our righteousness, this, this is the Gospel! All else is philosophy and vain deceit. A penal death and a perfect righteousness imputed, the one for pardon and the other for acceptance—these are the things which make the Gospel glad tidings of great joy.

The spiritual heirs of Dabney and Thornwell continued to enunciate this world-shaking deed of God until the 1939 General Assembly unanimously declared that acceptance of the doctrine that Christ offered up Himself a sacrifice to satisfy Divine justice and reconcile us to God is involved, among other things, in our ordination vows.

Of course this does not mean that there are not other facets to the ineffable wonder of Christ's work for us. That He has victoriously vindicated the justice of God even in forgiveness is the assurance of Christ's triumph over legalism, sin, Satan, death and Hell. Preachers like Gregory the Great and Martin Luther proclaimed both the "Latin" and the "classical" view of the atonement. In Christ's offering of Himself in our stead, Thornwell sees the supreme act of worship and the beautiful spirit of the true priest. For Thomas Smyth, the background of the atoning work of Christ was the justice of God, but the foreground of the picture—the place where his preaching delighted to dwell—was the love of the Lord.

Daniel Baker bade his son remember that "the sermon which does not distinctly present Christ in the beauty and glory of His mediatorial character, is no better than a cloud without water, a casket without a jewel, a shadow without the substance, or the body without the soul. You ask why my preaching is so much blessed ... My plan is incessantly to preach Christ and Him crucified."

God in Justification

On the day of Pentecost the disciples were vibrant in their testimony to the mighty acts of God in Christ. And foremost among all those acts was the unapproachable manifestation of God's power in the raising of Jesus Christ from the dead on the third day. God acted in visiting upon Christ our substitute the whole guilt of our sins; and He died crying that the whole debt is paid, "It is finished!" Then God raised Him from the dead in the blessedness of pure righteousness. In raising from the dead our representative, Jesus Christ, God implicitly justified His body in Him their head. Moreover, the ascended, reigning, living Christ is busy making this potential justification actual in regenerating those whom He has redeemed; and in calling them to faith and repentance through the preaching of His Word. Today we speak of Christ proclaiming Himself through Christian preaching, confronting men—and bringing them to decision. Our fathers were equally conscious of Christ's direct action by His Spirit working faith in their hearts and uniting sinners to Himself in their effectual calling. Indeed, their glorious emphasis on justification may well give a content to God's encounter with men that is sometimes lacking in our preaching.

As a student at the College of South Carolina, James Henley Thornwell picked up a copy of the *Westminster Confession of Faith* in a second-hand book store and found the organizing principle of this great book and of all theology in the Reformation doctrine of Justification.

For R. A. Webb of Louisville, "There is no more important doctrine, no more distinguished blessing, in all the Christian system than justification." For Dr. Wm. S. Plumer, Pastor of the First Church of Richmond and later Professor in Columbia Seminary, "Justification by Christ's imputed righteousness is the centre arch of that bridge by which we pass out of time into a blessed eternity."

In his class instruction at Columbia and later at Louisville Seminary, Thornton Whaling was never tired of reiterating that Christ's bearing our sins in His own body on the tree closed for us the gates of Hell. But the sinner needs not only his guilt imputed to Christ and done away in His Cross; in addition to having his debts paid, he needs a positive righteousness that he may have access to Heaven. Now as our sins were laid upon Christ and all their fearful punishment endured in His cross, so also was His whole holy obedience imputed to us. By the one the doors of Hell were closed, by the other the gates of Heaven were opened. And all this is the work of grace through faith.

God in Reviving Grace

At Pentecost the immediate reference to the mighty acts of God was the coming of the Holy Spirit. This centennial year is the time to remember that God has visited and does visit His people with seasons of saving grace bringing "revivals in the midst of the years." He does not always speak in the whirlwind or the tempest, but with a still small voice as the Spirit uses the Word for the conversion of sinners and the edification of the saints.

Two centuries ago, as our American tradition was being formed, God led the Presbyterians to share in the Great Awakening when the Spirit mightily used the preaching of Jonathan Edwards, George Whitefield, Freylinghuysen, the Tennants, Samuel Davies and Devereaux Jaratt. Despite the fanfare and cavalcades for evangelism, this last year saw the lowest increase on professions of faith in five years, the greatest number of losses, and the lowest net gain. These shocking statistics ought to send us to our knees that we may know God's way with His people today. Perhaps, there is a word for this year in the account of the revival God granted through John L. Girardeau's ministry in the Anson St. Presbyterian Church of Charleston where nine-tenths of the five hundred members were Negroes.

The greatest event in his ministry was the revival in the later eighteen fifties. This began with a prayer meeting that constantly increased until the house was filled. Some of the officers of the Church wanted him to commence preaching services, but he steadily refused, waiting for the outpouring of the Spirit. His view was that the Father had given to Jesus, as King and Head of the Church, the gift of the Holy Spirit, and that Jesus in His sovereign administration of the affairs of His Church, bestowed Him upon whomsoever He pleased, and in whatever measure He pleased. Day after day, therefore, he kept his prayer addressed directly to the mediatorial throne for the Holy Spirit in mighty reviving power.

One evening, while leading the people in prayer, he received a sensation as if a bolt of electricity had struck his head and diffused itself through his whole body. For a little while he stood speechless under the strange physical feeling, then he said: "The Holy Spirit has come; we will begin preaching tomorrow evening." He closed the service with a hymn dismissing the congregation, and came down from the pulpit, but no one left the house. The whole congregation had quietly resumed its seat. Instantly he realized the situation. The Holy Spirit had not only come to him—He had also taken possession of the hearts of the people.

Immediately he began exhorting them to accept the Gospel. They began to sob softly, like the falling of rain, then with deeper emotion to weep bitterly, or to rejoice loudly, according to their circumstances. It was midnight before he could dismiss his congregation. A noted evangelist from the North, who was present, said, between his sobs, to an officer of the Church: "I never saw it on this fashion." The meeting went on night and day for eight weeks. Large numbers of both black and white were converted and joined the various churches of the city. His own was wonderfully built up, not only in numbers, but also in an experience that remained in the Church. It is in such events that "Our God is marching on."

God in World Missions

As God has blessed His people with seasons of grace when the Holy Spirit was particularly close and powerful in their hearts, so He has led us into new appropriations of His marching orders for His body the Church. In 1831, John Holt Rice of Virginia, challenged the General Assembly to recognize that the Presbyterian Church is a missionary society the object of which is the conversion of the world, and that every member of the Church is a member for life of the said society.

In 1861 the General Assembly inscribed on the Church's banner as she first unfurled it to the world the Great Commission. And despite Southern poverty, every year of Reconstruction saw a new world mission opened: China, Italy, Brazil, Colombia—later the Congo, Japan, Korea, Mexico, Ecuador, Portugal, Iraq, Formosa. The fruit of these endeavors was evident at the 1961 General Assembly in the testimonies of fraternal delegates from most of these countries. What has been done adds its weight to the mission call:

> Where once the twisting trail in darkness wound
>   Let marching feet and joyous song respond.
> Where burn the fun'ral pyres and censors swing,
>   Make straight, make straight the Highway of the King.

Now unto Him who loves us, who redeemed us from our sins by His blood; and made us to be a kingdom, priests unto His God and Father, to Him be the glory and the dominion for ever and ever, Amen.

22. THE PLACE OF JESUS CHRIST
IN CHRISTIAN FAITH[1]

THE only message which is the power of God unto salvation is the Gospel of God. This means, of course, that we have the "audacity" to place our Lord Jesus Christ and the Gospel of which He is the theme in a different category from the best thought of the age. It means that we recognize the Bible's Christ and Christ's Bible as being each *sui generis* the Word of God. Christ is not merely a way; He is *the* way and His Word is *the* truth. "In distinction from all other forms of religion the Christian religion is faith in the one Mediator … For faith in the Mediator—in the event which took place once for all, a revealed atonement—is the Christian religion itself."[2]

From the very beginning Jesus has "had a place assigned to Him by Christian faith which is distinct in kind from that assigned to other men; He has been believed to be, both to God and to the human race, what no other is or can be." "He was and is to both God and man who no other can be," so that "all divine and human relations are determined by Him."[3]

We give to our Lord this unrivalled place because we find that this is just the place which He assumed for Himself and the place His authorized apostles gave to Him: "No man knoweth the Father, save the Son and he to whom the Son will reveal Him." "No man cometh unto the Father, but by Me." "I am the way, the truth, and the life." "He that believeth on the Son hath everlasting life: and he that believeth not the Son shall not see life." "I am the living bread which

[1] WCR, *Our Lord—An Affirmation of the Deity of Christ*, 173-83.
[2] Brunner, *The Mediator*, p. 40.
[3] Denney, *Jesus and the Gospel*, pp. 143-144, 151.

came down from heaven: if any man eat of this bread he shall live forever: and the bread which I will give is My flesh which I will give for
the life of the world." "I am the door: by Me if any man enter in he
shall be saved." "The Son of man came not to be ministered unto, but
to minister and to give His life a ransom for many." "Neither is there
salvation in any other: for there is none other name under heaven
given among men, whereby we must be saved." "There is one God,
and one mediator between God and man, the man Christ Jesus."
"How shall we escape, if we neglect so great salvation; which at the
first began to be spoken by the Lord." "And the Lamb shall overcome
them: for He is Lord of lords and King of kings."

The New Testament frankly maintains the conquest, or if you
please, the imperial concept. "The intention to conquer is characteristic of the Gospel. This was the aim of its youth when it went
forth among the religions that then surrounded it, and with this aim
it must enter any field in which old religions are encumbering the
religious nature of man. It cannot conquer except in love, but in love
it intends to conquer."[1] This concept grows out of the very essence of
the Christian faith as being the only saving Word of God, a message
which makes all the difference between life and death. And it is only
when the distinctiveness and exclusiveness of the Christian religion
have been allowed to fade to a certain extent out of men's minds and
the compulsive attraction of the Christian faith is less felt that syn-
thesis is consciously possible.

Missions and the Christian Heart

The expulsive power of a new affection is realized in all its potency
when the guilty soul sees that the love of Christ has snatched it from
the gates of hell by the shedding of His own precious blood. When
the native witness of the heart is "He is the propitiation for our sins,"
the immediate inference is "and not for ours only, but also for the sins
of the whole world." The love of Christ constraineth us to judge "that
if one died for all, then were all dead, and He died for all, that they
which live should not henceforth live unto themselves, but unto Him
which died and rose again." Yea, the love of Christ constrains the

---

[1] Clark, Wm. N., quoted by Speer, R. E., *The Finality of Jesus Christ*.

truly apostolic heart to reckon itself the bond slave of the Lord and His debtor to carry His Gospel to the Jew and to the Gentile. When Christ enters lives that had been seared with sin, and cities that had been neglected in the ministrations of God's truth, the response from saved hearts is "This is indeed the Saviour of the world."

The love which saves us is the love of the Father who withheld not His only-begotten Son, but sent Him to be the propitiation for the sins of the world, and the love of the Son who loosed us from our sins by His own blood. That love constrains us to lay down our lives that others may know this glorious Gospel of the laying down of His life. Hence the history of Christianity has been a history of great hearts yearning for and marching into the regions beyond. This love carried Alopen to China, Patrick to those who had previously enslaved him, Boniface to the forest of Germany, Peter Waldo to the poor of Europe. It overflows in these words of Francis of Assisi, "May the glowing and mellifluous power of Thy love, absorb, I pray, O Lord, my mind from all things which are under heaven, that I may die from love of Thy love, who has deigned to die for love of my love." And in the midst of that holocaust, misnamed the Crusades, it shines from the life and in the sentiment of Raymond Lull, missionary to the Turks, "He who loves not, lives not; he who lives by the life cannot die."

With the recovery of the Bible the world vision leaped from the Scotch Confession of 1560, "This glad tidings of the kingdom shall be preached through the whole world for a witness to the nations." God put into the heart of John Eliot a compassion for the souls of the Indians and a desire to teach them to know Christ and bring them into His Kingdom. And Eliot's remarkable ministry proved his motto, "Prayer and pains through faith in Jesus Christ will do anything." David Brainerd took up the torch crying, "O that I could be a flame of fire in the service of my God."

A German nobleman meditated on the wounds of Christ until his heart responded, "I have but one passion, it is He," and Zinzendorf organized the Moravians under the single aim, "Our unwearied labor shall go through the whole world that we may win hearts for Him who gave His life for our souls." The Moravian Church today boasts three times as many members in the foreign as in the home field: while its service in leading Wesley from the Arminian work-righteousness to Luther's great doctrine of justification can never be forgotten.

A consecrated cobbler in England, a group of college boys who gathered about a haystack to pray in America awakened the hearts of the English-speaking peoples. In the South, J. L. Merrick reminded us that, "The motive which led the Redeemer to leave His home in the highest heavens, and to journey far down to this ruined world was no other than that powerful spring of action, which has acquired the name Missionary Spirit … It is nothing but the pure religion of the Gospel, in its most amiable and active forms."

Speaking before the General Assembly of the Old School Presbyterian Church meeting in New York, James H. Thornwell took up the refrain, "It has grown into a proverb that the spirit of missions is the spirit of the Gospel." As made priests by Christ, "we must be animated by the same principles which pervaded His offering. Zeal for the Divine glory, love to God, and compassion to men should stir our souls and move our feet." "When a world says, Come, and pleads its miseries; when God says, Go, and pleads His glory, and Christ repeats the command, and points to His hands and His feet and His side—it is enough to make the stone cry out of the wall and the beam out of the timber to answer it."

Why world missions? When Sam Lapsley was studying at the McCormick Theological Seminary, his classmates came to him and urged him to give up his plan to be a missionary. They assured him that his gifts would carry him to places of high honor and prestige in America. To their appeals at first he said nothing; but when a second night they plied him for an answer, the young Alabaman replied, "You have asked why I insist on going as a missionary. Here is my answer: I am going to Africa because of the nail prints in the hands and the feet and the spear thrust in the side of my Saviour."

Missions and the Christian Mind

The Great Commission (*Matt.* 28:18-20) also speaks to the Christian reason or common sense. Jesus began the great commission with a statement of His own position: "All authority hath been given unto

Me in heaven and on earth." Jesus' authority extends to the farthest corner of this earth. Mission dollars and mission loved ones can never go where He does not rule. Beyond earth He numbers the stars of the heaven, ordering their courses, while angels worship Him, and do His bidding.

More than that, Jesus puts Himself into the center of the Name of the living God. In the Old Testament the Name of God was just God revealed. The Hebrew thought of "Name" not as an external symbol, but as the adequate expression of the innermost being of the bearer. We read of "this glorious and fearful name, Jehovah thy God" (*Deut.* 28:58); that "behold the name of Jehovah cometh" (*Isa.* 30:27). The Old Testament vision of missions is, "So shall they fear the Name of Jehovah from the west and His glory from the rising of the sun" (*Isa.* 59:19). In the hour of their need the Hebrew saints cried that the Name of Jehovah had been named upon them. For the Christian community Jesus gave a new name for Jehovah, that is "the Name of the Father and of the Son and of the Holy Ghost." In the heart of this Name of the living God sounds the trinitarian Name of our Lord, "the Son."

Again, in the Commission Jesus authorizes His precepts to be taught to the ends of the earth and to the consummation of the age. Heaven and earth shall pass away but His words shall not pass away. No clime and no age will find them obsolete. His words are eternal truth, they will never need revision. They are the final truth of earth and heaven. And with His words Jesus promises His own presence. His is a presence that reaches across time and space to accompany every one of His disciples as scattered to earth's remotest bounds they severally obey His missionary orders. Only He who is God can be the final and ultimate revelation of God, everywhere present with those who teach His commandments.

In other words, the "marching orders" are preceded, interpenetrated, and followed by manifold affirmations of our Lord's own glory. And this is just the matter which calls for a reasoned consideration. Is it reasonable to believe that the all-powerful Lord of heaven came to earth on a mission smaller than the world? Can one reasonably believe that the second person of the Triune Jehovah came to this planet to be merely the Saviour of the Nordic peoples? The glory which our Lord Jesus ascribes to Himself in the great commission compels us to recognize that He came to save the world. "The outbreak of missionary thought has as its correlative the redemptive Lordship of Christ in all the world." One cannot believe that Jesus is the eternal Divine Person the Great Commission represents Him as being and claim for Him anything less than the world. The Lord Jehovah who created Betelgeuse and marshalleth the spiral nebulae did not come to this planet merely to occupy a niche in a pantheon along with Buddha, Confucius, Mohammed, and Miki.

And if a reader is tempted to furl the colors of the Lord of Glory, may the writer venture a personal word? If you deny the Lord that bought you, you at the same time forfeit the salvation He purchased for you with His own precious blood. You and I are sinners, great sinners. Sin is against the great God of heaven and earth. It is an infinite evil. Only the blood of an infinite Redeemer can pay our awful demerit of guilt. Only the Lord Himself hath power to lift us from the pit of sin's pollution into His own pure likeness. Give up the infinite Saviour, the Lord of glory, and you sink into that eternal perdition from which He alone can save you. Paul said that if righteousness could come even from the law of Moses then Christ died for naught. A Jesus small enough to march shoulder to shoulder with Lao-Tsze could never save your soul from Hell. It takes an infinite Jesus to save my sinful soul and your sinful soul; but an infinite Saviour will not be less than the Saviour of the world. Even common sense, then, demands that the Christian continue to proclaim Christ for the world. It is not reasonable to claim less than the world for the One who is infinite and who must needs be infinite to redeem one soul—my soul, or your soul—from the infinite demerit of its sin. Thus, a consideration of facts of such importance that a reasonable being has no right to neglect them gives the dilemma: *either* give up the salvation of your own soul, give up an infinite Saviour, *or* hold on to the Christian evangelization of the world. For, "the measure of a man's interest in foreign missions is an expression of his valuation of Christ."

It is not Christian common sense for me, a minister of the Gospel, to become so engrossed in the acquisition of learning or so absorbed in the application of principles to society, as to forget that I am the sinner for whom Christ died. Perhaps a story that the late Wm. M. McPheeters enjoyed telling on himself will illustrate the point. It occurred when he was a young professor in Columbia Theological Seminary. At a faculty gathering someone raised the question, "What would you be, if you were not a Christian?" The young professor ventured to suggest, "If I were not a Christian, I think that I would be a pantheist." "If you were not a Christian, my young brother," answered J. L. Girardeau, "you would be a lost sinner."

During a recent outbreak of anti-foreign nationalism in China, when the lives of many missionaries were endangered, Dr. Donald Richardson was fired upon. On his arrival in America, he told the Synod of South Carolina that he was not willing to return to China merely to teach the Chinese a new philosophy, they already had many philosophies: that he would not go back just to inculcate a system of ethics, there were numerous ethical systems in the Orient; but that he coveted the privilege of going back to tell those who had sought his life:

> There is a fountain filled with blood
> Drawn from Emmanuel's veins,
> And sinners plunged beneath that flood
> Lose all their guilty stains.

The infinite Saviour is the only Saviour for the preacher, for his American congregation, and for China's perishing millions. There is no salvation in socialism, or Buddhism, in Hinduism, nationalism, or internationalism, in idealism, Confucianism, or secular prosperity. "He that believeth on the Son hath eternal life; he that obeyeth not the Son shall not see life, but the wrath of God abideth on him."

Whenever those who receive this Saviour think out the implications of their salvation, as John and Paul have done under the inspiration of the Holy Spirit, or as Calvin, Kuyper, and Hepp[1] have done under the guidance of Holy Writ, they realize that "this is indeed the Saviour of the world" and "the Lord of all." It is not enough to say,

> God has other words for other worlds,
> But Christ is the Word of God for this world.

[1] Calvin, *Institutes of the Christian Religion;* Kuyper, *Calvinism;* Hepp, *Calvinism and the Philosophy of Nature.*

Rather, "All things have been created through Him, and unto Him, and He is before all things, and in Him all things hold together." "All things were made through Him, and apart from Him was not anything made that hath been made." For, "In the beginning the Word was, and the Word was in abiding fellowship with God, and the Word was God" (*Col.* 1:16-17; *John* 1:1-2). He who satisfied the infinite guilt of my sin is an infinite Saviour, the Sovereign Jehovah, in His immeasurable grace fulfilling His promise to visit and redeem His people.

Missions and the Christian Conscience

Moreover, it has gradually dawned upon the Christian Church that missions are not only a matter of heart and reason, but of conscience. This ought, at any rate, to be clear to the Calvinistic Churches. We profess to believe in the sovereignty of God. Our sovereign Lord hath commissioned us to carry His message to the ends of the earth. His Divine authority is our right to preach salvation everywhere. We have our marching orders, our credentials stamped by the Lord of Glory, we do not need them re-stamped by any laymen's committee.[1] On His authority we proclaim repentance and remission of sins at home and abroad. In His name we invite men to turn from sin to God, to believe on the Lord Jesus Christ that they may be saved. At the same time we repeat His solemn warnings to those that refuse the cup of salvation drawn from His expiatory death.

God wills missions! Among those who accept the Scriptures as God's special revelation there can be no ground for doubting this assertion. But what a mighty forward step would ensue if the Church simply realized its truth. When Pope Urban II addressed the Council at Clermont, November 1095, on the situation in the Holy Land and urged a crusade to save it from the Moslems, the chivalry of Christendom responded, *Deus Vult!* This cry, *God wills it,* loosened Europe from its foundations and for two centuries hurled it upon Asia. One of our Lord's most solemn and final commands is, "Go

---

[1] The Laymen's Foreign Missions Inquiry conducted a reappraisal of the mission motives and methods of American Protestant missionary work. It resulted in a report published in 1932 as *Rethinking Missions*.

ye into all the world and make disciples of all nations." And His solemn warning is, "Not everyone that saith unto Me, Lord, Lord, shall enter into the Kingdom, but he that doeth the will of My Father which is in Heaven." "Missions is the mission of the Church." When the Southern Presbyterian Church was organized eighty-five years ago, she properly inscribed the Great Commission on her banner in immediate connection with the Headship of Christ, regarding this as the great end of her organization and the indispensable condition of her Lord's promised blessing.

More than a century ago John Holt Rice faced the American Presbyterian Church with a challenge to declare that: "The Presbyterian Church in the United States is a missionary society, the object of which is to aid in the conversion of the world, and every member of the Church is a member for life of the said society and bound, in maintenance of his Christian character, to do all in his power for the accomplishment of this object." Just a century ago, the Synod of South Carolina and Georgia declared: "The Church, by the very elements of her Constitution, is a missionary society, that it is enjoined upon her as a duty to impart to others the blessings which she has herself received, that the great Head of the Church has constituted her the appropriate channel through which the light of the Gospel is to be offered among the nations, and that her organization is such as to embody her strength and call forth her resources and bring them to bear to the best advantage upon the world's conversion to God." And, if the reader from another section will allow another bit of local history, it is just a century ago now that the body of Mary Jane Smithey Wilson, from the First Presbyterian Church of Richmond, Virginia, has slept under a syringa bush in the Transvaal, near Johannesburg, South Africa; while for almost as long a period the body of her husband, Alexander Erwin Wilson of North Carolina, has slept in West Africa. These missionary proto-martyrs and those that have followed in their train, remind us that missions is the will of our Lord.

The purpose of this chapter is not to elaborate all the functions of the Church; but to insist that, however much difference of opinion there may be as to whether certain other things are or are not the function of the Church, there can be no question but that our

Lord hath laid this tremendous task upon His Church. When men are inclined to shift the emphasis to the more tangible and visible social problems, the Southern Presbyterian remembers that it was just the men who sought most to maintain the sole Headship of Christ and obey His missionary commission that the Head of the Church rewarded, not only with precious souls, but also with noteworthy accomplishments in the fields of social service, for example, J. Leighton Wilson in the suppression of the African slave traffic, B. M. Palmer, Jr., with the cessation of the Louisiana lottery, and Hampden C. DuBose with the prohibition of the Chinese opium trade. An interesting recent comment to a similar effect is the testimony of Gabriel Mistral, the Chilean poetess, "My passion for the Bible is perhaps the only bridge that unites me to the Anglo-Saxon race, the piece of common soil on which I find myself at home with this race … Only in the word of God do we meet and enjoy a common emotion; the rest is pure tragedy in difference."[1] The Church that seeks to do her Lord's will because it is His will, finds in the doing thereof many fair flowers, by-products of missions, beautifying her path. But the Church which turns from her Lord's will merely to cultivate such flowers as appeal to her tastes will miss the most beautiful flowers of earth and the brighter joys of fellowship in Heaven with souls from many lands which she has reached with His Gospel.

This is written with the special hope and prayer that God, the Holy Spirit, may be pleased to bless the present Presbyterian Church in the United States with an increasing measure of the faith which characterized the organizers of that communion, faith in the Holy Scriptures, as God's unique and sufficient rule of faith and life, in the Westminster Confession and Catechisms as the system of doctrine taught therein, in world evangelization as the great end of the Church's organization.

As she held this faith with some degree of steadfastness, God has honored the testimony of the Southern Presbyterian Church until in eighty-five years she has grown from seventy thousand to over six hundred thousand members in America, and more members in the foreign field than she had in the home field when she was organized.

[1] Mackay, *The Other America*.

The highway upon which such notable progress may continue is not the primrose path of inclusiveness, but the straitened way over which Jesus Christ, seated on a solitary throne, reigns as the alone King, Head, and Lord of His body, the Church.

23. CHRIST IS OUR RIGHTEOUSNESS[1]

The message of the first tract written in behalf of the Reformation for England was brief and clear. When there was no room in England for William Tyndale to translate the Bible, he fled to the protection of Martin Luther. There in Germany, Luther's associate John Bugenhagen wrote this word for the English people: "We have only one doctrine: Christ is our righteousness." That sentence states well the fruit of Luther's own agonizing search for a gracious God.

In peril of his life, young Martin Luther vowed to become a monk, thinking that only in that way could he do enough to make God gracious to him. He kept the rules of his order with a strictness which earned for his monastery great praise. He diligently attended the seven sacraments. He confessed his sins for hours at a time. He listened to sermons on sin, law, duty, merit, fear and penance but found no Gospel in them.

He tried to climb up to God by the three ladders offered by the medieval Church: the way of merit or moralistic piety, the way of thought or rational scholasticism, and the way of ecstatic piety. But when he was unable to climb up to heaven by his own efforts, God came down in Christ and did for sinful man what he could not do for himself and what he cannot do without.

Little monk, you can never do enough to make God gracious; but you can start with the living God who is so gracious that He has wrought out for the sinner the righteousness of God in the perfect human life and the sacrificial death of Christ. By raising Christ for our justification, God declared that Christ had satisfied all of His holy requirements for our complete forgiveness.

[1] WCR, *Presbyterian Journal,* February 4, 1976, 11.

And this righteousness of God is communicated to me, the sinner, as I put my trust in Christ. By the obedience of the One are the many justified.

The Holy Spirit opened to Luther this blessed truth as he was studying Romans 1:17: The one justified by faith is the one who shall live. God in Christ has done and obeyed and suffered enough to justify you. He is the end of the law for righteousness.

As Luther wrote in his *Commentary on Galatians:* "Righteousness is given in the Word of the Gospel through which Christ comes and gives Himself to me so that I can lay hold upon Him in faith, as the ring lays hold upon the precious stone ... Therefore let us turn our eyes wholly to the brazen serpent, Jesus Christ crucified, and assuredly believe that He is our righteousness and life."

> For in the whole Gospel nothing else does Christ do but take us out of ourselves and put us under His wings that we may trust wholly in His satisfaction and merit ... As chickens are covered under the wings of the hen, so we should shroud ourselves and our sin under the covering of the flesh of Christ, who is our pillar of cloud by day and our pillar of fire by night.

Luther also wrote, "God does not give grace freely in the sense that He will demand no satisfaction, but He gave Christ to be the satisfaction for us."

The best righteousness which sacraments, service, right thinking, and kind deeds can work in us will not suffice. "All for sin could not atone; Thou must save, and Thou alone."

Christ is our righteousness. All that He did and bore for us on Calvary and through His whole life is the righteousness of God given for and to sinners—imputed to us and received by faith alone. This is no cheap grace. It cost God. It cost Christ. It costs the Holy Spirit to bring it to us, to work faith in us and thereby to unite us to Christ in our effectual calling.

ALSO PUBLISHED BY THE TRUST

'OUR SOUTHERN ZION'

OLD COLUMBIA SEMINARY (1828–1927)

by David B. Calhoun

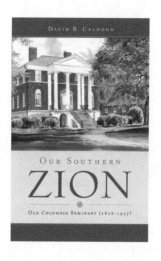

ISBN: 978 1 84871 172 3, clothbound, 408pp.

I have long admired the historical/theological writings of Dr. David Cal-houn (of Covenant Seminary) because he has the rare gift of combining historical accuracy, wide and deep cultural perception, theological insight and best of all, the fragrance of Christ and his gospel. His most recent volume on the first century of Columbia Theological Seminary (then in South Carolina), 1828-1927 exhibits all of these qualities in a beautiful combination.—DOUGLAS F. KELLY

PRINCETON SEMINARY

VOL. 1: FAITH AND LEARNING (1812–1868)

VOL. 2: THE MAJESTIC TESTIMONY (1869–1929)

by David B. Calhoun

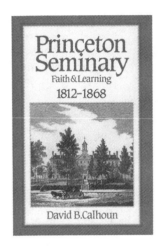
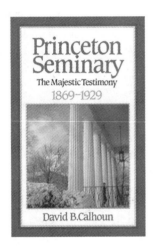

Vol. 1 ISBN: 978 0 85151 670 7, clothbound, 528pp.

Vol. 2 ISBN: 978 0 85151 695 0, clothbound, 592pp.

This splendid, thoroughly researched, two-volume history of Princeton Seminary reads like a novel. It tells the story of one of the key institutions that shaped the transformation of post-colonial, adolescent America into a world power, and that for the first time made the Christian faith global, carrying it literally to the uttermost ends of the earth. Calhoun has 'the gift'—he makes historical characters spring to life. His story is more than the story of a theological seminary; it captures the essence of a whole century and a quarter (1812-1929) of the coming of age of America.—SAMUEL HUGH MOFFET

The Banner of Truth Trust originated in 1957 in London. The founders believed that much of the best literature of historic Christianity had been allowed to fall into oblivion and that, under God, its recovery could well lead not only to a strengthening of the church today but to true revival.

Inter-denominational in vision, this publishing work is now international, and our lists include a number of contemporary authors along with classics from the past. The translation of these books into many languages is encouraged.

A monthly magazine, *The Banner of Truth,* is also published and further information about this and all our other publications can be found on our website, or by contacting either of the offices below.

THE BANNER OF TRUTH TRUST

3 Murrayfield Road,   PO Box 621, Carlisle,
Edinburgh, EH12 6EL   Pennsylvania 17013,
UK   USA

www.banneroftruth.co.uk